The Making of a Gay Asian Community

Pacific Formations: Global Relations in Asian and Pacific Perspectives
Series Editor: Arif Dirlik

What Is in a Rim? Critical Perspectives on the Pacific Region Idea, 2d edition
edited by Arif Dirlik
Chinese on the American Frontier
edited by Arif Dirlik with the assistance of Malcolm Yeung
Voyaging through the Contemporary Pacific
edited by David L. Hanlon and Geoffrey M. White
Inside Out: Literature, Cultural Politics, and Identity in the New Pacific
edited by Vilsoni Hereniko and Rob Wilson
Teaching Asian America: Diversity and the Problem of Community
edited by Lane Ryo Hirabayashi
Encounters: People of Asian Descent in the Americas
edited by Roshni Rustomji-Kerns with Rajini Srikanth and Leny Mendoza Strobel
After Postcolonialism: Remapping Philippines–United States Confrontation
by E. San Juan, Jr.
Surviving the City: The Chinese Immigrant Experience in New York, 1890–1970
by Xinyang Wang
Displacing Natives: The Rhetorical Production of Hawai'i
by Houston Wood

Forthcoming Titles

Pacific Rim Becomes Borderless
by Xiangming Chen
Born in the USA: A Story of Japanese America, 1988–1947
by Frank Chin

The Making of a Gay Asian Community

An Oral History of Pre-AIDS Los Angeles

Eric C. Wat

ROWMAN & LITTLEFIELD PUBLISHERS, INC.
Lanham • Boulder • New York • Oxford

ROWMAN & LITTLEFIELD PUBLISHERS, INC.

Published in the United States of America
by Rowman & Littlefield Publishers, Inc.
4720 Boston Way, Lanham, Maryland 20706
www.rowmanlittlefield.com

12 Hid's Copse Road, Cumnor Hill, Oxford OX2 9JJ, England

British Library Cataloguing in Publication Information Available

Library of Congress Cataloging-in-Publication Data

Wat, Eric C., 1970–
The making of a gay Asian community : an oral history of pre-AIDS Los Angeles / Eric C. Wat.
p. cm. — (Pacific formations)
Includes bibliographical references and index.
ISBN 0-7425-1109-X (alk. paper)—ISBN 0-7425-1110-3 (alk. paper)
1. Asian American gays—California—Los Angeles—History. 2. Asian American gays—California—Los Angeles—Social conditions. 3. Gay communities—California—Los Angeles—History. I. Title. II. Series.
HQ76.2.U52 C38 2002
305.8950794′94—dc21 2001041928

Printed in the United States of America

∞ ™ The paper used in this publication meets the minimum requirements of American National Standard for Information Sciences—Permanence of Paper for Printed Library Materials, ANSI/NISO Z39.48-1992.

for Dennis Akazawa (1949–1989)

A tribute to Dennis Akazawa in a Gay Asian Rap Group newsletter. Dennis died of AIDS complications in 1988. He was also a member of A/PLG in its early days.

Contents

Acknowledgments

It is not easy to go into a stranger's house and start asking questions, many of which are quite personal, and not know what to expect. But I imagine it must be much more nerve-wracking to have a stranger come into your own house not knowing what kind of questions he is going to ask. All of the narrators gave more than I had ever expected. They were kind, forthcoming, and patient. I thank each and every one of them for making this a much easier process than I had anticipated: Paul Bautista, Reggie Bogan, Andy C., Charles Chang, Paul Chen, Doug Chin, Prescott Chow, Chris Gaynor, Terry Gock, Dean Goishi, David Hong, Leo Joslin, Roy Kawasaki, June Lagmay, Steve Lew, Patrick Mangto, Harry Park, Hoang Phan, Stanley Rebultan, André Ting, Tak Yamamoto, Stan Yogi, and four others who chose to remain anonymous.

I was also privileged to have worked with my thesis advisors, John Ibson, Art Hansen, and Terri Snyder. They gave me the space to roam freely and to entertain unusual ideas. Yet when necessary, they set their collective feet down and challenged my assumptions or offered a reality check. In times of uncertainty, I could count on them for a shot of self-confidence. Their enthusiasm taught me how to be excited about my own research. With them, I felt completely free to share my half-baked ideas. It was the best gift for any budding academic.

I was blessed with other more informal advisors: Alice Y. Hom, Michael Steiner, Steven Shum, and Eric E. Reyes. Dale Murakami introduced me to some narrators in the beginning, and Milt Owens opened up the Asian/Pacific Lesbians and Gay archives where I found a collection of the organization's earliest newsletters. Both were indispensable in helping me get started.

Special thanks to the staff at the Oral History Program at California State University, Fullerton, where the tapes and transcripts of this project are archived. Because of the topic, a lot of the secondary sources were difficult to find. Fortunately, I benefited from a few institutions that specialize in keeping rare documents: The ONE Institute in Los Angeles, the International Gay and Lesbian Archives in San Francisco, and the Asian American Studies Center Reading Room/Library at University of California, Los Angeles. A special thanks to Terry Chiu for his help in preparing the photographs. I would also like to thank Matthew Hammon, Renee Jardine, and Susan McEachern at Rowman & Littlefield, who turned this book into a reality.

Finally, I want to thank my parents. When I was young, I told them I wanted to be a writer. They took me seriously and said I should write what I know best. Their tacit encouragement the last few years enabled me to write with as much courage and integrity as my frail soul could muster. Theirs was the best advice to a son, to a writer, and to a man.

Introduction

The title of this book, *The Making of a Gay Asian Community*, derives from that of E. P. Thompson's *The Making of the English Working Class*. In the introduction of this 1963 classic, Thompson explains the use of the word "making" by arguing that class formation is "an active process, which owes as much to agency as to conditioning. The working class did not rise like the sun at an appointed time. It was present at its own making."[1] He continues,

> If we stop history at a given point, then there are no classes but simply a multitude of individuals with a multitude of experiences. But if we watch these men over an adequate period of social change, we observe patterns in their relationship, their ideas, and their institutions. Class is defined by men as they live their own history, and, in the end, this is its only definition.[2]

Likewise, there is a tendency to define "community" as just an aggregate of individuals, as an ahistorical "category." For instance, we measure the strength of a community sometimes by the sheer number of members who claim to belong to the community or whom the community claims, with little regard to the multiple relationships that exist within the community or between it and another community. Surely, number is a factor in the way that a community is shaped. But there is no magic number after which an aggregate of individuals becomes a community. Like class formation in Thompson's case, I want to look at the gay Asian community in this study not "as a 'structure,' or even a 'category,' but as something which in fact happens (and can be shown to have happened) in human relationships."[3] A community cannot be understood with an atomistic epistemology. How it comes to be is a historical question.

There has not always been a gay Asian community in Los Angeles, although gay Asian men have lived in the city for a long time. As this oral history unfolds, one does not have to look very far back in history to find a time when gay Asian men did not relate to each other as gay Asian men. Many of the narrators[4]—people whom I have interviewed for their life histories—agree that there was not a sense of community before the formation of Asian/Pacific Lesbians and Gays (A/PLG) in late 1980, although there had been venues, especially gay bars, where gay Asian men could congregate in large numbers in Los Angeles in the1970s. A/PLG was the first formal organization representing the interests of gay and lesbian Asians in Los Angeles. By the end of its first year (1981), its officers assessed the state of the organization in its newsletters and gave their own perspectives on how A/PLG had fulfilled or failed their expectations thus far. One of the officers wrote:

> I think I came to the first meeting of A/PLG because I was intrigued by the idea of an organization that was both gay and Asian. I was interested in knowing how to deal with both being gay and Asian. I wasn't sure it was possible to do this in a very compatible manner. I guess I also wanted to meet new people and possibly even to cruise. Through this, I got to meet many wonderful people I would not have been able to meet any other way—certainly not in the kind of lifestyle I had been leading. In many ways, it has been a tremendous growth experience for me.[5]

One can detect in this statement a transformation that the officer had not expected when he first joined the organization. At least for this officer, A/PLG had changed how he looked at his own racial and sexual identities and in turn how he related to other gay Asian men. His statement echoes the life histories of many narrators who credit A/PLG for their leadership development and self-esteem. The late 1970s and the early1980s, then, represent a disruption in the consciousness of gay Asian men in Los Angeles—from a lack of a community to self-identification, in which the formation of A/PLG played an important role. This "adequate period of social change," or what I am referring to as the "pre-AIDS years," is the focus of the book.[6] The officer's statement raises certain questions about gay Asian life before A/PLG: Why was it difficult for him "to deal with being both gay and Asian . . . in a very compatible manner" before A/PLG? How were these identities kept separate? What "lifestyle" had he been leading? And how did it prevent him from meeting people the way he had met other A/PLG members? How were these relationships different? What were the "many ways" that A/PLG contributed to his growth? By looking at the years before and immediately after the formation of A/PLG, one can better answer these questions.

Like most changes in history, this first transformation of gay Asian consciousness did not happen smoothly. In the course of my research, I was both troubled and intrigued at first by the degree to which gay Asian men had subscribed to a racial hierarchy of desire. In the 1970s, how gay Asian men related to each other can be summarized in two general points, both of which could be observed most saliently in gay bars, then the center of social life for many gay men, Asians not excepted. First, gay Asian men were often segregated into their own respective ethnic cliques. Second, gay Asian men did not find each other desirable as sexual partners, the corollary of which was that white and Asian was the more natural coupling. These two points are the most consistent themes in all the interviews; most narrators brought them up even without provocation. These were the challenges that A/PLG took on in its first years, with mixed results. Although the racialization of desire was not a new idea to me,[7] I find these two general points very troubling because they contradict the individual memories of the narrators. Many narrators grew up in racially segregated neighborhoods at a time when many Asians, because of restrictive covenants and job segregation, were still barred from many parts of our cities. Some had lived in Hawaii or Asia where Asians were the majority. Therefore, as they were beginning to discover their attraction to other boys and men, they directed their desire to members of the same racial groups. Asked why he wasn't attracted to Asians, narrator Ernest Wada*[8], a Japanese American who grew up in East Los Angeles after World War II, says,

> I never thought about it actually. At school, when I used to have these crushes and physical attraction, it was a mixture of Asians, Mexicans, whatever turned me on. But once I became gay, I guess I was looking for . . . I don't want . . . I want someone that is masculine.

Contrary to the stereotype, the narrators who had sought white sexual partners were not ashamed of being Asian. All had a very strong sense of Asian identity, some having grown up in predominantly Asian communities or neighborhoods. A few even occupied leadership positions or were otherwise active in Asian American organizations. Every one of them enjoyed the company of very close Asian friends, sometimes even preferring an all-Asian social environment to others. That a majority had still subscribed to a white beauty myth demands a more complex analysis than that of a popular or conventional psychology, which pathologizes them and their relationships as markers of self-hatred, helplessness, or low self-esteem. They were proud gay men, and they were proud Asians, but this had not translated into a coherent gay Asian identity. Identities are not additive. Some narrators had believed that these two identities, both intact, were irrelevant to each other. Ernest's testimony implies the contradiction of having racial pride and not perceiving members of one's own racial group as sexual subjects is a product of a learning process, albeit an unconscious one. Without his recognizing it, his childhood desires were erased and replaced by something else as he entered the gay community, or "once [he] became gay."[9] This clearly contradicts the notion that gay Asian desire toward white gay men is "natural" or changeless, a sort of *laissez faire* attitude adopted by some gay men, both white and Asian, even today. When we don't question how our desire is constructed (or controlled) and instead give a lazy, essentialist explanation of "what makes one hard," we run the risk of perpetuating an unbalanced power dynamics on which this desire construction is based. As Judith Butler writes, "If sexuality is culturally constructed within existing power relations, then the postulation of a normative sexuality that is 'before,' 'outside' or 'beyond' power is a cultural impossibility and a politically impracticable dream, one that postpones the concrete and contemporary task of rethinking possibilities of sexuality and identity within the terms of power itself."[10] The assumption that my research makes—and indeed argues for—is that desire, at least the form that it takes, is anything but innate.

At this point, I must caution readers from inferring from any part of this book that every white–Asian relationship is first and foremost a manifestation of problematic power dynamics. Even in relationships where the two partners do not share equal power, genuine emotions can develop: Witness most heterosexual couples. Furthermore, I do not imply that something is necessarily negative because it is not "natural." Gay men and lesbians had suffered too many times under the "nature" argument that I have no interest in perpetuating here. Human relationships are not organic lettuce; natural does not mean better or healthier. Neither do I want to leave readers the impression that desire between two Asians is more "authentic." In fact, as my research in this history of organizing among gay Asian men in Los Angeles suggests, such desire is also learned. As Ann Laura Stoller explains, "For Foucault, there is no 'original' desire that juridical law must respond to and repress, as for Freud. On the contrary, desire follows from, and is generated out of, the law, out of the power-laden discourses of sexuality where it is animated and addressed."[11] My task here is to describe these "power-laden discourses of sexuality" that both incite and excite our desires, while at the same time to explore the human agency in shaping our desires to the kind of people we want to be.[12] In other words, I want to examine how much freedom we have—as gay Asian men, but perhaps just as human beings—in making erotic choices.

I have another ambition, a perhaps less academic one. The racialization of desire, the same that the narrators in this book have experienced, is still very much alive in the gay community today. What is different, no doubt owing in part to the existence of diverse gay Asian organizations in Los Angeles, is that there is now an alternative discourse. If, when I came out in the late 1980s, I didn't want to go to A/PLG, there were other organizations that I could and did belong to, like Gay Asian Pacific Support Network (GAPSN) and Mahu, the gay and lesbian Asian/Pacific Islander (API) student organization at UCLA where I was an undergraduate. (Unlike A/PLG, both GAPSN and Mahu have an exclusively Asian membership policy.) Exactly because my generation was able to come out into an established community ready to provide support, we often assumed that the community was always going to be there. I have heard it said that a generation in a gay community spans only about five years, and in many ways, A/PLG is "generations" ago. It is hard to imagine a time when there were no gay Asian organizations in Los Angeles and easy to take what is available now for granted.

My own commitment to this research goes beyond my intellectual interest in retrieving the past. I believe that recovering this local history is essential to organizing the gay Asian community in Los Angeles and helpful to other communities in other locations. It's not just the mistakes that we can learn from. If we can understand what it means for ordinary people to take charge and change their environments to make their lives a little better, maybe we would not take this community for granted and wait idly for history to "progress" in its due course. If I succeed in portraying this community as owing itself to the agency of dedicated individuals, maybe we would understand that nothing was handed to us on a plate and we, too, could become a little more active and involved. As Gary Okihiro writes, "Oral history is not only a tool or method for recovering history; it also is a theory of history which maintains that the common folk and the dispossessed have a history and that this history must be written. . . . [It] is the first step toward ultimate emancipation; for by freeing themselves from the bonds of a colonized history, they will be able to see their true condition, their own history. From that realization and from an understanding of the majority group and their institutions, minorities can proceed to devise means for their total liberation."[13] The present and the future constantly disappear and become the past, but, as Michael Schudson writes, "in the notion of humanness is a temporal dimension, a necessary orientation both to the past and to future, an understanding of self for which a sense of the past is not instrumental but defining."[14] Our vision of who we want to be is arrived at through a learning process: We learn from our past, and the past is our collective "anchor for imagination,"[15] our imagination of our future before us.

I also want to contribute to a growing literature that focuses on desire as a legitimate force in moving history and organizing community. Desire, as opposed to lust, is not a mere personal preference. As the following narratives show, it shapes communities and institutions. In other words, desire influences how we relate (or don't relate) to each other. At the same time, the relationship is dialectical: How we envision communities and how we pattern institutions to carry out this vision can also influence the different forms in which desire can manifest itself. Because it is about building relationships, this also has significant implications for community organizing. For example, in a very broad sense, organizations like A/PLG and GAPSN in Los Angeles were spaces created for the coming together of gay and bisexual men from various Asian ethnic groups. While A/PLG has always opened their membership to everyone regardless of race, GAPSN is very clear from its beginning that it should be an organization exclusively for and by gay and bisexual Asian men. These divergent policies reflect, in general, the different relationships that either organization believes gay and bisexual Asian men should engage in with other people and communities, on both personal and institutional levels. As each organization recruits and involves its memberships in its programs, it is in effect promoting its own vision and shaping the community according to it. Therefore, desire cannot be divorced from how history is made, and from how community organizing is to be done effectively.

I want to enter a caveat in this introduction before we begin. The format in which this oral history is presented relies heavily on excerpts from the life history interviews I have conducted. While I have tried my utmost to solicit narrators' feedback to ensure the final presentation of their words adheres to the spirit in which they were spoken, I do not present this as history undistilled. Although most of this book is written in the narrators' own words, I have edited, severed, and sequenced the narratives in a manner that is compatible with how I want to tell this history.[16] History is not linear or always progressive. I am confident, though, that my arrangement has not compromised the complexity of their experiences for the sake of coherence or drama.

One issue did get sacrificed by the way I have framed this history, and it deserves some explanations. From the very beginning, I have been clear about this being a document about the history of gay Asian men in Los Angeles. The development of the Asian lesbian community has a separate history, though the two communities did intersect at certain points, as in the case of the early years of Asian/Pacific Lesbians and Gays. However, approaching the formation of A/PLG within the context of organizing among gay Asian men can have an unfortunate and false implication that Asian lesbians were absent or passive in the organization. That is not the case at all. The internal controversies that preoccupied the organization, especially those about the role of non-Asian members in the organization and the cruising that went on at meetings and events, alienated many women, and their number remained only a handful despite the organization's staggering growth in its first few years. I do address the participation of lesbians in A/PLG in this book, admittedly in part to illustrate the tension these controversies, which were specific to the men, had created. By 1984, the Gay Asian Rap Group (GARP) had developed exclusively to address gay Asian men's issues. In turn, many of the women chose to organize separately. It took a few more years of hard work by Asian lesbians and bisexual women to form and incorporate Los Angeles

Asian Pacific Islander Sisters (LAAPIS). At the same time, the participation of lesbians in A/PLG declined over the years to a point where the organization finally changed its name to Asian/Pacific Gays and Friends (A/PGF) in 1997 to better reflect its membership profile. The historically low interest and participation by women in A/PLG illustrates the extent to which the white–Asian dynamic dominated the organization in its early years. I do not pretend to write this history "as is." In fact, writing a history of A/PLG that focuses on the needs and issues of Asian lesbians will yield a very different product than this. I hope, though, that my neglect is not attributable to chauvinism.

I also had trouble thinking about how to begin this history with all these random individuals coming together. How do you begin this history with so many beginnings? Although the narrators grew up in different times and in different parts of the world, I connect them in chapter 1 through their self-awareness of race and sexuality in their childhood and young adult lives. I also focus on a handful of narrators whose life stories will become more central as the history develops. Chapter 2 describes the various places in Los Angeles where gay men congregated before and during the 1970s, such as bars and bathhouses, and how Asians fit or didn't fit into this gay scene. Although gay bars and bathhouses were centers of gay life at that time, Asians were so scattered in these establishments, either because of number or discrimination, that they were not able to come together yet. In the 1970s came River Club and Mugi's, bars where many gay Asians and their "admirers" would frequent. The development of these "rice bars" is discussed in chapter 3. The concentration of gay Asian men in these spaces allowed for possibilities of organizing. But, as chapter 4 shows, it took a political consciousness on the part of a few individuals to envision a community. Gay Asian men's experience in political activism gave them a critical ability for analysis as well as access to networking and resources in forming Asian/Pacific Lesbians and Gays. Chapter 5 details how the A/PLG founders strengthened the infrastructure of the organization at the same time when they were trying to resolve conflicts generated by the different agendas people brought to the nascent organization. While the leadership saw A/PLG as an opportunity to develop more gay Asian leaders and educate the larger gay community and Asian American community about their issues, many members regarded A/PLG as a dating service, a more benign alternative to gay bars. Although these differences were not completely reconciled, the debate raised consciousness for a new generation of gay Asian men as the community itself became more visible and diversified. Chapter 6 traces the beginning of this second transformation a few years into A/PLG just as the AIDS epidemic began to take hold in the community in the mid-1980s.

My parents were rather reserved people. Perhaps they were saving their stories for their old age. But as a child, I got my stories from my grandmother. She lulled my brother and me to sleep with Chinese folktales that never failed to extol virtues like perseverance and fraternal love, rewarded us with other equally exemplary stories if we had finished our homework without fuss, or repeated them on a lazy afternoon when there was nothing else better to do. In moments of wistful self-awareness, she would recall her own life episodes, as a young widow, as an upstart nurse, as a single poor working mother to her four young children, in a time of war and its aftermath. Although I don't plan to have children, I always imagine myself repeating these stories to my nephews and nieces with the kind of pride that invokes one's belonging and completeness. Because of my grandmother, I always see myself as part of this family, this history, these myths. It was not until I started this project that I realized I never had that as a gay Asian man. Being gay is almost an ephemeral thing. What have I inherited and to whom can I pass it on? I have never thought I owe anything I did as a gay Asian man to an earlier generation, and I never accepted responsibility for the generations after. But as I am looking back to these twenty or so interviews, I have an image in my mind of myself as a child, propping up my head with one arm, looking up and listening attentively to my grandmother. This time, I have written the stories down.

NOTES

1. E. P. Thompson, *The Making of the English Working Class* (New York: Pantheon Books, 1963), p. 9. See also Joshua Gamson, "Must Identity Movements Self-Destruct? A Queer Dilemma," *Social Problems* 42, no. 3 (August 1995): 390–407. Gamson writes, "Identities, in rational-actor models (before they came under increased critical scrutiny) are typically conceived as existing before movements, which then make them visible through organizing and deploy them politically; feminism wields, not creates, the collective identity of 'women.' " New social movement theory, on the other hand, conceives collective identity as a "continual process of recomposition rather than a given." This process is characterized by establishment of differences, usually between the group and its dominant counterpart; by the development of consciousness; and by symbols and action that the group employs to resist or restructure existing systems. Despite the differences in emphasis, both models presume the agency of individuals in the process of identity and community formation.

2. Thompson, *The Making of the English Working Class*, 11.

3. Thompson, *The Making of the English Working Class*, 9.

4. For a list of the twenty-five narrators interviewed for this oral history and their biographies, see Appendix I.

5. *A/PLG Newsletter*, January 1982, issue 1B.

6. By 1984, another gay Asian organization—Gay Asian Rap Group (GARP)—had emerged in Los Angeles, and the AIDS epidemic had already begun wreaking havoc on the community and bringing many gay men closer. These two phenomena changed the

gay Asian community significantly and gave rise to a new generation in Los Angeles. Although they fall outside the "adequate period of social change" I have designated for this study, in the last chapter and the afterword, I make some cursory suggestions on how we can begin to look at these two phenomena.

7. See Eric C. Wat, "Preserving the Paradox: Stories From a *Gay-loh*," *Amerasia Journal* 20, no. 1 (1994): 149–60.

8. The narrators who chose to remain anonymous for this oral history have selected pseudonyms to be used throughout the book. On first mention, the pseudonym is denoted with an asterisk (*). Appendix II, which gives a brief biography of each narrator, also indicates pseudonyms with an asterisk.

9. I'm reminded here of Lisa Lowe's comments about Franz Fanon's *Black Skin, White Masks*. See Lowe, "Decolonization, Displacement, Disidentification: Writing and the Question of History," *Immigrant Acts* (Durham: Duke University Press, 1996), 97–127. She writes:

> In alluding to the paradoxical fluency of the colonized subject in the colonial language and culture, Fanon astutely names the twofold character of colonial formation. The imposition of the colonial language and its cultural institutions . . . demands the subject's internalization of the "superiority" of the colonizer and the "inferiority" of the colonized, even as it attempts to evacuate the subject of "native" language, traditions, and practices. Yet the colonized subject produced within such an encounter does not merely bear the marks of the coercive encounter between the dominant language and culture, constructed as whole, autonomous, and disinterested, and the specificities of the colonized's group's existence. Such encounters produced contradictory subjects, in whom the demands for fluency in imperial languages and empire's cultural institutions simultaneously provide the grounds for antagonism to those demands.

The lack of coercion makes it difficult for the "native" to identify and name this colonial encounter. Yet, the contradiction that colonization demands of the "native," if revealed, provides the impetus for resistance, as in the example of organizing around A/PLG.

10. Judith Butler, *Gender Trouble* (New York: Routledge, 1990), 30.

11. Ann Laura Stoller, *Race and the Education of Desire: Foucault's* History of Sexuality *and the Colonial Order of Things* (Durham: Duke University Press, 1995), 165.

12. The two are not incompatible. See Stoller, *Race and the Education of Desire*, 192. As Stoller states, "While it is clear that production of these desires was not indifferent to the taxonomies of rule, they did not always uphold them. We may reject, with Foucault, a notion of primordial drive but still explore a space for individual affect structured by power but not wholly subsumed by it. . . . Rather it acknowledges a wider range of transgressive sentiments and cultural blurring that informed what was unspeakable and what was said."

13. Gary Okihiro, "Oral History and the Writing of Ethnic History," in *Oral History: An Interdisciplinary Anthology*, ed. David K. Dunaway and Willa K. Baum (Walnut Creek, Calif.): AltaMira Press, 1996), 209–10.

14. Michael Schudson, *Watergate in American Memory: How We Remember, Forget, and Reconstruct the Past* (New York: Basic Books, 1992), 55.

15. Schudson, *Watergate in American Memory*, 155.

16. For a more detailed discussion on methods and methodology, see Appendix I.

I

Before the Beginning

AS SISSY AS THEY COME

In the beginning, there were little hints of a connection among this random assembly of individuals. They did not live in the same neighborhoods, the same cities. Their families belonged to different walks of life. They adhered to traditions specific to their respective cultures and local histories. In their young lives, most of the narrators tried to be as "normal" as those around them, doing what was expected of teenagers at that time: going to school, joining clubs, dating girls. Even if they shared a similar attraction to their own sex, that remained a fantasy caged in the corners of their heads. There were, of course, innocent encounters with other boys who would grow up a different way or brief moments of recognition on forbidden pages. Other cruel children might whisper unkind words that frightened and worried them. Later on, some would feel the excitement of seduction and the confusion that followed the next day. But for the most part, with all the pains of growing up that every child or young man endures, these narrators did not expect to organize their lives around their desires. There is a line between behavior and consciousness, a threshold where doing acquires meaning and doubts are replaced by courage. Much of this history of the gay Asian community in Los Angeles began at this threshold. Their unwavering conviction of who they were—or better yet, the potential of what they could be—was the driving force behind the formation of this community.

Tak Yamamoto

I can't tell you that much about Westminster [Orange County] where I was born [1938] because we went to Poston, Arizona, during the relocation [Japanese internment during World War II], except that it was a farming community back then and most of the other people there were white. When we came back to [Los Angeles] California, we lived in Little Tokyo for six months. Then my father found a small three-car garage and converted it for us to live in. It was in East Los Angeles, one of the few places that we could've gotten into at the time. In that era, there was still restrictive housing; Asians couldn't move into West L.A., for example. East L.A. was primarily Jewish and Hispanic at the time. I would say my interaction was primarily with the Mexican kids and smaller groups of Japanese kids who came out of the camps after the War. They were who I saw in school. When I was in high school, I felt dating was an important feature that we needed to do. So I dated a girl. I liked her, but there was nothing sexual. I think at that time I didn't really understand where I was coming from. And so I thought the attraction to the opposite sex would all develop at some point. But here I was, seventeen years old, and there was no attraction at all. I really can't say I was attracted to men either. It was a no-no thing. So even if I felt it, I would've denied it.

When I was in high school, I worked in a five-and-dime, and there was a guy, a Hispanic man, who used to come in there powdered up. I mean, he looked like a mannequin. I thought to myself, "If that's what being homosexual is, that's not what I am because I don't see myself going in that particular direction." And that was my first exposure [to homosexuality]. Then I saw a couple of people that were especially super-nelly in high school. People laughed at them. Now I think they were the strongest ones because they were saying, "The hell with you! We know who we are." But at that time, that was offensive to me because I didn't relate to that. I said, "Gee, you know, I must be the only freak in nature because there isn't anybody else I could relate to." I mustn't be gay, but I felt uncomfortably straight. I really didn't know where I fitted in. And I think one of the things that kids today still feel is that there is no place for them to fit in, and there's this idea that suicide is a way out because there is no group to be supportive of you. That was exactly how I felt, but this was more real in the 1950s because there truly wasn't any place that you could go. I think that was the scary part.

Ernest Wada

I was born in Terminal Island in 1935. It was largely a community of Japanese living there. A fishing community, too. Most of the people who lived there were fishermen and their families. I was about six years old when I went to the camps. Life in the camp for kids my age was no different than outside the camp. Kids at six years old pretty much adapt to situations. Besides, we were protected from adversities such as the ones my older siblings and parents had to endure. We had elementary schools from first to sixth grade and high school from seventh grade to twelfth. The teachers were predominantly Caucasians. In this respect, our education was not disrupted. You see, if you're living in an entirely Japanese community, it's almost like a homogeneous society. Right? So, making the transition from an all-Japanese Terminal Island to an all-Japanese Manzanar [relocation camp in eastern California] was not a big deal for me. Actually, the only change that I was aware of was that we relocated from a fishing community to a desert community. As for contact with other ethnics, the only contact with whites I had up until then were teachers, provisional doctors, firemen, etc. I had no idea what the war meant.

When we came out of the camps, by then, Terminal Island had become a naval base entirely, with the exception of a few private concerns, such as Starkist Tuna. My father was a fisherman before. When we came back to L.A., he started working in produce. We moved to East Los Angeles, right in the heart of the barrio. You know Aliso Village [a housing project]? We lived right across the street from Aliso Village. This was a very new and traumatic experience for me. This area of Los Angeles had a preponderance of Latino Americans of the Mexican variety along with whites and blacks. Housing was short during this period, and most Japanese returned to similar areas scattered around Los Angeles. There were very few Japanese American kids in my school. Beside myself, there was only one other Japanese girl in my fifth-grade class.

I am the youngest son among four sisters. No brothers. Since I have no brothers, I grew up with an absence of male role models. Because most men were fishermen, they were out to sea a great deal of the time. Up until then, my role models were my sisters. I was brought up with all of these sisters and other women. I actually thought I was the fifth sister. I had very feminine traits. The Latinos never made an issue of this. The kids I ran around with were all Mexican Americans. They were very sweet. Right from the start, they just took me under their wings and never expressed any kind of bias. Based on my experience, Latino boys are very sexually mature at an early age. They just have a healthy attitude toward sex and in many cases are not discriminating about engaging in sexual activities regardless of the partner's gender. They taught me a lot. Oh yes, my Latino buddies taught me how to masturbate and perform masturbation on them. When things became heated (even at this age), they'd enjoy penetrating me anally. Being so feminine, I thought all of this was natural. I recall an experience where I engaged in sex play with a special friend who was a couple of years older than I. Before he penetrated me, he kissed me in a manner that made me swoon. I really developed a big-time crush on him. Can you believe this behavior at age ten? Because of them, I discovered my sexuality as far as preference for males only. Being as sissified as I was, the horny boys would always single me out for their sexual release. They were also very protective of me. For instance, the black boys used to terrify me by calling me a "slant-eyed Jap." The Latino boys always came to my rescue.

I also dated girls. Girls had crushes on me, but to me, I was always looking at the guys. Never a question. Because when I went out with these girls, I would like their boyfriends in their circle.

Why would you be dating them if you knew that you were only attracted to guys?

See, you're asking this question from a very liberated point of view. In those days, you had to do that. Otherwise, immediately they'd think you were queer. I mean, you're as sissy as they come, but if you date girls, somehow it seems that maybe you're not queer. It's a guy thing. Even at that point, you were trying to do the right thing to be accepted.

Doug Chin

I was born in 1949 and grew up in a basically middle-class neighborhood in Hawaii. Our neighborhood was racially mixed in that we had whites, blacks, Puerto Ricans, Filipinos, and the different Asian groups were also there. I was in private school from sixth grade through high school. In my high school days, we had more white influence because of the military there. They tended to send their kids to private schools. Growing up, [my knowledge about homosexuality] was very limited. It was not something that was spoken of around the house. My first homosexual experience was with my neighborhood friend, actually a cousin of a friend who was visiting. As children, we just played and we were interested in each other's parts. So that's how it started. I must have been about twelve.

I also dated girls. I remember going to four different proms my junior year. I mean, I was actively dating. And you know, necking, we used to go out and kiss. I learned about gay people through friends, straight friends, in high school. They wanted to taunt them. So they used to drive by a transvestite club and make fun of them. I went a couple of times, until I knew better.

Roy Kawasaki

I was born and raised in Hawaii in a very small cane planters' community. My father was a cane planter. Mother was a seamstress. I am the youngest of six children. I grew up in a very tight-knit Japanese community because most of the families were all Japanese cane planters' families who worked for the sugar plantation. Eventually I ended up, like all of my friends, working in the cane fields. I attended a small community elementary school. We had three teachers. Each teacher taught two grades. And there were like fifteen students in fifth and sixth grades. So they were really small classes. I think out of the whole school, there were maybe fifty to sixty students. Very small. Everyone knew each other's business.

It was basically all Japanese. We had few Hawaiian families, few Filipino families. And the Portuguese that attended our elementary school lived with his family in a dairy community just below my home. Growing up, I really enjoyed my childhood because we were very close. Everyone got involved in sports. Everybody played baseball during the summer. Of course, I was really terrible at it. I just had no athletic skills at all. So I always felt threatened when baseball season came around. I think at an early age, I knew I was somewhat different. I liked certain boys in my neighborhood. And when I went to high school, I became friends with a few people. They were kind of the oddballs. And that's where I put myself into, the oddball category. My high school years, I really felt lonely, although I did know some boys. But yet I just never felt comfortable with them. I guess because I knew there was something different about me. I just wasn't sure what it was at that time.

Then I came to Los Angeles in 1961 to attend L.A. City College. I was twenty. The reason I ended up in L.A. was to pursue an education, which my parents couldn't really afford. So they said, "Why don't you go to Los Angeles? There's your brother and your sister living there. You could stay with them." So I decided to do that. I was an art major then.

Being away from Hawaii was like having a burden just lifted off my shoulders. I didn't have to hide anything. I could be here and be anonymous. I made friends with a few guys also from Hawaii. We became very, very close friends. I don't know how it came about. I guess we were all lonely, away from home, so we kind of supported one another.

I remember this one person—he was Asian—someone that I really liked and felt an affection for. I didn't know what was happening. I just fell in love with this guy. I remember going to one of my art instructors and telling him about this, not realizing that the problem that I was having was my sexual identity. Why I picked my art instructor to reveal this to, I have no idea. I also saw a psychologist in the school. But after two or three sessions, he was transferred. So I stopped. The person I was in love with ended up joining the army. That's when everything for me stopped. But I knew there was something inside of me that I had to find out: What was wrong with me? Why did I feel like this? I was so naive then.

Then I transferred to Cal State L.A. I really didn't think about my sexuality and was just concentrated on my studies. Then I met this guy during a coffee break. We became friends. He invited me—he was a senior and I was a junior then—over to his home. It was one of those really rainy nights. I was seduced and we had sex. Really it was just one-way kind of sex because I wasn't sure what was happening. I felt so guilty and dirty the next morning. I went home and I just felt very, very strange. But then as days passed by, I began to think about the experience and said, "You know, I really enjoyed it." But I was still angry with him. I guess he really felt bad about it, too. He gave me a little gift, a necktie pin, as a friendship thing. I still have it now. We are still friends today. But, you know, that was my first experience.

Paul Chen

I was born in Jacksonville, Florida. I'm actually fourth-generation Chinese on my mother's side and second-generation Chinese on my father's side. My great-grandparents on my mother's side moved to Northern Florida in the 1890s. So my Toisan is actually a hundred years old. I speak very strange Toisanese.

My parents met at the University of Minnesota. They were the only Chinese there, and because of anti-miscegenation laws, they had to date each other. During World War II, my father actually worked for Chiang Kai-Shek. When Chiang Kai-Shek had to make the move to Taiwan, my father no longer had an education. So he followed my mother back to Florida to her family. That's why I was born there.

In Florida during those days, the 1950s and the 1960s, we were considered colored. I think technically the law was that anybody more than one-eighth non-white was considered colored. So we had to go drink out of colored water fountains and sit in the back of the bus. My parents couldn't buy a business anywhere else except the black ghetto. So my father had a grocery store in the black neighborhood when I was growing up.

I remember one time we had to get our car fixed and had to ride the bus. My mother just sat down on her seat, and this lady came along and she started screaming at us at the top of her lungs because we weren't sitting at the back of the bus. And my mother said to us in Chinese, "Just ignore her. She's a crazy woman." I remember this vividly.

My father didn't come to the States until he was forty, forty-one. So he never dealt with prejudice before. Of course, it wasn't a fun thing to do. He didn't like Northern Florida. I guess my parents wanted to shield us from prejudice. So he picked us up and moved us to Southern California when I was in fourth grade. We settled in Fullerton.

Did you experience the same prejudice in Fullerton?

Fullerton? Well, you know, we were exotic. People tried to relate to us and desperately tried to say something nice. A lot of people used to say something like, "I have rice a lot." The prejudice is nicer. It wasn't necessarily less. There was in elementary school, I think, one Japanese girl in my grade. In high school, there were two that were the same age as I was. Aside from that, it was very white. I got beat up a couple of times in elementary school because I was different. Plus, I was obviously feminine all the time. I was really different, being Chinese and being gay.

I knew I was interested in men, but I rarely concentrated on those feelings. It wasn't that I even thought good or bad about them. It was just there. I don't remember having crushes on my classmates. No, at that time, I had crushes on people like Sean Connery. I guess I defined myself as not heterosexual, even though I didn't have words for it. I do remember in junior high learning a lot of sexual terms, going through puberty. Of course, it was the first time I got to see naked bodies because of gym.

I learned the word "homosexual" when I was in seventh grade, I think. I remember stressing out about it because I identified with it and obviously it wasn't something that people thought was good. I was laying in bed thinking about it a lot. One time I got out of bed and told my mother I was homosexual. Then she said, "You don't know what you're talking about. Go back to bed." So I thought, Okay, if you're not going to be concerned about it, I won't be either.

When I was fifteen, the school had a field trip to a museum up in L.A. I snuck out of the museum and I found one of those newsstands that you put a couple of quarters in, you pull it up and you get a newspaper. Well, the *Advocate* was in this one. So I put my fifty cents or a dollar in and bought it and hid it in my backpack and took it home and read it. I suddenly knew there was somebody for me. I mean, it was a newspaper for people like me. And after I got my driver's license, I would get into the family car once a month and drive all the way to that same little newsstand. So by the time I got into college, I knew I was gay. I've been reading the *Advocate* for a few years.

ALL ABOUT BUTCHING UP

For many gay Asian men who were born in the 1940s and graduated from high school in the 1950s and 1960s, higher education was often not an option. Some might have attended community college or vocational schools, or obtained a bachelor's degree later in life. This was a time before affirmative action and liberal admission policies that opened the doors of American colleges and universities to many working-class and middle-class people of color. Since the 1970s, campus organizing, which led to the formation of many gay and lesbian student organizations, helped many gay and lesbian students discover their sexual identities and politicized them as well. Asians, as we shall see later, were no exception. Without access to higher education, however, an earlier generation of gay Asian men enlisted in the military as an alternative. Although many, like Doug Chin, who was in the Army, "did not join the military expressly looking for homosexual experience," it was something that many of them found, perhaps due to the homosocial nature of military life. Not only did the narrators engage in some of their earliest homosexual activities in the military, but many also began to adopt the gay label itself and decided to live the rest of their lives as gay men. From this informal and underground network of gay men, they shared knowledge and information of the gay community that they were able to use after they were discharged and returned to or settled in Los Angeles and other metropolitan cities.[1] And in some cases, their gay experiences heightened their racial difference and raised their consciousness as people of color.

Ernest Wada

I just turned nineteen when I enlisted [mid-1950s]. At that time, it was mandatory that you had to meet your draft obligation when you turned eighteen. I didn't have any college exemption. (Besides, I don't know if they had written in college exemptions in those days.) So rather than waiting for them to call us, many of us just volunteered right after high school for the draft to be called earlier to get our obligation out of the way.

I took basic infantry training. After that, it was mandatory to go on to advanced infantry training, which was all in Fort Ord in California. And right after the two—which were eight-week cycles of both basic and advanced infantry training—they gave me a short leave and then immediately stationed me in Korea. My entire active duty was sixteen months.

Two of my closest friends with whom I associated in the military were an Italian from Boston and a Caucasian of Polish extraction from Long Island, New York. We were of the same mind set, and we became really good friends. This was a very fortunate experience for me because it enabled me to see that good people are essentially people, regardless of ethnicity. Both got married right after, and they each sent me an invitation to their weddings. So that's how they felt about me. By then, I was aware that I was a homosexual, but I was still closeted. I wasn't out to them, but I'm sure in their case, it wouldn't have made a difference.

But I saw a lot of gay guys in the military, blatantly gay. A lot of them were like in clerical capacities, in medical capacities and so forth. The line soldiers, the infantrymen, there might have been some, but I couldn't tell. I tried to butch it up by then because you were not going to survive if you acted like a sissy under those circumstances. In the military, it was all about butching up. You had to. I was going on these bivouacs. That means you go out of your station compound and in the field, sleeping in pup tents with other guys. We each had what you called a shelter half. It's on your backpack. It's your half of the tent that you're going to put up. You put up one half and I put the other half and we push in. So they call them shelter halves. The local prostitutes knew when the men were going out in the field and they would follow the campers. That was their best chance to get out there and sell their work. So I was in bivouac this one time, setting up tent with this guy from Hawaii. He brought in a prostitute, a very pretty girl. And after he got through, he said, "Take some. I'll pay for it." And no way! But this is just one of those butch things that they did that I had to be subjected to. I didn't participate in that aspect, but all the other things I had to. Training itself is just a man thing. I don't see how these females survive in the military now.

Although I was not out, I was having rendezvous, but not with gay guys. They were with straight guys. These were just guys that, I guess, knew what they were doing, but they didn't view it as they were being queer. It was just sexual release. I would initiate these encounters. I mean, I was not entirely reckless about it. You find somebody who's attractive to you, and then you get to know the person and they get to know you. They find out you are decent and so forth, and then you wait for the right moments and see if they'd submit to it. And ninety percent of the time, they would.

So you were pretty sure they wouldn't tell on you?

No, they came back for seconds.

Tak Yamamoto

Well, I think I had an inclination prior to my going into the service. I was already eighteen years old, but no sexual experience. When I came to the question on the application to enter the military—"Do you have homosexual tendency?"—I halted there for a minute. I thought, "Well, I never acted on any of these feelings. So how would I know if I have homosexual tendency?" So of course I just answered no. When I had been in the service for a couple of years, I got to meet some gay kids. I felt comfortable around them, and I told myself, "You know, maybe this is who I really am."

My first sexual experience was when I was twenty, when I was stationed in Germany. When I was in the service—it was 1957 to 1961—there was no "gay pride" or anything like that. We had to meet under the cover of darkness. Or off the base. We would meet in town. I got to meet people who told me about some gay bars, or quasi-gay bars, in Germany, and I would go to them. But we still couldn't be overt off the base because there was always this fear that the military special investigation group would be looking for us. Sometimes they would pose to be gay. I guess that's what we'd call entrapment now. But they would do that then and kick the guys out of the service. I wouldn't say that happened frequently, but I knew several cases. So even though I went to these bars, I wouldn't do anything overt.

I think coming out in the military worked for me because I wasn't here in the United States. Being in Germany, I think, gave me a certain amount of freedom to act out. But also when I was there, I was beginning to try to understand that I wasn't white. There just weren't many Asians in the service. You probably could count us in one hand. So as a Japanese American, it was very difficult: You couldn't talk to anybody about just being Asian. Instead, you had to develop kind of a white attitude to fit in.

What would that attitude be?

In this case, I don't think you found blame [with white people]. You did what you needed to do to get the work done. You catered to the white majority. You didn't think about someone being put down because they were black because that didn't somehow affect you. I mean, after all, I was white in my mind. So whatever I did, I was looking for acceptance by them more than anybody else. So I was basically a banana, I guess—yellow on the outside, white on the inside. That's what I did for a long time, until I became actively gay—"actively gay" meaning I would go to town and meet these people in the bars and realize that I'm not white and the person they're seeking is obviously an exotic one because that's what I was [supposed to be] back then. I was not in demand. There were very few Asians, and there just weren't that many Germans that got turned on by us. I probably met about ten or twelve.

The interesting thing was the parents of my German lovers—almost always the mother—didn't quite understand who I was because I wasn't white, black, or Hispanic. And I had to explain to them, I am American because I was born there, but I'm Japanese. And yes, all of us in the United States have all these possibilities. But the Germans only saw Americans as white, black, or Hispanic. I was a novelty.

I think at that point, I got to understand that, in order for me to get along, I really had to broaden my base.

My best friend then became this black guy, P. K.—the sweetest guy you ever wanted to know. When I got out in sixty-one, we kept in contact. Once he came and visited me at home and got to know my Mom. My Mom didn't speak English, and he didn't speak Japanese, but they would communicate in some kind of way. When I got home from work and asked P. K., "Ah, P. K., what did you guys talk about today?" And he would tell me. And when I asked my Mom, she would say the same things. And it was a lot of different, complicated things. How did they talk to each other, you know?

Prior to my going into the service, I was only eighteen. So I wasn't aware of any gay places in L.A. When I was in the service, I talked with different people who had been in Los Angeles, and they gave me information on how to find these gay bars. They said, "Oh, you got to go to the Red Raven" or "You got to go to the House of Ivy and you got to go to this place." They gave me all these names, and I would look them up when I got home, to see what they were all about. After P. K. got out of the service, he moved here. He lived about a mile from here. We would start running around the city, going to bars and parties. From then onward, I knew I didn't have to take that white perspective of things because I was never going to be white.

Doug Chin

I was in the U.S. Army for three years. My tours started in Fort Ord for training. Then I was sent to Japan for two years, in Tokyo, Camp Oji and Camp Zama. I completed my tour of duty in Fort Lewis in Washington, in the Tacoma-Seattle area, and then returned to Hawaii in early 1971. It was a few months after that I identified myself as being gay. I had two homosexual experiences in the military, one with a gay male, one with a straight male. We kept it very clandestine. It wasn't until I was almost discharged that I started doing any kind of [homosexual] activities. And it was purely by accident how they happened. I mean, I was approached. I enjoyed the experience—the closeness, the touching, the feelings. I didn't keep in touch with either one of the two men. The service ended and we broke. That was it. But it was after I'd come out of the military, started working and going back to school, that I adopted a gay lifestyle. I was dating people. That was when I met Jim through mutual friends, and we started dating. Jim had been affiliated with a company [whose] corporate headquarters was actually in Washington, D.C., with an office in Southern California. He was on assignment [when I met him] as an attachment to the military, servicing the strategic computer equipment that they had in Hawaii. He had been doing this for a number of years. He was sent to Vietnam during the Vietnam War era to service the computers there. So he had pretty high clearances. Eventually he asked me to become lovers with him.

THE FUTURE IS IN AMERICA

History and culture play a significant role in how homosexuality is manifested differently in Asia than in the United States. Although many people believe that American culture is more open to different forms of sexuality, the 1950s witnessed the harrowing red-baiting of Communists and homosexuals that drove many gay men and lesbians back into the closet. Even with the sexual revolution beginning in the 1960s or after the Stonewall Rebellion in 1969, sexual politics continued to be an unending violent battleground. But ironically because of this virulent repression, there is also an organized resistance on the part of lesbians and gay men to defend themselves.[2] On the other hand, in most Asian cultures, sex in general was not a common topic for conversation. Unless one was openly challenging the dominant sexual mores or flaunting his or her "deviancy," most people tolerated homosexuality with one eye open and another closed. This silence actually afforded some space for Asian men and women to explore same-sex sexuality. A lot of behavior that would be derided as "gay" in America would be acceptable or even commonplace in many parts of Asia. Narrator Terry Gock, an immigrant from Hong Kong, recalls,

> As I was growing up, it was okay to hold hands with guys. It was okay to be much more physically close with guys than what is apparently appropriate here [in the United States]. So when I had those feelings [same-sex attraction], I didn't feel anything particularly wrong with it. Coming over here [in 1970 when I was nineteen], I felt sort of inadequate, especially in the early years, because the rules had changed all around me. But I came from a culture where we [Asians] were a majority. (If anything, we were guilty of beating up on those non-Asians.) Through my growing up, there was enough foundation to buffer some of this inadequacy.

Many immigrants were surprised to find the United States not as liberated sexually as they had imagined. Some narrators who had lived in Asia even suggested that it was easier for them to lead a gay lifestyle undisturbed in Asia than in the United States. Racial prejudices and stereotypes were also something new to them. This would have some bearing later on when both immigrants and American-born Asians came together to establish a sense of gay Asian community in Los Angeles. Although some immigrants might not readily identify with the history of racism and resistance in this country, their strong sense of who they are was an asset to a group of people who were still shaping their identity.

When talking about the differences between American-born Asians and Asian immigrants, one must be careful about generalizations. When asked whether or not these differences exist, Bill Matsumoto, a gay Asian activist in the Bay Area during the 1980s, responds, "Yes, but I hesitate to make generalizations about either because there are such varying degrees of assimilation and attitude among both. Some foreign-born Asians can be very aggressive, while some American-born Asians can be very quiet. But then you'll find persons for whom the opposite is true. It's really difficult to generalize."[3] The narrators, both immigrants or American-born, sometimes do speak in generalizations on this issue, at times with qualifications. After all, it is human to recognize patterns and try to make sense of them. I also feel that it is both important and possible to look into different factors that shape the complexity of our community without taking away the complexity of the individual.

Andy C.

I could say I was a late-bloomer. I didn't get really involved until I was seventeen or eighteen. It's just like how families were back in Malaysia. You never talk about sex. I think I had the feeling then, but I was a little hesitant, maybe a little bit afraid, too. Although I didn't quite understand the word homosexual yet, I knew I was different. When you're different, you always get into the negative side of things, instead of being positive. I was always worried about what would happen to me. The same questions always popped up in my mind.

When I was in college in the 1950s, we used to go to the live animals science lab in the school. It was a room with all kinds of facilities. When they were showing slides once, this classmate of mine said, "Come sit in the back with me. Come sit in the back with me." I kind of had an idea [what he meant], but I still wasn't sure. I went with him to the back. That's where it happened. When the room darkened and the slides were on, he would pick my hand and put it to you-know-where. That's how it all started.

After I graduated and left college, I started moving around. I found a job in another state, and I was there for about a year. Then I moved to Penang. Penang was, more or less, the capital of gay life. It was more gay than most parts of Malaysia, with the exception of Kuala Lumpur, which was kind of low-key. Penang was more up front. I got to know more people there, and we used to do things and party together. But still, on a quiet scale. When I was younger in Malaysia, there were no clubs like in the States. That came later on—I would say about late 1960s or 1970s. But still, they were still under a lot of pressure because they were closing them down faster than they sprang up. Before that, it was more like private gatherings, friends introducing friends. You'd get into a closed circle and move around. So we would do things quietly and make arrangements to go out. Surprisingly, back home, people didn't put much emphasis on homosexual behavior unless we were overbearing. I think in most Southeast Asian cultures, you have a reasonably sized community of bisexuals. If you behave somewhat effeminately, you might be labeled gay. But if you live quietly, nobody would say much. You wouldn't be crucified. That's how the gay life existed, somewhat on a quiet scale, but we did a lot of things. They were mostly hush-hush. We just had to use our own discretion.

At one point, though, when I was in my twenties, I was kind of dressing up in the other sex, doing a little bit of stage work. From there, I was going to contests and functions. I think my mother knew about it. She didn't see me personally, but she had heard from a lot of friends, family friends. She didn't really object to it. I felt she was worried about me more than anything else because I was different and she could see what it was coming to. What's going to happen when I grow old and can't take care of myself? How will I survive? My Dad was a little disappointed. He's got three boys, so it wasn't a big worry for him. I think the most disappointed part for my Dad was that he had this expectation of me to follow up the family business, but I took off after graduation. Although he didn't say anything, I knew he was disappointed that I didn't follow through or communicate with him my intention to leave home, the latter I knew I just couldn't.

I worked in Penang for a few years before I left for Hong Kong in 1967. Going to Hong Kong was like a steppingstone for me. By then I had in mind of coming to the States to see how much further I could better myself. My employer was the First Secretary of the British Consulate. I made an agreement with him that I would work for him for two years. And after two years, should I choose to go to the States, he would have to release me. My thinking was, if I traveled far enough from my family, that was one way of proving to myself that I could be independent and not rely on them. If I didn't go far enough, there was always the choice of running back home. I needed to put myself to that test. Also, at the same time, if I ever get out of my own family circle, that would give me a chance to be my own person and the opportunity to build my character.

André Ting

I was born in China, and I moved to Hong Kong when I was three years old. When I was thirteen to nineteen, I was in Malaysia. I had my junior high and high school education in Malaysia. And then after that, I went to Brazil. I wanted to see more of the world. I thought I was going to live in Brazil for good. But I was restless. So I applied to two universities in the United States. I was given scholarships to both of the universities that I chose. One was in Austin, Texas. So I ended up in Austin, Texas. It was a private university called St. Edwards University, run by the Holy Cross brothers, who also ran Notre Dame in Indiana. So I heard that it was a good school.

Like I said, I went to Malaysia for my high school education. All the textbooks were in English. So for me to start everything anew in Portuguese [in Brazil], it would be very difficult. To go from an English-speaking country, such as Malaysia, to the United States would be easier. That's why I picked the United States. I mean, everybody heard about the States, heard about all the good schools. So that was always in the back of my mind.

Maybe it was a very eventful decade, as you know, the 1960s. I did not know my sexuality. I was a hard-working student, just trying to get good grades. Eventually I did go to protests, like anti-war protests and so on. One could not help not being influenced by the sexual revolution of the decade. I was influenced deeply. I became more open-minded. For the first time in my life—I was brought up in a Catholic background where sex was considered dirty—I looked at free love as something that you can enjoy. I was raised by brothers. I was taught for years by nuns and brothers, who were very conservative and very puritanical, to say the least. When I was in high school, for example, in Malaysia, one student brought some pornographic pictures to school and later on when he was discovered, he was expelled immediately from the Catholic high school. So I was profoundly affected.

After the three and a half years at the university, I went to Houston, Texas, to study for my master's degree. That's when I came out. I'd been reading a little about homosexuals and sexuality. When I was living in the dorm, there was another graduate from St. Edwards University. He came to see me several times in my dorm, and we talked, and talked, and talked. He suspected that I was gay, because he knew that I did not have a girlfriend, that I was by myself. And eventually he said to me, "Let's go out to a bar and have some fun." So he took me to a gay bar. I think it was in 1970. The minute I walked in, I realized that's where I belonged.

I was over-dressed. I had a sport jacket and a tie, but they were the completely wrong attire for that club. People were in very casual clothes. And for the first time in my life, I saw men dancing with men. I felt completely at ease. It was a revelation to me. My whole life changed.

After that, we were going out a lot. In fact, shortly after discovering that bar, I became a bartender at that bar, even as I was doing my thesis. At that time, in Austin, Texas, there were only two gay bars. One is called the Pearl Street Warehouse. It's a disco that caters to a younger crowd. That's the one I worked in. At the Pearl Street Warehouse, there were whites, Latinos, blacks, and very few Asians. Maybe I was the only one at that time. And then the other one is called the Apartment, which catered to an older gay crowd. There was no lesbian bar at that time.

I just discovered my sexuality, and I tried to find out more about the gay culture. The only thing that I found was the [sobs] . . . I'm sorry, I'm very emotional. . . . The only paper I found was the *Advocate*. And I read it. I read every page. I felt that those are my people, you know. And I found that it was published in Los Angeles. If a place could have a newspaper like that, that place must be a very nice place to be. And I said, you know what, that's where I'm going. I'm going to L.A.

Paul Bautista*

I was born in 1960 in Quezon City in the Philippines. I grew up in an upper-middle-class community. Mostly those communities had high walls. That's how you could tell when you were in a nice neighborhood—nothing but walls. I went to a very strict Catholic school. I think we all got up at six A.M., in school by seven and out of school by four. We did our homework from the time we got home from school until dinnertime. You got to watch maybe half an hour of T.V. and then you were back to doing homework. Then you were in bed. That was Monday to Friday. I remember the only shows I watched as a kid were *Hogan's Heroes*, *The Jetsons*, *The Flintstones*, stuff like that.

From watching T.V. or just looking at the world, I started gravitating toward what males I thought were handsome or cute. I guess especially back then, because it was a Catholic school and there weren't any girls. The only women were the teachers. You don't want to be called teacher's pet, although I'm sure I was. I remember I was always smaller than the other guys. At this school, there was always this thing where the bigger, bullier guys were after the cute ones. I remember sitting in front of the class on somebody's knees, one of the bigger boys in my class, so I could copy the homework off the board. It was totally normal. It was as if I was his girlfriend, but it wasn't like that. We were very affectionate. We always hugged or held hands. You know, you'd see that when you go back to Asia. These Asian kids, they walk around and they hold hands, or arm in arm, like girls do here. It was nothing weird, and that's very much the society I grew up in. All that affection with kids was absolutely normal.

At the same time, in the Philippines, homosexuality was very negative because the only gays that were labeled as gay were hairdressers. I remember there was this hairdresser . . . I forget what his name was . . . he had this huge Afro—because of the times—and was very slim, had tight pants and all that stuff. He was such a strange creature to look at. It was sort of a Filipino version of Quentin Crisp. Very effeminate, very affected, and dressed in a very unisex way. As a kid, it scared the hell out of me. I thought that was what I might look like because I was attracted to guys. So I decided, "I know I am attracted to men, but I'm not him. So I'm not gay. I know what gay is—it's that hairdresser. And I'm not him." The world was pretty black and white then.

In 1970, when I was nine years old, we came to the United States. At first, we kids thought we were just going to be here for the summer. I remember them saying, "We are going on the Jumbo Jet." It was the maiden voyage of the 747 in 1970. It was Flight 01 or something. The plane was so big it couldn't land in Manila. It had to land in Tokyo. So we had to fly to Tokyo to meet the plane there. We all got excited. I remember inviting all of my elementary school friends to the airport so they could wave good-bye. We just thought it was like a fun thing to do.

When we got here, we found out we weren't going back. It was a little tough. Mom and Dad had decided that this was the best place for them. Dad had wanted to be in politics in the Philippines ever since he was very young; he was groomed to be a politician. Then when he got a taste of it, he didn't like it and became badly disoriented. It was so unethical back there, a lot of hand-shaking, under-the-table kind of politics. He couldn't take it.

We had this idea of what the United States was supposed to look like, from the movies and all the T.V. shows that we saw, like *Mission: Impossible*. Everybody was blond and blue-eyed Caucasians. We didn't know there was such a thing as minorities in the States. And when we came to Los Angeles and we saw all these other nationalities, it was so neat because you didn't feel quite so alone. It was like we were all in this thing together.

In junior high and high school, I dated girls. It's funny. You know, when you go to the prom and the dances, you have to get your pictures taken, and they give you these wallet-size photos and the five-by-sevens for the girls to keep. Well, Mom kept all the wallet ones for all the dances that I'd been to, all the girlfriends that I'd had. There were quite a number of them. The only explanation I could give her was that, I wanted to go to the dances and you had to have a date. So I dated a lot. I think I treated all my girlfriends nice. I probably taught ninety-nine percent of them how to kiss. But I never went to bed with any of them. That was something I wasn't going to violate. It seemed like if it was going to be their first time, it would be unfair to have to be a first time with someone who was faking it.

Did you come out to your family eventually?

Yes, but I can't take full credit for it. There was this kid in my boys' choir in high school. I was a senior and he was a sophomore or junior. He had a crush on me. I allowed him to hang out with me because I knew he was gay. He was incredibly effeminate, and so he didn't have anybody to hang out with. A couple of weeks after I started my freshman year at USC [University of Southern California], I was working at 20th Century Insurance at night, and so I would get home like at one-thirty, get in bed, and I would get up in five hours. I would get up at seven to make it back to USC on time. So seven o'clock, I was just getting up to get to school. Dad came in to my bedroom and said, "Well, these parents called us last night. They were crying on the phone and they said that their son is gay and that you have turned him gay."

I was wondering. . . . First of all, I was wondering whether I was awake. And he said, "That's ridiculous, right? Do you know this kid?" And I said, "Ah . . . yes . . . he was in the boys' choir with me. I didn't turn him gay. He was gay when I met him." And Dad said, "But you're not gay, right?" And I said . . . I stopped for a moment. It dawned on me that that was my big opportunity. It was just a split-second decision: I could've so easily made the decision the other way and denied it. And things would've been very different in my life.

But I didn't. I fessed up and I said, "Yes, I am."

And right away, Dad said, "No, you're not." He said, "I want you and your brother here tonight, so we can have a family talk." And what my brother had to do with it, I had no idea. My older brother was just one year older. At that time, he had moved in with his roommate because he was going to Cal State Long Beach, I think.

That night we were there. . . . We walked in, and Mom and Dad were awfully serious sitting in the library at home. Mom was already crying. I mean, her eyes were already swollen. It was like she had half a day of this already. Of course, my brother was starting to sniffle, too. First, I had to come out to my brother. And he started crying. He said, "How come you never told me?" We hadn't talked for years when we were in high school. We had this tension when we were growing up. We saw each other coming down the hallway, and one of us would duck into one room so the other one could pass by. It was horrible.

On that night when I came out to him, it was like something new had begun. It was like all of a sudden we were talking for the first time. Mom started the conversation. She turned to my brother. She basically asked him if he was gay. My brother couldn't even get the words out. He just kind of nodded. Then she asked him, "Are you happy?" And he answered, "Yes. I'm very much in love with Marvin"—who was his roommate. Mom and Dad had already met him. He was a nice guy and worked for the bank. Mom said, "Well, your Dad and I just want you to be happy." That was it.

That was it!

And the rest of the evening they pointed the gun at me and said, "Now, you, what's all this bullshit about?" I had never been berated by my Dad so much in my life. "What about your girlfriend? What about all these girls you went out with? Are you doing this because we didn't let you study in France?" (Before college, I desperately wanted to study abroad.) I was trying to explain to him that I always knew who I was. I was trying so desperately to explain to him how different I was from the gays that they knew from the Philippines—like the hairdresser—that they pointed at, because I would've been embarrassed to have people look at me that way, to have them think I was like that.

I think my brother was a lot happier that evening than I was because all of a sudden I had so much to prove. My parents had come to expect that of my brother because of the way he had carried himself. I think he dated once when we were in school. When he was younger, what he wanted for his birthday was a cookbook and a cake mixer. He was baking carrot cakes when he was eleven years old. We shared a bedroom for a while before we really got on each other's nerves as teenagers. And there was this invisible line down the middle of our room. I kept my side of the room neat, but it was still a teenager's room. His side of the room was glass-chrome attaché, contemporary furniture, the latest module of furniture from the early 1970s. It looked like a showcase, and he was fourteen years old! He was an interior designer in the making. It was so prissy. [Laughs] There was no way they could've mistaken him for anything else.

Virgil Vang*

I was born in San Francisco in 1950, raised in a fourth-floor tenement in Chinatown. I remember dried fish and laundry hanging on a clothesline between apartments. A lot of traffic coming from the street. Music from the Chinese record stores, also, playing old Chinese tunes, Cantonese tunes, from Canton or Shanghai. A lot of old men and old women and young families all mixed together. It's sort of like being fermented. My family was kind of a lower middle class, but with definite middle-class aspirations, as far as education [was concerned]. We ate pretty simply, like cabbage, tuna fish, sometimes those *lep-chaun*, those sausages, Campbells soup over macaroni. But that was fine. We just put our energies elsewhere. I went to Chinese school. I didn't like it because the Chinese school at that time was controlled by *Kuomintang*. They didn't talk about China at all, just Chinese history until 1949 and all the provinces of China. That was it. American school was all Chinese with white teachers mainly. That was okay, too. If you grow up under these conditions, you really have no alternative. You don't know anything else.

I lived in Taipei for a couple of years in the early 1970s. I was pretty promiscuous and exposed to gay life in Asia. For me, it was quite liberating. All my lovers were Asian. I got around quite a bit. I had some lovers in Hong Kong and Taipei, different places. They ranged from airline stewards to journalists, to hustlers, waiters, all kinds of people. I think it's actually in Asia when I came out. When I came back here and moved to L.A., it was different. I felt separated out more: I'm an Asian American here, and then gay here, and this and that. You're just much more aware of all these differences. In a way, it was sort of a letdown here.

This is very different from what most people would think of homosexuality in Asia. They would think there's much more taboo or separation back in Asia.

I think people just have different stereotypes of Asia that are not based in any kind of reality. When I was in Asia, really more important than sexuality, even gender, was probably class. If you're from upper middle class or working class, that really makes a big difference in who you would hang around with and your [life] expectations.

Let me give you an example. In Taipei once, I was sitting by the railroad station, smoking a cigarette. This guy came up to me, an older guy. He sat next to me. He had a leather belt, *pei-dai*, and he was rolling it and unrolling it in his hands. We were talking Chinese. He said, "This is for export. It's real leather." Blah, blah, blah. He thought I was a country boy or something. I didn't really need the belt, but then I was curious. So I got on his motorcycle and we went off to some Japanese part of town where they had these old Japanese houses. We made love. Then he dropped me off somewhere else in his motorcycle. That's one kind of encounter.

The other is, I would go to these fancy hotel bars and sit there and drink. And I would run into people. That was usually the middle class. In any case, I found it easier to be gay Asian in Asia. Maybe because I was younger.

I mean, let's face it, I was privileged. I was middle class in Asia. I could speak English and Chinese. It gave me access to all kinds of groups. I was sort of a free spirit, young and good looking. I usually would have older Chinese lovers, like in their forties. But I also would have younger ones, people my age, in their twenties. It really didn't matter. But here, when I came to L.A., older white guys and younger Asian men and this and that, it was all very . . . a little more set, less mobile, in a sense.

Hoang Phan

My childhood in Vietnam was actually quite wonderful. I was from a middle-class neighborhood. From Western society, that would be considered poor. But in Vietnam, it was sort of in the middle. I remember the war, the threats of it all the time. I remember friends. I went to a private boarding school to become a priest. If you were a Catholic priest, you wouldn't have to go to war.

My Mom was a housewife. My Dad was working for the U.S. government. His boss was a major in the army. He was like his gofer, almost like a personal assistant: He took his boss around and did errands for him. Dad drove the car. It was always a neat thing because you didn't see cars back then. He'd give us rides in his automobile. I was exposed to American men, much, much more than women, in the military. I thought they were extremely attractive. I found the American men to be extremely sexy because they were bigger and they were taller. And I was always attracted to older guys, rather than younger men. I associated hair with maturity, body hair, like the sense of becoming a sexual being. The weird thing was that I never consciously thought about it. It's just one of those things that is instinctual. You react to it, rather than being told what it is.

That was all during my sexual awakening period, even though I had a wonderful relationship with another Vietnamese boy in the boarding school that I went to. He was a soccer captain—hence my fascination with soccer players. I remember very clearly the day I met him. I was walking across the field, and he and his athletic friends were playing soccer. He would literally stop the game, make everybody stop and wait until I passed the field. Then they would resume playing. Then I would notice more frequently that he would be where I would be. We got to know each other. I remember this: If we got back from recess and if he didn't bring me a present, I wouldn't talk to him for a week. That's how I was.

Our relationship started to progress into a physical level. If you could imagine this beautiful chapel that had benches where you sit and things to kneel on. I would be sitting like this on the bench [sitting with head back] and he would be kneeling [from the pew] behind me and blowing little kisses on my neck. I thought that was the most sensuous thing. I didn't really associate it with sex, but with tenderness. I didn't really think, "Okay, this is gay or this is not gay." I didn't know that it was not natural, that I was not supposed to do this, that this was supposed to only happen between men and women. What I was feeling for this man is what I think women or men should be feeling for each other. I knew that I was attracted to men, but I didn't say to myself, I'm a *gay* person, because, well, I wasn't funny-looking. I didn't have two sexes, and I didn't dress up in women's clothing. I didn't have these characteristics that we associated as being gay. I didn't make the connection that being gay just means that you're loving or you can love a person of the same sex. I thought gay was something more negative.

After that, we forayed into kissing. He knew what to do. But we never progressed into the sexual arena. Coming from a very traditional, Catholic background, I told him that we couldn't do anymore because we weren't married yet.

Then my family left Vietnam in 1975. My dad's boss basically told him that Saigon was going to collapse and the Communists were going to take over. He then gave my father a choice, either to stay or to leave the country. I had a lot to do with the departure of the family for two reasons. I always wanted to go to America to study. I had the grades, but we didn't have the means to do so. And second, it had to do with being gay [my attraction to men], believe it or not. I knew that in America it would be easier to be gay. I didn't know why. I was fifteen. It wasn't like I read books about America. So I told my parents, "You know what? You can stay in Vietnam and all of us would be sent to concentration camps and all the education you put us through would be a total waste. The future is not here. The future is in America."

Notes

1. These narrators' experiences support what many historians have suggested to be the military's contributions to the growth of gay communities during and after World War II: "Postwar L.A., seemingly all sunshine and surfer boys, epitomized the American dream. Many a gay serviceman moved to L.A. or San Francisco instead of going back to his hometown. Gay bars sprang up everywhere." George Haggerty, ed., *Gay Histories and Cultures: An Encyclopedia* (New York: Garland Publishing, 2000), 548. See also Allan Berube, *Coming Out Under Fire: The History of Gay Men and Women in World War II* (New York: Free Press, 1990); John D'Emilio, *Sexual Politics, Sexual Communities: The Making of a Homosexual Minority in the United States, 1940–1970* (Chicago: University of Chicago Press, 1983); and George Chauncey, *Gay New York: Gender, Urban Culture and the Making of the Gay Male World, 1890–1940* (New York: Basic Books, 1994).

2. See also D'Emilio, 1983.

3. Felix Racelis, "Bill Matsumoto Finding Community, Fighting Discrimination," *The Advocate*, no. 363 (March 17, 1983): 25.

2

Caution and Abandonment on the L.A. Nightscape

WORK WAS WORK

Lacking knowledge and information about gay life in their own city, an earlier generation of gay Asian men had to rely on an informal network of friends and acquaintances to gain access into the gay world of Los Angeles. In 1964, before Roy Kawasaki became familiar with the gay scene in L.A., he was living with roommates at an apartment that was only half a block from a bar called The Castaway (corner of Virgil and Monroe). One hot summer day, Roy decided to go down to the bar and have a beer. As he walked into The Castaway, he noticed that the clientele was all white. He said to himself, "My God, there are only men in this place." Perhaps shocked by this realization, Roy walked right out of there. It was only years later that he found out that The Castaway was one of the more popular bars that gay people went to. At that time, he simply didn't know what a gay bar was. A year later, Roy met a gay Hispanic man in school. Together, they went to different bars all over the city: Red Raven (on La Brea at Melrose), The Klondike, and The Crown Jewel, which populated a much livelier Downtown L.A. then. "He was the one who opened the doors for me to the gay bars and the bathhouses," Roy said. "I slowly came out that way."

Harry Park moved to Los Angeles in 1958 from his hometown, Honolulu, Hawaii, when he was twenty-three. At that time, he was working for American Airlines. Harry was no stranger to the travel industry. In Hawaii, he had worked as a messenger for a travel agency and later a steamship company. In fact, he came to L.A. by ship and docked in Long Beach. According to Harry, being in the travel industry, he was able to meet quite a number of gay men, some of whom became his companions as he went to various bars all over town.

Working in the field of social work in the 1970s, Charles Chang, also a transplant from Hawaii, met a few co-workers who were gay. "One of them introduced me to the gay community," he said. "He was a lot younger than I was, but he'd been out. Having lived in California, he knew where to go. So he took me to my first bathhouse, my first bar, which was Ripples [in Long Beach]. We discovered other bars, here in Long Beach. Some of them are still here, like the Mindshaft, Silver Fox. And some other bars just disappeared, went out of business."

Although gay Asian men like Harry and Charles were able to make gay acquaintances at work (a majority of whom, by the way, were non-Asian), they also saw a clear delineation between work life and social life. Many of them felt the need to keep their private lives separate from work to avoid gossips, but sometimes also to protect their livelihood. And at a time when dancing with another man and holding hands in public could get gay men in trouble with the police, they had to be careful even in gay environments. Harry Park remembers, "Oh, it was terrible in those days. You couldn't touch anyone. You couldn't walk around with a drink. You couldn't do things that are normal, and I mean normal even for someone who was straight. It was just primitive." Caution was a way of life. The process by which they came to reveal themselves to both gay and straight co-workers (or to be discovered by them) could be a clumsy one.

Charles Chang

When I first came to L.A., I wasn't really sure what gay life was about. I just wanted to play it day by day and see what would happen, see where my life would take me. I was working at the Metropolitan State Hospital at that time. Interestingly, I met a co-worker who wanted a roommate, and we decided we would get a place together. It was funny: Later on when I talked to people after I left the hospital, I found out the gossip was that we were lovers because he was very effeminate. He was the one who got married to a woman. I was the one who turned out to be gay!

I'm not sure if this line of work [social work] draws a predominantly gay population because it's a helping field, because it's a people field. At work I met three co-workers who were gay. We weren't openly gay. Everybody was in the closet at work. One was an older fellow. He was probably in his fifties by then. He lived with his lover, but I think it wasn't spoken. We had office parties at his house, and his lover wouldn't be there.

At work, it was like "Don't Ask, Don't Tell." Yes, there would be discrimination. I know a lot of my clients or their relatives probably wouldn't work with me if they knew I was gay. The clients I worked with were mental health patients. They had enough to deal with already. And that's not something that I needed to put between me and them, one more perception of alienation they had to have.

Roy Kawasaki

I was still struggling with my sexuality when I started teaching for the LAUSD [Los Angeles Unified School District]. At that time [late 1960s], work was work, and my personal life was my personal life. That's how I kept it. I got along fine with the faculty. There was just no reason to reveal my sexuality.

There was this principal, I remember. I was teaching sixth grade at the time. He was always coming into my room and just harassed me about my teaching style or whatever, you know. He was always on top of me. Being so insecure to begin with—I was still a novice—I was getting so nervous, to the point of having a nervous breakdown from this man. One time, he came up to me and said, "Oh, Roy. Come here. I want you to look at this. Someone has drawn a penis on the wall." And he made a point that I saw that. He wasn't asking me to do anything about it. He just said, "Look at this." I mean, why should he take the time to show me that it was there? He should've called the custodians. I felt he was always harassing me.

Fortunately, I left the school not too long after to pursue my special education credential. But do you know I found out later that this principal turned out to be gay? He had three or four marriages and a daughter. He came out around the time he was to retire. Back then, some people talked about him, but then they always said he was married. I got to think maybe what he was trying to do was to find out something about me.

During the early years of my teaching career, there was a fear about being discovered about being gay. In one of my educational classes, my professor brought up the fact that there was this one person who was picked up [arrested] for . . . I don't know what he was doing . . . but he was gay. He was cleared eventually and was able to get his teaching credential. So she said, "If you have something like that, please let us know. We can clear this up." So I thought it couldn't be that bad. But I think, during those early years, you just didn't know what would happen if you were found out, because people weren't really sophisticated enough then about gayness. Everything was still closeted. The vice squads were always out there, wanting to pick people up.

I did meet several gay teachers. One of them I met in my first year teaching—I forgot how we got to know about each other—but we're still friends today.

At that time, did you have conversations about being gay or what you did over the weekend or outside of work?

Yes, I think we discussed things like that, as long as there was no one around us. [Laughs] We did, or we would go out and have drinks together after school.

André Ting

I came out in 1970 in Texas. When I came out to the Los Angeles area, I was still trying to discover myself or trying to make up for lost time. So I was going out every night, mostly partying. Like seven nights a week. It was like a double life, yes. In the daytime, I was working part-time as an instructor. I would dress conservatively as an instructor. I'd take a nap in the afternoon and every night I went out to party. I would put on the fashionable bar clothes at that time, which would be tank tops and things that are revealing because, you know gay people, especially when they were just discovering themselves, they really want to let down their inhibitions. It's one time they can let their hair down. So I would say, yes, at nighttime I would live it up, with loud music and dancing for four to five hours a night. At that time, I lived in Orange County, but I partied everywhere, all the way from Orange County to San Fernando Valley. I hit all the bars.

The 1970s were really a leftover of the 1960s, more or less. The period of the 1960s was a sexual revolution; it was a time when young people discovered free love. They had sex for fun, and not for relationships or any commitment or emotional ties. And the 1970s were an extension of that. So after the bar, we would just say, *your place or mine*. So we would go home and have sex. I don't mean to brag, but I did work out. I did wear tank tops. I did have compliments. No, I never had any trouble. In fact, I had too much sex at that time. I used to keep a diary of every person that I went home with, the names, the age, and so on. But after one hundred partners, I quit. I kept doing it, but I just did not keep a record. After a few years, there were just too many. It was just too wild at that time. I would quickly make friends with the people in the bars, friends of all races. At that time, we were all young. We just became very good friends. We socialized not just in the bars, but later on outside the bars, too. For example, when I applied for U.S. citizenship, they needed to interview somebody who knew me. The person who came to testify about my conduct is a gay man I met in a bar.

Tak Yamamoto

When I worked for the federal government at one point in the 1960s, there was this deal about not revealing any of your lifestyle or you could be fired. You'd hear other gay people say the same thing. We always used a different pronoun. We never said "he"; we said "she" while we talked about our date over the weekend because you didn't want to reveal to your co-workers that you were gay or you had a lifestyle other than this job.

I got the job that I have now in the Voters Registrar's Office in the late 1960s. I think after a while, the women in the office had the inclination that I might be gay. And they talked with the supervisor—oh, it was probably about twenty women that I had to interact with—and they had a little meeting about whether or not Tak was gay. The problem that they sought out in the end was, Did it matter that I was gay? At that time, I had to go and check out on different things for the elections. I had to go and meet other people in other departments. I had to work with County sheriffs because of our operations, [like] securities, transportation. . . . They were wondering if I would be able to talk to the butch sheriff types, you know, because after all, I was gay and I was flamboyant. So they decided to let me do it and find out if I could. So I did it. It worked out fine. It had no repercussions. I talked to a woman that I knew well afterward. She said, "You know, we had this little meeting, and this all came up. And they said, 'Well, he does okay, and so what difference does it make if he is gay or not?' " In this case, they couldn't have fired me for being gay, but they had to acknowledge the fact that being gay was not an obstacle in working with straights, in this case, straight cops.

So you think most people would understand . . .

Well, I don't know about understand. I think most people are willing to take you on with that part of it anyway. They were looking for people to do stuff. I mean, counting bodies was more important than what his difference was. I'm sure we'd never be friends, but that's not my problem. It's, Can I be an effective manager? Can we plan this together? Are you going to have a problem with me directing you? That worked out.

I know, for a promotion, it did make a difference, though. I was at the department, then, for seven years. I got all the promotions for the intermediate level, and I trained everybody for the top level. I never got it myself. So finally one year, the personnel officer—Peter, he knew I was gay and I knew Peter was gay—and his associate, who was the training person, decided that they would train me to fill this position. I went through the whole training, but the same attitude came up again. But Peter and his associate said, "No, why don't we instead put Tak in that position now and not bring somebody else and see if he works out?" I worked out fine. They had no reason then to hold me back. So I was thankful for the personnel officer and his associate because I would not have gotten anywhere with the management.

ALL THE INFORMATION YOU EVER WANTED

Things began to change as the gay community in Los Angeles became more institutionalized and visible. One of the signs of this was the flourishing of gay publications, especially the local-based community periodicals that informed readers of sites and events of interest to them. While the informal networks continued to be an important source of information, many gay Asian men also relied on these "gay rags" as a map to discover places that would otherwise remain underground to them. In addition, they took advantage of the classified section to meet new friends and possible lovers, much as later generations of gay men flood the Internet nowadays.

Just as importantly, for those gay Asian men who lived too far from metropolitan hubs of gay activities, these publications validated their same-sex attraction as something that was shared by others, thereby creating an imagined community at a time when a physical one might be out of reach for some. For example, in the early 1970s, Leo Joslin was a teenager growing up in (and out of) Atascadero, a small town in the central coast of California with a population of about twelve to thirteen thousand. The town was so isolated that Leo remembers that, for driver's education, they had to drive ten to fifteen miles to Paso Robles just to practice on stoplights because Atascadero didn't have one for a long time. "We didn't have a movie theater, either," says Leo. For information about gay communities in the more metropolitan areas of the state, he had to rely on what he calls "underground papers," particularly the *L.A. Free Press* and *Berkeley Barb*. Like Paul Chen, who traveled from Fullerton to Los Angeles to buy a copy of the *Advocate*, Leo also had to travel a great distance to catch a glimpse of gay life on paper. "I was able to get both [the *Free Press* and the *Barb*] through a local newsstand in San Luis Obispo," he says, which is fifteen miles away from his hometown.

Besides these community publications, many gay men also found validation in novels with gay themes and characters. When Hoang Phan was in high school, he was a new immigrant, and to improve his English skills and to sate urges that he couldn't yet name at that time, he read romance novels, such as Andrew Holleran's *Dancer from the Dance*. Unlike the "gay rags," Hoang could read these novels freely at home because his parents, being limited in English, did not suspect the contents of these books. "I read all the trashy, romantic, Harlequin novels, but it's gay subject," Hoang said. "No pictures, though. I would tear off the covers. It was safer that way. They [his parents] had no idea what I was reading. They would assume that I was reading school work. So I got away with a lot of stuff." Stanley Rebultan confesses that he "cried so many times when I read the novel *The Frontrunner*," by Patricia Nell Warren. "I wrote a letter to her," he says. "I asked her the question, When will I find my dream lover? This book is so realistic to me. I never got a response from her, but that was an outlet of my yearning at that time. So I always have this fantasy about having someone on a regular basis or maybe even living with somebody." Until gay men like Hoang, Stanley, and Leo could find an actual community, these words and images would have to suffice.

Stanley Rebultan

I came to the United States in 1972 [from the Philippines]. Right after I arrived here was when I got married to this woman I was engaged to. It lasted for a long time until I started discovering what I really wanted. I had the feeling [of being attracted to men] even when I was in the Philippines, but I didn't explore it. I had a different kind of life at the time, but there was this feeling nagging inside of me. About three years after my arrival here—you know, you meet people, you're exposed to what you see, what you feel—I got my first copy of the *Advocate*. At that time, it was at every corner of the street. And I was like a thief, putting those quarters—I think it was fifty cents or seventy-five cents at the time—in the machine, in case someone I knew might see me pulling out a copy.

I started reading what was going on in the gay community. I learned that there were pockets of groups of people all over the country who had been organizing, who had started this resistance movement way back in [1969] that is called the Stonewall riots. I read the *Advocate* on a regular basis and I was becoming aware of all of this. Later on, I jumped to the classified ads, and that's how I started meeting people. Now I did this all secretly. I was sneaking around [behind my wife's and my brother's back], although I had not done any kind of sexual activity. It's like I was preparing myself for a steppingstone or something.

Pretty soon [in the mid-1970s], I started friendships with people that I met. They were like my peer group, people that I hung out with. And then all of a sudden—this was the beginning of the disco era—I found myself going out dancing with these people. Now, at the time, although I would love to do it, I was paranoid dancing with another man. But you get used to it. Prior to this, the manager whom I had worked for used to bring me to this topless dancing bar. We used to go there and get drunk. The gay bars were like a 180 degree change. That was the first time I saw two guys kissing. I thought I would like to do that. I was very innocent at the time. My feelings were well suppressed. . . . You know when you look at mustard for the first time, you know it's mustard because you've read about it. You know it's for hot dogs. But you see how it looks on a plate and you say, "It looks like shit, like baby shit." And then you taste it. Now you can never eat a hot dog without mustard. So that's how it was. [Two men kissing] looked nasty at first, but it was good. Okay? Once I tried it, it was good. Now if I look at mustard, I forget what it reminded me of the first time I saw it. Because I already accepted it.

Did you meet a lot of gay Asians through these ads? Did they take out ads?

No, because, you know, my penchant at the time was this Nordic type—blue eyes, blond, muscular. It has changed a lot now, but that was my ideal. . . . It was not really idealism; it was a fantasy. You cannot just find that Nordic type, especially when you're older. You don't have that attraction anymore. Now, the ideal is a good person, someone who understands me, someone I can communicate with, someone who has similar likings. That comes first, rather than the looks. The looks are just superficial. There're no more raging hormones.

Where do you think that Nordic type fantasy came from?

You're looking for something different. So the fact that my upbringing in the Philippines where I came from, there was no blue-eyed, blond, white person over there; it was like my fantasy. Exotic. But over here, as they say, if you're exposed to the plenty, you're looking for that plenty. So I think I had neglected my appreciation of Asian–Asian love. When I was in Yokohoma [at an international AIDS conference in 1994], I was so intrigued by the way Japanese guys looked. See, that was the plenty. "My God," I said. "What was I thinking before?" Over here, if there were this nice-looking Japanese guy interspersed with all the other people, I wouldn't have paid him any attention.

Paul Bautista

My brother would take these incredibly long showers. One time, when he went to the showers, I went to his drawers. I don't know what I was looking for, maybe something that I thought he had taken from me. I pulled the lower drawer down, and there were all these *Playgirl* magazines that he had. (That's kind of how I figured out early on that he was gay, too.) So it was like clockwork. Anytime if I was home and if I would see him go to the showers—I knew he would be in there for two hours—I would have at least two hours to go through his magazines. I would take the ones from the bottom or the middle, so he wouldn't know they were missing, in case he pulled out of the showers before I could get them back in there. He paid for all these issues of *Playgirl*, I'd say, for a good year. I read all of them.

At some point, they mentioned the *Advocate* being a gay magazine. So early in my senior year [in high school], I was in Hollywood and I made a point to look for this magazine at the newsstand. Back then, the *Advocate* was like a throwaway newspaper. The ink would rub off as soon as you touch it. (It wasn't like a slick magazine like it is now, all done in color.) So I picked this thing up. There it was—all the information you ever wanted. It really scared the hell out of me. I would've never dreamt it. I thought if I were to be able to go to bed with a man once or twice in my life, that would've been fine. That would've been to me worth living, waiting for those moments. I would've gotten married and had kids, and if somewhere along the line, I would meet someone and fall in love with him and have an affair, that would've been fine. The idea that people actually lived their entire lives with the person they actually loved was—ah—it was better than Santa Claus.

In the middle of this issue [of the *Advocate*] was a humongous, three-dimensional diorama of different places where kids hung out and so forth. There was this place called the Odyssey where kids went to if they were over eighteen but below twenty-one. I wasn't eighteen, but if you're not eighteen, you pretend you're eighteen. Once you're eighteen, you pretend you're twenty-one. So I snuck in there one time, drank juice for the most part. There were a lot of straight kids there as well, a real mix. I met people like David Cassidy, and somebody told me that there was this really neat place that played much better music. It was called Studio One. So a couple of weekends later, I went there. This was like 1977. At Studio One, I met this guy who told me about this place where Asians would go called the River Club. And the River Club was just right on Riverside Drive, just east of Los Feliz Boulevard. It was really a neat little place. I mean, it looked horrible in the daytime. But at night, they had a whole patio area, couple of pinball machines and a pool table, and a tiny dance floor. It really wasn't all gay Asians. Half of the bar was Latino. The other half—most of the patio—was the Asians.

Remember I was telling you I was stealing magazines from the back of my brother's drawer. He actually had this one issue of the *Advocate*. (I don't know whether it was an earlier issue than the one I got.) It had this layout of this incredible bathhouse called the Hollywood Spa, with little cartoons of guys walking around in towels through mazes and rooms and gym rooms and so forth. And I thought, "Gym rooms—I could at least get to that." So once again, I took my fake I.D. and went in there and pretended I was a student and I lived nearby and I wanted a gym that I could work out in. Of course, I'm sure the bouncer knew I was all of seventeen, but he let me in anyway because I was good for business. So I went in there. I couldn't believe it. All these guys were actually walking around in towels. Some of them were just totally naked! It was such an overload to a point where it scared you. They were playing David Bowie's "Young Americans" over and over again. To this day, when I hear David Bowie's "Young Americans" I still think of the Hollywood Spa. Everything smelled new that evening; I think they just re-carpeted. There was this huge grand staircase and there's this porn star—I don't remember his name—putting on a show for everyone, and people were just oohing and aahing. It was like out of a dream. It was amazing. Yet at the same time, you felt so . . . because I hadn't discovered the River Club, I felt that everybody was so white and buff and bigger bodies and I was just this scrawny kid that no one was going to want. Boy, was I wrong! [Laughs]

It was an eventful night. It was a scary, exciting, and eventful night. I had sex. I remember going down this maze, getting pulled in somewhere. Before I knew it, I was inside someone. At first I thought I was getting a blow job, but all of a sudden, his feet were over my legs. I was so confused, but I was enjoying it anyway. And when I finally figured out what was going on—it was very dark—I realized that someone was not sucking me. I was in it. I was expecting him to be in pain. When I had seen pictures of intercourse, I thought the guy on the bottom must be really putting up with this or getting paid for it or something. But this guy was not moaning in pain. He was really, really enjoying it. And pop, he was done, and I didn't even have time to cum. He was gone. I remember he wiped me off and shoved me off his module or whatever that little space was. And there I was, just standing there, wondering what the hell happened.

I went to the showers and then walked around some more. Got into one of the rooms and it was like an orgy going on. A lot of oral sex. It was so bizarre. By that time, my stomach was churning so badly that I had to get home. I knew Dad would get home at eleven, and I wanted to beat him to it. I didn't want him to miss me or notice the engine was hot and ask me where I'd been. I hit the Hollywood Freeway at 10:45. I was so sure that I was going to see Dad's car on the freeway. There were thousands of cars going on the freeway at any second, but I was so sure that he was going to see me. I was that paranoid! I was so afraid that I had to turn off and go to a gas station and throw up.

And of course, I went to school the following morning, looking for signs. Back then, it was VD [venereal disease]. I mean, we saw so many things about syphilis and gonorrhea. I looked at myself and I was just waiting for my peter to hurt. I was looking at zits on my back, anything, you know, I could find. I was so scared that I was going to come down with VD. It was at least three months before I had enough nerve to go back to a gay disco.

David Hong

In high school, because school was in a different part of town, we would have to take the bus. Well, I stopped at a newsstand because it's the place I always walked by to buy newspapers. And I happened to see some gay literature there. I saw magazines. Pictorial magazines. I would buy the newspaper and ask to buy that. The newspaperman very, very discreetly wrapped it in the newspaper and I made my purchase. It's kind of like telling me that he knew of my discretion and helped me along with it. Every so often, I would go there and buy it. They [the magazines] had these mail-order things. So I sent for them. Being stupid, I used my real name and everything. Well, that stuff came to the house. One day, I had a piece of mail that came. And it was already opened. And whoever opened it—my guess is my mother because she gave me the mail—didn't say anything at all. So I opened it in my privacy and saw what it was. There was literature to buy more magazines, et cetera. Why would she have given it to me and not say anything? Typical Asian parents, you know. So my guess is, growing up young, she's probably known, but there is denial.

[At some point,] I went to North Carolina. At Duke [University], there were no gay Asian students that I identified with. When I went to the clubs, I was the only Asian at the time. I met people from University of North Carolina, Chapel Hill. There were clubs in Raleigh, and we'd go over there as well. So I met people from North Carolina State and et cetera. Eventually, during my rounds, I met other Asians: but only two other Asians, one Filipino and one Chinese. The Filipino, I can't exactly remember where he's from, but the Chinese guy was from Savannah, Georgia. He was maybe second-generation Chinese. He was raised in the South, yes. He was a music major. I lost touch with him. But anyway, my very first sexual experience with another Asian was with him. All my sexual relationships back then—or I won't say relationships, but sexual encounters—were with whites and blacks. He was my first Asian. I enjoyed it so much that what I did was to seek out other Asians. But in North Carolina, that was it. There were no others. Just two or three of us.

I moved to L.A. in May of 1981. Being already exposed to the gay community through other cities that I'd been in, my first notion was of course to identify the activities here in Los Angeles. I wanted to find out if there were any gay rags. Obviously the places to find out were the adult gay bookstores. At the Pleasure Chest, I found the *Frontiers*, and it tells you about Circus Disco, the Odyssey—which was by the Beverly Center—Studio One, et cetera. So I went to these places.

From reading the *Frontiers*, they talked about the upcoming Christopher Street West gay pride events [in June], which was seeking volunteers. So I called. I met some key people there who assigned me to running the placards for the groups, which had to stand on Crescent Heights [Avenue, where the parade begins] to form themselves in an order according to a numbering system. So it was my task to monitor the groups. And on the day of the event, I had to put the signs up, get the groups in order to start them off.

So interestingly enough, A/PLG was a contingent in the parade. When their turn came, some of them saw me and asked me, "Come and march with us." I said I couldn't. So they just talked to me about who they were, what they did, et cetera. They also told me about the upcoming Fourth of July picnic that they had in Griffith Park every year. So I went to the picnic and I met more A/PLG people there and got to know what the organization was about. It interested me because it was my first exposure with other gay APIs.

I'VE NEVER SEEN YOU GUYS

Before gay Asian bars like the River Club (which was owned by a Caucasian man) or gay Asian organizations like the A/PLG came into existence, there were few places where one could find a significant congregation of gay Asian men. Reggie Bogan, a Caucasian man who in the 1980s became active with the A/PLG and was employed as a bartender at Mugi's, a gay Asian bar in Los Angeles, ran a bar in Hollywood called the Stopover from 1973 to 1977. He did not recall seeing any Asian patrons during that period. In fact, even Reggie, no stranger to the bar scene in Los Angeles and a one-time bar-owner himself, didn't become "aware of Asian gays until I started going to Mugi's in the early 1980s [as a patron before he joined the staff]." Of course, gay Asians have been frequenting bars for decades, but in the 1970s, their presence was scattered and they seldom traveled in groups of even just two. The few who eventually found each other did so often through mutual non-Asian friends, particularly the rice queens, those who have an exclusive sexual interest in Asian men. Nevertheless, old-timers often comment on how rare it was to find another gay Asian man in a gay establishment. So startling was such an encounter that often they didn't know how they should react. Should they nod or wink in acknowledgment of their commonality? Dare they approach each other to make conversation? Perhaps not certain what this racial commonality could mean in a gay context, many simply looked away.

Ted Hune*

One of the friends I met through the [personal] ads was a rice queen, Randy. We didn't hit it off sexually, but we became good friends. He moved in and became a roommate of mine. And then through Randy, because he dated a lot of Asians, I met other Asians. They were friends of his, and since we were roommates, I started hanging around with them, too. I remember we went to the Office once. It was a dance club in the [San Fernando] Valley. We were the only Asians there. I remember there were five of us in our group—one Chinese, two Japanese, a Filipino, and myself. I was kind of standing on the side; I wasn't dancing at the time, and this Caucasian guy came up to me. He said, "Where did you guys come from? Are you all related? Because you're all so cute." Because we were all young at the time. So I said, "Oh, Thank you. No, we're not related. We're just friends." He said, "I've never seen you guys." "No, we don't come to this club very much."

And then I started going to the River Club with them. Actually at the River Club I met one of my closest friends, Nguyen. This is 1975. I went to the River Club with my roommate Randy and some of his Asian friends. As soon as we walked into the River Club, Nguyen got eye contact with Randy. All the time we were there, Nguyen was really cruising him like mad. Because I'm not a night person, I drove myself. So I left early. The next morning, when I woke up, there was Nguyen. In my place. Randy was still sleeping. And then we started talking, and we became friends. Well, Nguyen was in a relationship. Only his lover was living in Thailand at the time. He was in the [American military] services. So Nguyen was here by himself. He was the first Vietnamese gay person that I hung around with. This is 1975. So he came over just before the fall of Saigon. He stopped dating Randy obviously, and Randy didn't want to get serious with him because he was already in a relationship. So we became close. We're still friends right now.

Andy C.

In 1969, I came to L.A. as a student because, in the beginning, I wasn't sure if I wanted to stay or not. I was in a business college. At the same time, I was also going to a beauty school. You know how people back home talked about America from all these things they'd seen on television. You know, a lot of the foreign-born Asians looked at all these T.V. shows and movies and thought, "Oh, they [American men] are so caring." It's like hero-worshipping. America is, oh gosh, what a place to be, like heaven, Shangri-La, whatever. But when I got here, I realized that it wasn't a bed of roses. The first year was the worst year for anyone who came alone, not knowing anybody, not knowing how to drive, not knowing all the streets and so forth. That was frightening. I remember the first year I was here, it was worse than El Niño.[1] Getting into the cold and rain, I ended up practically sick with cold and fever for at least three months. By the end of the year, I almost went home, but I stuck on because of pride. My parents would help me, but because of my own determination to come here, I was not going to ask them for anything. I almost called them to say I was ready to go home to Malaysia. They would send me the ticket. They'd be glad to.

So after the first year, I applied for a green card. The immigration officer who interviewed me at the time told me I had to quit beauty college. I thought it was strange at first. I said to myself, "Could they really be that direct to me?" Then I understood what caused it.

Being in beauty college means you're gay?

More or less. It was probably not acceptable here, although I thought the States to be so open-minded, so easy, with so many things going on. I was totally surprised when that came up. Back home, I would walk with my male friends, and we would hold hands in the streets or hug or something. No one would think anything of it. But when I got to L.A., if you were seen holding hands, they would crucify you, like calling you faggots. It was a little hard for me to accept.

What about your social life?

Those days were kind of restricted too, until I got my citizenship in 1976. You have to realize that I was not a green-card holder in the beginning. I couldn't get in trouble. So I had to be very cautious. I had a friend from Penang who was here maybe a year or two ahead of me. We used to room together in the beginning. We were leaning on each other for strength, so we dared go places and not be alone. He had a few friends. I'm more of an introvert. So I used to go with his friends, and once in a while, we would go to bars. We would go to Oil Can Harry's, Queen Mary on Ventura Boulevard, and the Redwood Room in L.A. I was more cautious than him, I guess, because I always felt, gee, this is a big city and you have to always be cautious in a big city. I wouldn't say that I didn't talk to anybody, but there was always the thought of being caught in a raid and what would I do then? Most of my friends then were from Thailand. I had one or two Malaysian friends. That was about it. I did have another friend from Hong Kong. They were pretty wild then because they'd been here much longer than I had. Their attitude was a little different because they knew eventually they would be going back home. This created a "couldn't care less" attitude somewhat.

After the first few years, I more or less knew what was going on and how to adapt myself, how to get around. When I got my citizenship, I felt more at ease, that I could do things that I didn't have to worry about, like being raided in a bar or being at the wrong place at the wrong time. I was never in a raid, but once I was at a bar right after a raid. That was enough to scare me. I heard some yelling. I wouldn't say loud screams, but carrying-ons like somebody probably didn't know how to handle the situation. Some rough-housing and things like that. It was enough to frighten me. I still remember those moments.

At times, I would go to drag contests and shows, most of the major ones, like the national cotillions. For a while, I won quite a few contests. In fact, one of the reasons I finally decided to move out of the circle was, after a while, I felt there was a lot of jealousy in these contests, even among my Asian friends who used to compete with me. And I had enough. I was always happy for them when they won. But if I won, I'd hear all kinds of negative talk. So eventually I backed out. I had my time. Let somebody else have theirs.

Andy C., Doug Chin, Roy Kawasaki, and Tak Yamamoto

[The following is an excerpt of a conversation I had with Andy C., Doug Chin, Roy Kawasaki, and Tak Yamamoto about the gay scene in L.A. during the 1960s and 1970s.]

Roy: There are two raids that I remember. One was at the Cannon Club. It was a private club on Topanga up in the hills.

Eric: You had to be a member to get in?

Roy: Yes, white men.

Tak: The membership of the Cannon Club was white. You could be invited by a white person. It was owned by a policeman.

Roy: They were dancing. And then somebody announced something. A light flashed and they all changed partners. Gay women and men would partner up. And the other one that I remember was a house party. After the bar sometimes, people would pass out addresses where they would be having a party. This was somewhere in Hollywood. I guess the noise was too much for the neighbors and they called the cops. Somebody mentioned the police, and we all fled. The whole house just cleared out, going for the doors. That was kind of interesting.

Tak: I have to say the same kind of thing. I went to a bar on Slauson in a black area. It was also a cop who owned it, so he was probably alerted before. They also had that big red light on the ceiling. Before the cops came in, the light would go on. I also went to several of the parties in the Silverlake area. Once I went with my friend Ernest, and I parked my car in an area that I knew I could get to. Once inside, Ernest and I looked around to see where our escape was going to be if we had to run. You just did that automatically. You didn't run out of the front door because that's where the cops were going to come in. So we tried to figure out how close to the back door we were and if we could run down the street. Twice I can say for sure they were going to bust us, but we were the lucky ones. We got out in time.

Roy: Also the bar scene you had to be careful at the time about the vice squad.

Tak: Remember what they would call entrapment. They [the vice squad] would go to the john, and the queen would come out later busted. She said, "He showed me everything. He was in there shaking it up. What was I supposed to do?" But that wasn't the way the cops would report it, "He approached me, and he touched me."

Roy: I remember sometimes when I went to the bar and buy a drink, they [the bartenders] would say, "Be careful. There is a vice squad in here. So don't . . ."

Eric: (To Doug) You didn't have that kind of experience?

Doug: When I first got here, it was about 1972 [two years before he moved to L.A. permanently]. Jim and I went down to Laguna Beach, and there was a sign post in the bar: No Touching. That's all.

Tak: I used to frequent Main Street in L.A., and that's where there were lots of drag queens. There was a time in L.A. when drag queens could go into the street in drag. This is in the mid- to late 1960s. The thing they would require to have was three pieces of male attire, which I thought was strange. So they could wear undies or bras as long as they had three pieces of male attire. And in Hawaii, I think they had to wear something that said, "I'm a boy," right? I don't know what good that did anyway. Over here, the three pieces of male attire just cracked me up. The drag queens looked pretty good. And most of them were Hawaiian types, big girls.

Andy: I didn't know they had a law like that because I didn't go like that. I went straight as a woman. [Laughs]

Tak: Please! They would've busted you, honey. That's where the fun was [Main Street]. It's no longer anything anymore.

Roy: See, at that time, Downtown was really vibrant. People went to town. It was really an exciting place. They had this place called Harold's.

Andy: Rough Trade, too.

Tak: Yes, there was another one. I can't think of it. Fifth and Sixth, there was this whole gay bars area in Downtown. There was another place on Eighth Street, too, near the Ambassador Hotel.

Andy: Redwood Room. There were more Hawaiians there.

Eric: There were a lot of Asian drags?

Roy: Yes, there were a few Hawaiian Asian drags: Kulei . . .

Tak: Brandy was the one I remember. She was very pretty. Brandy Lee.

Doug: They really applied the sense of being a drag queen. They really put on the make-up, compared to the other drag queens. When you go to drag shows and you see a white drag queen, they looked terrible. They don't do anything or much of anything.

Roy: The Hawaiian drag queens were really serious. They wore expensive clothing. When they went to a contest, they really looked good, the make-up, their hair, whatever they did.

Tak: The ones that I got to know at the end, they started from Friday night and stayed in drag until Sunday morning or Sunday evening or until they went back to work on Monday. One of them worked for Tokyo Florist or something. She was the delivery person. Of course, her eyebrows were still plucked, but she didn't really look that feminine. She looked like a big butch guy when you saw her. But on Friday night, she couldn't get more feminine if your life depended on it.

Andy: How can you stay three nights like that?
Tak: They had pills and everything, sweetheart. They used to ask me, "Oh, would you care for some Black Beauty?" I said, I don't think I want any of that stuff. I think that kept them going.
Eric: (To Andy) You were doing some contests, too.
Andy: In Hollywood and the Ventura area. Never down in Main Street. No way.
Tak: Oh, baby.
Andy: Excuse you. [Laughs] I have walked a few blocks in the street. One time I remember I walked like a few streets down the hill by Alvarado. I got stopped a few times.
Tak: They thought you were working. [Laughs]
Eric: You were actually propositioned?
Andy: Oh, yes.
Doug: (To Andy) You mentioned C'est La Vie. So did you go there escorted? Were you escorted by that guy who was into transvestites?
Andy: Oh, no, this was a real guy.
Eric: So these were like straight guys who would escort drag queens?
Andy: Yes, they are straight, but they could be bi[sexual] or gay.
Eric: But they didn't identify as gay men.
Andy: Uh-huh.
Roy: They were gay.
Andy: Not gay like me.
Tak: Nobody is like you, sweetheart. [Laughs]
Andy: You can be.

Ernest Wada

Before I went into the military, I bumped into this particular guy who was gay. He felt me out. In fact, he made a point of seducing me. He was always going to the Red Raven. I heard about the bar from him. And through that seduction—I wasn't even twenty-one then—and knowing him, he educated me about what was going on as far as being gay was concerned.

What did you feel the first time you went into a gay bar? Were you scared? Were you anxious?

All of it. All of it. I was just standing there, taking it all in. You see, I feel that the whites set the standards of everything in this life. Whether we realize it or not, we tend to follow those standards and emulate them, which was no different in the gay circle at that time. The selective process in the bar scene was just deadly because the whites were going for other whites at the time, and Asian types were not a commodity. I don't know if it is now even, is it? I mean, the whites at that time, I feel, viewed us as more of the subservient types. They expected us to be submissive—this is an extreme analogy—a geisha type. We were supposed to wait on them hand and foot or something.

And then as soon as we opened our mouths and started talking, they discovered that we were just as Americanized as them. Then they felt intimidated. Or they came off condescending or patronizing. Of course, you could see through that and you took it. On the one chance that somebody might be attracted to you, you went along with it and thought, "Well, okay, let's see where this'll go." But after a while, it just became too ridiculous and it became apparent that they were either stupid or ignorant. Then you let them have it. They didn't know what was going on because, well, *he's an Asian, how come he is behaving this way? He's just like the white queens, vicious, just as vicious.* Well, we learned.

I mean, you didn't have a chance [in the bars] if you were an Asian. That's the way I felt about it. And you know how gay kids are competitive to begin with. They'd stab each other's back to get what they want. Well, it wasn't quite that bad, but it was bad enough. This was compounded by this idea that white people were interested in whites and they didn't know what to make of the Asians. We were just a novelty they might try or something. That's the type of prevailing feeling we [Asians] had when we were in the bar environment or the gay scene. I wasn't a troll or a reject. I was reasonably attractive in my younger days. I could have suitors and so forth, but I never got that satisfaction [from the bars]. You'd have to be really exceptionally beautiful or something for them to give you the time of day. And rejection is the keyword here. The fear of rejection was really my biggest fear. Going to the bar scene, I would never approach anybody because I couldn't take the rejection.

Were there a lot of Asians when you started going to bars in the 1950s?

Not at all. In fact, they were so scarce that if you saw another one, you really stuck out to each other. I didn't meet Tak until the 1960s. I was still associating with my friends from high school, who are straight. And by then, these guys were getting married and having their families. I was really leading a dual life.

So your gay life was relegated to the bar scene only at that point? Were there other things that . . . ?

Well, okay. I'm glad you asked. The bar scene was what I described mostly. But then I said, I had to have my sexual gratification, too. So I went to the tubs a lot, the bathhouses. Indiscriminate sex with whoever you choose. To me, it was expedient. It was a pretty regular scene. You just walk around, walk around, walk around, checking rooms, checking rooms, checking rooms. . . . These guys were in their rooms with their door wide open playing with themselves. And if you saw one that you were attracted to, you went in. If the interest was mutual, they wouldn't turn you away. But if they were not interested, then they just waved you off.

And then there were the gloryholes [in public restrooms]. Again, this was just strictly, strictly anonymous sex. You just saw the hole [on panel between stalls]. And if the guy was looking through it and if he wanted you to put yours in, they'd finger or give you a sign. If you wanted to, you'd do it. If you didn't, you'd just ignore it. I used to go to this one particular restroom when I was living in Montebello. It was the May Company on Whittier Boulevard. It was very active. There were always takers. I particularly liked that one because the crowd that came in there were either Hispanic or white. No Asians. I think I was the only Asian there. A lot of guys were married. I'm sure these guys were married and just engaged in this just to get their release. I guess they had the same idea. They had to get their gratification. So they just came to get sucked off or whatever.

I also went to the parks. Griffith Park was very, very active. I used to go there a lot. All of this stuff just to have sex for expedience. I would rather go to these places than to the bars. That way you didn't have to go through this tiresome thing of drinking drinks you didn't want, and talking and talking. Everybody knew what they were there for under those circumstances in the parks. I mean, they were not there to get a drink. They were not there to engage in conversations. They wanted sex. And that's what you went for. I was relatively successful on that turf.

Did you meet other Asians in the bathhouses?

Oh, yes. But I wouldn't be interested in them.

What type of men were you looking for?

[Pause] You mean other than Caucasians? My physical attraction is whoever turns me on. It's just not a specific type.

But not Asians?

No, no. For one thing . . . I never thought about it actually. In high school, when I used to have these crushes and physical attraction, it was a mixture of Asians, Mexicans, whatever turned me on, you know. But once I became gay, I guess I was looking for . . . someone that is masculine. I'm not saying Asians were entirely a turn-off to me. There were some really nice, attractive Asians in those days that I wouldn't have any qualms tricking with. In my earlier days, though, when I was active in the social scene, that was how I felt. But not now. I see all these Asian American types that are just out there and doing things, and holding responsible positions, and really just integrated into the strata of leadership. I see that now. They hold good jobs. They are educated. See, I didn't see much of that when I was growing up. Most of us were the pioneers because our parents definitely weren't going on to universities. They came here and started working, and then they went to the camps. There were no bars like Mugi's or Chopstix or Xanadu [gay Asian bars] that you hear about now. There was no place that was exclusively Asian at that time. Maybe gay Asians have come into their own now. But all my experience of being gay, up until now, was trying to be the white boy, gaining their acceptance and trying to be as white as they were. I don't want you to leave here thinking I was just another Asian person trying to be white. I was just never comfortable about who I was. I suppose being Asian was a part of it. So we copied the whites. That's what I'm saying. Well, I don't have to go through that anymore because I've been through it. Been there. Done that. And in the wash, it didn't mean anything anyway. But back then, whether we realized it or not, we did. We followed the standards of the whites.

Charles Chang

My friend at work introduced me to the gay bar scene. He was more interested in picking up guys. So it was kind of a handicap to have somebody following him around. So after that, it was like I was on my own. I was very reserved in that kind of atmosphere. I don't know if that's because of the Asian in me or I'm not a very extroverted person. I would be just standing there and waiting for somebody else to take charge and make the first move. I did get picked up in a bar by a white guy. That's when I had my first sexual experience with a man.

Very rarely, though, would I get asked or picked up. That made me feel like, Well, people don't like Asians. I don't know if you can call that discrimination. It could be just people's personal taste.

I never saw myself as a sexual being. Well, maybe if I was straight, I'd be attractive to a female Asian. We'd get married and have babies and something like that. But being Asian in the gay community, I didn't see that I could be attractive to anyone. And if they were sexually attracted to me, then it was like, Wow, there's something wrong with them. [Laughs] What's with this guy, you know?

Did you see other Asians in the bars you went to?

Hardly. Hardly.

Paul Bautista

Going to the bars in those early years was pretty scary. I remember showing up at Studio One for the very first time with a three-piece suit because I was so intimidated. I was on the debate team in high school. That was the only time I felt I was in command because I would get these awards for my debates. Studio One, hell, I'm going to have to walk in there wearing something jazzy. I felt like I was in control until I walked in and I realized nobody was wearing a three-piece suit. [Laughs] That was interesting. That was the best polyester three-piece suit JC Penney had back then.

It was nerve-wracking. I would say from the time I parked my car to the time I left—I was there for three hours—my comfort zone was probably like ten minutes. The whole time I was just busy trying to figure out if I'm holding my drinks right, if somebody's looking at me. Am I drinking too much? Why don't I like the music? Is someone going to see me?—which was the worst one of all. I'd come up with a thousand excuses not to do it. But for those ten minutes it was fun.

Back then, there were very, very few Asian couples because of the density. There wasn't that much of an Asian population around yet. You didn't have the high migration, coming in from Southeast Asia and Korea back then. Basically the two groups that were here were the Chinese and the Japanese. Filipinos weren't even a dent yet. We just started. I think it wasn't until the mid-1980s that you started seeing Asian couples. Most of us who grew up here grew up being attracted to Caucasians because that was the standard on T.V. and in school. I mean, the kids who we grew up in school with who had the best dates, they were all Caucasian kids. They didn't look like us.

The only gay Asians that were foreign-raised that we saw were the ones who were effeminate. Back then, a lot of effeminate Thais showed up in the picture. A lot of screaming Filipinos, too. I think maybe out of every six effeminate Asians that came in, there would be one butch guy. That was a horrible, gross generalization, but that's the way it was. They [effeminate Asians] had nothing to lose. This was like gravy, like a candy shop for them when they got here. Do you know what I mean? They could be themselves and not be made fun of.

The ones who were compelled by society to be straighter[-acting], they weren't visible. When you're obvious, you've got nothing to lose. If you're not obvious, what you want to do is fit in here first, get the American mold down pat, get your career going, your schooling done. The last thing you can afford to do is muddy the waters and become labeled as a pervert or a deviant. There wasn't this empowerment. There was no March on Washington yet. There was no AIDS. So all they really had was this formula, which was Mom's and Dad's formula. This was how the straights did it and they were happy and normal. They had to follow that mold. So they either got married or they were in the closet. These were the two formulas. There wasn't anything in between.

Leo Joslin

I left Atascadero at eighteen and went to Occidental College in L.A. L.A. was a lot different. It was neat living in the city, compared to living in the country, because there was a lot more to do. I was actually able to go out and meet guys, which I wasn't able to do in a small town. Actually went out and cruised.

I didn't know where to find guys. I knew Hollywood Boulevard was where gay people would go and cruise in the early 1970s. This is like summer of 1973, going into 1974. I went and hung out on Hollywood Boulevard. There was a coffee shop there called the Gold Cup. That was where I could meet other young gay guys, but that was also where the hustlers went and hung out. I didn't know where else to meet guys, so I went there, you know. Everyone thought I was a hustler also, but I wasn't hustling. I was meeting all these guys that were hustling. My first couple of encounters in L.A. were with hustlers, male prostitutes. There was this guy named Priest, who was a white kid. He was young. I met another guy named Mike, a Mexican. I remember them being a couple of people that I first was hanging out with or having sex with casually. Through them I found out about this place called Gino's, which was on Melrose. So I went and checked that place out. It was a juice bar. They didn't serve alcohol, which is why they would let people in who were under twenty-one.

That was my first gay bar, and from there, I found out another place in San Fernando Valley called the Outer Limits. They had this thing called the Chicken Night. On Wednesday nights, if you were under twenty-one, you could get in free. They would open until 5 A.M. So every Wednesday night, I would drive my car out to the Outer Limits. It was on Magnolia in North Hollywood. The place would be packed, mainly with young kids, an under twenty-one crowd. That was in 1974. So in 1974 and 1975, I'd be down there every Wednesday night. Friday and Saturday also. I kind of lived there.

I started letting people in college know that I was going to the Outer Limits. Everybody knew it was a gay bar. So people would know that I was either gay or bi[sexual]. College was tough because nobody was out. I lived in a dormitory. What started happening was when I would go in and take a shower, everyone would leave. [Laughs] It's like they were really homophobic. That bugged me. So I just decided to move off campus and forget about it.

Once I was walking across the front lawn in front of the dorm, someone was screaming out the window, "Look at that faggot." It was really awful. So my whole social life switched from college just to the people I was meeting up with in the gay community. When I look back, I wish I could've gotten more involved with my college peers. But I didn't. I didn't really give them a chance after those experiences. I just decided that I didn't want to have anything to do with them. I kind of went into this total immersion trip where I said that all my friends had to be gay. No heterosexual friends.

At the places you were going to, did you see other Asians there?

No, mainly whites, Hispanics, and African Americans. Of course, they didn't call themselves African Americans back then. The only place I started seeing Asians was the place called the River Club. But that wasn't until 1977 or 1978.

THREE PIECES OF ID

Before and even as gay Asians began to organize themselves in the 1980s, the management of some mainstream gay bars and bathhouses found ways to curtail Asians from patronizing their businesses. This in turn discouraged many gay Asian men from even trying to get into these places. Dean Goishi, for example, still doesn't visit West Hollywood all that often "because I had a very bad taste of going into West Hollywood bars, where Asians were carded and asked for three pieces of picture I.D.s and all that good stuff." Stories about gay Asians who were discriminated against circulated through the community. Even those who had no trouble gaining entrance regarded them as urban legends. Most found them credible since, once inside even those bars that did not practice discrimination at the door, many of them experienced discrimination of a different sort. As Harry Park recalls, "I've seen people give dirty looks to someone when they walked in because of their race. I've heard snide remarks, just bitchy remarks. *What's that nigger doing here? How come that chink is here?* Dirty looks. Facial expressions. Turning their backs. You name it. It was there." Later on, in the early years of A/PLG, some of them even led protests against some of these bars that had discriminated against Asians.

Tak Yamamoto

In the 1960s, there was a West Hollywood, but it wasn't boys' town yet. You know, it was just part of the County, which was not under the city of L.A., so you had a little more leeway. The sheriff might not have enforced the rules as much as the L.A.P.D. did. So West Hollywood was a little more open for us to be in. But a lot of the bars were still kind of catering to white males. I would go to a bar, and afterward, a coffee shop. Coffee shops were a rarity then, but P. K. and I went to this after-hours coffee shop, which was primarily white. I knew the owner and we had no problems getting seated. But there was a client there one time who made a noise about the fact that he could sit here but P. K. [who is black] couldn't. I called the waiter and I said, "Could you get the manager?" The manager came out and he took the other person out because he was just too disruptive. At the time, it didn't have a policy of white-male dominance. They were looking for a kind of a community that they hadn't had yet because West Hollywood was still not fifty percent gay.

Roy Kawasaki

When I first started going to different bars [in the mid- to late 1960s], I didn't see that many Asians yet. The Crown Jewel, one of the bars that I went to, was strictly more Hispanic and white, and the Klondike was white. Most of them were white. There were very few Asians in between. There were [Asian] people who were gay, but they were so spread out. Like Roy T. Maybe I'd see him in this bar one night and then I wouldn't see him for the longest time. Suddenly, he would pop up again. Same thing with other guys, because they had their own [non-Asian] friends or social scene. When I did see them in a bar, some would kind of avoid eye contact with me. I remember this one guy. . . . What was he, a doctor? A dentist? . . . Very nice looking. He was the one I saw a lot. I know he would avoid contact with me. I just felt that this person just did not want to be bothered with Asians. He was "white."

Did you feel strange in these bars because of your ethnicity?

You know, it was almost like—how should I say it?—that the people there were gay and I was not, they were the queers and I was not queer, because of my being different. I don't know how to explain it. I didn't feel like I was part of it because I was an Asian. I think part of it was my denial because I thought one day I'd be married. But I also don't think I was accepted warmly by the non-Asians. We were too foreign to them. We didn't fit the white [gay] model. Those who were attracted to Asians were either familiar with the culture or older men. A lot of the older men that we knew were attracted to Asians because of their experience, not so much here, but probably in Japan or some other parts [of Asia].

There was this one time when I felt a bartender just ignored me. I went for a brunch, and it was empty. I was there early to meet some friends, and the bartender was talking to somebody down at the other end. He saw me walk in. I sat down and waited for him to come up and say, "Oh, yes, what can I do for you?" or "What would you like?" But he never came down. He just kept on talking and just completely ignored me. So I thought maybe I should yell at this guy or something. That's one time I felt like maybe it was because I was an Asian.

There really wasn't any other place to meet Asians unless you went to a private party. The ones I went to were hosted by Caucasians. These were parties at their homes. As the years went by, I met some other Asians in these parties, older Asians than myself, like Ed. He must be in his eighties now. And there was John, who is Filipino. He must be in his mid-seventies, maybe.

I guess as you meet one Asian, then you'd get to meet another. It's sort of like a chain reaction. You get introduced. By the early 1970s, I began to meet more Asians like Tak, and I thought, "Oh, wouldn't it be nice to have a club? Here we are. We are gay and we should have some kind of club to come together and just have fun." Other people were saying the same thing. That's when people were already thinking about some kind of support [for gay Asian men].

Stanley Rebultan

I used to patronize with my friends this place called Studio One. That place used to have discriminatory practices to exclude people that they perceived as not good for the business. They excluded older people. They excluded people they perceived as ugly. They excluded minorities, blacks, Asians, and I was subjected to that once. I believe it was 1978 or 1979 because I became a citizen in 1980. They asked for I.D.s, which was customary, you know. You could show whatever identification you had as long as it was legal. But those bastards over there at the time, you could show them a fake California I.D. and they would accept that. But a green card, they would not know shit about green cards. They'd say, "No, that's not an I.D." At that time, my identification was my green card, with a picture and everything on it. (I don't remember if I was already driving or had a California I.D.) They didn't accept it.

I said, "What? Do you know what you're looking at? This is a document that establishes my legality to stay here."

Then they said, "I don't give a damn. Give me your California driver's license."

"Look," I said this to the person at the door: "Either you're ignorant or stupid, or you're just discriminating. I want to talk to the manager."

And then he said, "No, the manager is not here."

"Bring him over here because nobody will get in this fucking door if I'm not getting in."

"Who the fuck are you?"

"Ay, I'm a customer here, and you're dealing in business here. And if I'm discriminated against, you're going to hear about this. You're going to be in deep trouble."

My friend at the time pulled my hand and said, "Are you creating troubles here? I'm leaving."

I said, "No, George, if you leave, I won't see you again. This is important to me. You just stand by me." I said, "I don't give a shit if they haul me to jail. I'd like to prove my point because this fucking place has been discriminating." It's been common knowledge.

So these queens lined up all the way to Santa Monica Boulevard. (The entrance was on LaPeer, a block south of Santa Monica Boulevard.) They said, "What's going on in there?" There was a commotion because it had been like two minutes already that I held up the line. So somebody with authority over there said, "Take him out of the door. Get him out." Which the bouncers tried to do. I held my position. And finally my friend George helped them dislodge my hand and pull the hell out of me, and people were starting to go in there.

I told George, "Fuck you! I'll never see you again. Get the hell out of here. Don't call me. I have nothing to do with you." I even belittled him. I said, "You're a shit! You don't know how to fight for your rights. I hope that you're subjected to the same discrimination. That's why you guys never progressed. Look at your attitude." (George was a Latino.) So my anger toward the establishment was vented at him.

But you know what? I think a week later, the whole gay community was picketing Studio One. I saw that in the news. On the second day, even though I had a job to go to, I found a way to go there in the evening. I made my own placard and went marching along with the group. I said, "Well, finally somebody spoke up the way I did." So eventually they changed their policies.

Leo Joslin

I don't remember seeing a lot of gay Asians back in the 1970s. I went to the gay parade in 1974 and 1976. I don't remember seeing any gay Asians. I'm sure there must have been some. They would've stood out. If I had seen one, I'd remember it. They might have been there in either of those marches, but I just didn't see them. I was dating a lot at that time, mainly white guys and some Hispanics that I met in MCC [Metropolitan Community Church] or the juice bars, like Gino's, Outer Limits, and the Other Side, which was on Highland. When I turned twenty-one, I started hanging out in drinking bars, like the Paradise Ballroom.

In 1977, I met Ross and we were actually together for many years. Our relationship evolved from open to closed, open to closed. He was Japanese. We were like an Asian–Asian couple, one of the few back then. We were considered an oddity.

Did people actually say that to you?

Yes, they were like, oh, how unusual. Then they'd always say, "Asians usually like whites." These were usually whites who said that. They called us lesbians. They were saying the appropriate relationship was a white guy and an Asian, and two Asians who liked each other were lesbians. Because there weren't that many of us to begin with, it was unusual for two Asians to be together back then.

Ross and I met at a bathhouse. There were some gay Asians in these bathhouses. Not a lot. The perception was, if you are Asian, you are passive. You are passive in bed. You like white guys. That was the stereotype. Not all of us fit that because I definitely was not passive. I think what attracted us to each other was that we were both Asians.

We were together, but we both would see other people on the side. That happened frequently. Then we closed the relationship. Then we opened it. During that period, there were a lot of things happening in the gay community. The bathhouses were really popular. Since we were in our early twenties, it was hard to stay out of those places. In fact, sometimes we ran into each other in the bathhouses. We would go out separately once or twice a week and stay up all night, and it was just a fun thing to do. People felt that open relationship was the way to go. It was a time of sexual liberation. You know, like we don't want to be tied down to the oppression of the mainstream. We want to go out and have as much sex as we want. We want to affirm our sexuality. So going out and having sex with a whole bunch of different people in one night was common for a lot of people.

There was one bathhouse that used to draw a large Asian crowd back into the early 1980s. It was called the Club Bath, I believe. It was right next to the Hollywood Freeway on Melrose. I remember there usually was a large presence of Asians there. Maybe twenty or thirty percent. I remember thinking that was kind of remarkable to have so many Asians there.

There was this other place called the YMAC. It was also on Melrose, near Fairfax High School actually. This was right before Melrose became the fashion center that it is. It used to be a real sleazy street and run-down. They had this bathhouse there that a lot of the hustlers used to stay at. I used to like to go there. I would take a nap, go to bed at ten o'clock and I set my alarm at two. And I'd wake up at two because I knew between two and six in the morning that was when there was a lot of sexual activity happening at these bathhouses. That's what I would do.

There were a lot of interesting places. Some of them were just huge. Huge and glittery. Others were small, little, dingy places. They each had their own character and drew their own type of crowd. So depending on what kind of crowd you're into, what you're after, that would dictate where you would go. My favorite bathhouses were the Club Baths, the Hollywood Spa, and the 8709 (which was on 8709 Third Street in West L.A.). That's where Gaetan Dugas used to hang out. You know, Patient Zero [in Randy Shilt's *And the Band Played On.*]. So who knows? Maybe I brushed elbows with him. The sex scene was really intense back then.

I remember the 8709 would be tough to get into for me. I think it was discrimination. The rumor was that, if you weren't white and really attractive, you couldn't get in. I did get turned away the first time I tried to get in. So I had to get a friend of mine to refer me. Even then, they asked for three pieces of I.D., which I had, which I gave to them. I did get a membership, but I think they were discriminating at the time.

THE CULT OF MASCULINITY

Images of masculinity have a long history in the gay community. George Chauncey traces the obsession with masculinity of the gay community back to the 1940s:

> The transformation in gay culture suggested by the ascendancy of *gay* was closely tied to the masculinization of that culture. Jeans, T-shirts, leather jackets, and boots became more common in the 1940s, part of the "new virile look" of young homosexuals. Increasing numbers of conventionally masculine men identified themselves as gay, in part, because doing so no longer seemed to require the renunciation of their masculine identities.[2]

The masculinization was a reaction to the "fairy" stereotype and to the conflation of femininity and homosexuality.[3]

Tracy D. Morgan documents the rise of the "physique movement" in the 1940s and credits the proliferation of "physique" magazines for making "men who were desirous of other men visible to each other, informing them about gay style, gay desire and gay language."[4] He writes, "Both [photo studios, Bruce of Los Angeles and the Athletic Model Guild (AMG),] were run by gay men and sought muscular models to pose for photographs. Bob Mizer, the founder of AMG, 'did all his recruiting personally, visiting local gymnasiums and male beaches in his search for men who fit the Athletic Model Guild image, which included chiseled muscles, a cleft chin, and, by and large, white skin.' "[5] Their clearly defined muscles, their choice of clothing (or lack thereof), their facial expressions and/or poses are often markers of American masculinity. This appeal of masculinity explains why these magazines flourished relatively undisturbed through the censorious 1950s when even less visually explicit gay publications were subject to obscenity charges. Morgan writes, "What gave many of these magazines their respectability, their ability to traverse gay and straight worlds with little or no opprobrium, was their glorification of a particular kind of masculinity: patriotic, strong, and white."[6] When done as camp, such hypermasculinization can mock conventional ideas of what a man is or should be. However, there is always a possibility of internalization. In fact, so pervasive and celebrated were these images of masculinity—cowboys, body-builders, construction workers, policemen, bikers, military personnel, or anyone in uniform—that hyper-masculine gay men were becoming known in the community as "clones." They have become *the* sexual icons of American gay community. Tim Edwards argues that as much as the clone culture is able to show the disruption of masculinity and heterosexuality, "equally, though, it was a semi-conscious acceptance or even an adoration [on the part of the gay men's community] of traditionally conceived male sexuality as many of these costumes and uniforms were and are worn for sexual as opposed to their original more instrumental purposes."[7] Even though the development of these masculine visual codes has the potential to subvert dominant society's negative stereotypes of gay men and offer a positively sexualized alternative for them to adopt, the way these images have been commodified presents a danger of conformism.

And commodification is the key here: Money can buy you the right look. It can give you access to membership in a gym. It can dress you with the right clothes and the latest accessories. And it can get you entrance into the right places to be seen. Capitalism works best when you can homogenize your consumers to make the marketing of your product easier. As John Champagne suggests, using pornography as an example, "The pornographic gaze's frenzied pursuit of the body is further complicated by pornography's status as commodity. Over . . . the competing versions of the gaze operating in pornography . . . , the commodification of pornography attempts to institute a universal, and thus commodifiable, gaze. This commodifying, universalizing gaze must find, in its increasing pursuit of consumers, a method of normalizing, or at least systematizing, the heterogeneity of the pornographic gaze."[8] Such commercialization—while affirming a politics of uninhibited sexuality—depoliticizes the community; the preoccupation of consumerism marginalizes issues of sexism and racism.[9] In fact, "the wholesale incorporation of the dominant definition of masculinity (which is unfailingly specifically white) is politically problematic for a group of people who have been oppressed by that definition."[10] This, of course, can include Asians, who have historically and culturally been excluded from this definition.

That still images could have such a powerful effect on our imagination to the point of influencing our desire is not far-fetched. As Marita Sturken argues, "Photographic images in general have a greater capacity than moving images to achieve iconic status. . . . [T]hey possess an ability to connote completeness and to evoke the past."[11] Unlike moving images which relate a continuous narrative, still images require more participation from the viewers, and therefore more emotional and imaginary investment in them. This is why, Sturken writes, "[M]odern discourse attributes to the photograph not only a neutral, empirical capacity but also magical qualities of expression and imagination . . . dual sense of imaging the unattainable and laying claim to reality."[12] In other words, still images invoke a mixture of reality and fantasy. In this case, by achieving iconic status, these masculine images became not only *the* ideal form of desire (fantasy), but also the standard by which the desirability of men would be judged (reality). The Greek pose in which the chiseled body invokes a sense of classical or mythical male forms, for example, can serve as a naturalizing agent, a "historical" proof of idealized masculinity.[13] In essence, this standard of ultra-masculinization—or the "clone culture"—presents a mythology that, though shared by all in the gay community, is a specifically white masculinity. This is still apparent today to anyone browsing through most gay publications with sexually explicit ads. Interestingly, even when other people of color are featured in these ads or magazines, the images still reflect the racial hierarchy in dominant society. Morgan finds that " 'Colored' bodies adorn the pages of bodybuilding publications [in the 1950s] in considerable numbers, but it is clear that Black and Latino men are only visiting Plato's world. If Black, they are en route from Africa to the New World as slaves. If Latino, they are framed as if in a postcard from the tropics. Both images are there to entice."[14] Even more than three decades later, filmmaker Marlon Riggs, in his documentary *Tongues Untied* (1989), echoes a similar criticism of the predominantly white images in gay advertising and art. Even in pornography that features muscled black men, they are usually portrayed as slaves.[15]

Gay Asian men endure a similar fate. While their images are not prevalent in mainstream gay "skin rags," there exists another genre of magazines, what Paul EeNam Park Hagland calls "rice queen magazines" or "RQ magazines," where gay Asian images proliferate.[16] (As we will see in the next chapter, this "ghettoization" of gay Asian men is replicated in the actual physical geography of "rice bars" in Los Angeles.) In the pictorials of these magazines, the Asian men put on display are masculine like their white counterparts, but with a twist. In their suggestive poses or captions, the Asian models are invariably boyish, innocent, and pliant. It is ingenious how these images of Asian men fulfill the superficial criteria of American masculinity and yet retain within the same bodies centuries of colonial fantasies about the Orient: The Rice Queen wants it both ways. Hagland summarizes this strategy in his analysis of one of the photos:

> The irony of this very butch, young man featured in generally butch poses is captured by the fourth in the series of photos, showing only his torso, buttocks, and legs from behind, with the tip of his glans [*sic*] hanging down as the sole conclusive evidence of his maleness; such a pose is clearly meant to show his vulnerability, his

> attraction as an object of anal penetration—the nonmasculine subject position in homosexual sex, at least as traditionally conceived. In the text created by orientalist discourse, this boy is both "man" and "woman," if by "woman" one means the passive partner of penile insertion. His masculinity, apparent from the rugged backdrop and masculine apparel of the photos, paradoxically makes the "femininity" of his pose for the camera all the more alluring to the unseen observer, who has reduced the boy to a "woman" by the penetration of his "gaze."[17]

Not only does Hagland's analysis of these RQ magazines include many examples of this, but he also finds a match between these images and the ideal gay Asian partners that the rice queens are seeking in the personals found in these publications. Again, fantasy and reality commingle.

These images are but a continuation of a long legacy of emasculation of Asian men in this country.[18] According to Yen Le Espiritu, "The exclusion of Asian women from the United States and the subsequent establishment of bachelor societies eventually reversed the construction of Asian masculinity from 'hypersexual' to 'asexual' and even 'homosexual.' The contemporary model-minority stereotype further emasculates Asian American men as passive and malleable."[19] The "asexual" or "homosexual" stereotype was used to justify a racially segregated labor force. Espiritu writes,

> The material existence of Asian American men has also been historically at odds with the traditional construction of "man." During the pre-World War II period, racialized and gendered immigration policies and labor conditions emasculated Asian men, forcing them into womanless communities and into 'feminized jobs' that had gone unfilled due to the absence of women. The existence of the Asian laundryman and waiter further bolstered the myth of the effeminate or androgynous Asian man.[20]

This stereotype is further exploited by media images. Summarizing research done in media images of Asians on television, Espiritu reports,

> More recently, such diverse television programs as *Bachelor Father* (1957–1962), *Bonanza* (1959–1973), *Star Trek* (1966–1969), and *Falcon Crest* (1981–1990) all featured the stock Chinese bachelor domestic who dispenses sage advice to his superiors in addition to performing traditional female functions within the household. By trapping Chinese men (and by extension, Asian men) in the stereotypical "feminine" tasks of serving white men, American society *erases the figure of Asian "masculine" plantation worker in Hawaii or railroad construction worker in Western United States*, thus perpetuating the myth of the androgynous and effeminate Asian man. This feminization, in turn, confines Asian immigrant men to the segment of the labor force that performs women's work.[21] (emphasis mine)

By repeating (or reenacting) visual images that affirm each other, as Sturken states, "memories are continuously re-written and transformed over time until they bear little resemblance to the initial experience."[22] Interestingly, many narrators report having crushes or affairs with other men of color, including Asians, when they were younger. This shouldn't come as a surprise because many of them, at the time of their coming of age, lived in racially segregated communities in America or in Asia where Asians were the majority. For example, Roy Kawasaki, a third-generation Japanese American born in Hawaii, recalls, "Growing up, my parents went to a lot of Japanese shows and movies, and I fell in love with the [Japanese] actors. So I think I have a very strong feeling toward Asians." It is only after they entered the gay community that they focused their desires predominantly on white men. Since then, the pursuit of this white masculine ideal became so central to their gay identity that many could not conceive the possibility of Asian–Asian love. Meanwhile, white–Asian coupling was accepted as naturally as heterosexuality itself, even though it bore little resemblance to their first childhood crushes. Those memories were replaced. In essence, through these persistent stereotypical images in the popular imagination, the feminization of Asian men is naturalized and their masculinity erased. In addition, as some of the narrators who were born and raised in Asia suggest, many Asian immigrant men came from countries where affection between men was part of the culture, and they found the American masculine standard foreign or even inexplicable. At the same time, what they used to subscribe to as acceptable behavior in their native country, such as men holding hands, was either frowned upon or exoticized as "feminine" in their new home. Feeling not so desirable themselves, it is no wonder that most gay Asian men felt inhibited or even alienated in mainstream gay bars. Their "passivity" unwittingly reinforced a cultural stereotype, becoming a self-fulfilling prophecy. When even gay establishments discriminated against them by keeping them out, that was just another blow to their self-esteem. And if they felt unattractive themselves, they would also find each other unattractive as well. They needed to find a space of their own to come together.

NOTES

1. El Niño is a weather condition caused by the warming of the Pacific Ocean, which brought a tremendous amount of precipitation to Los Angeles and other western coastal cities in the United States in 1998.

2. George Chauncey, *Gay New York: Gender, Urban Culture and the Making of the Gay Male World, 1890–1940* (New York: Basic Books, 1994), 358. See also Murray Healy, *Gay Skin: Class, Masculinity and Queer Appropriation* (London: Cassell, 1996), 58; and Tim Edwards, *Erotics & Politics: Gay Male Sexuality, Masculinity and Feminism* (New York: Routledge, 1994). Edwards identifies those gay men who embrace masculine dress and behavior as "masculin-

ists": "a cult of proponents of gay male machismo that took traditional or stereotypical forms of masculine display, posture or dress and pushed them to the extreme out in the open, partly as a positive expression of sexuality and partly as a counter-reaction to the stereotypes of effeminacy that had dominated the previous century at least" (46).

3. This is also what Judith Butler would call "collective disidentification." See Healy, *Gay Skin*, 9. Healy quotes Butler, "It may be precisely through practices which underscore disidentification with those regulatory norms by which sexual difference is materialized that both feminist and queer politics are mobilised. Such collective disidentification can facilitate a reconceptualization of which bodies matter and which bodies are yet to emerge as critical matters of concern."

4. Tracy D. Morgan, "Pages of Whiteness: Race, Physique Magazines, and the Emergence of Public Gay Culture," in *Queer Studies, A Lesbian, Gay, Bisexual & Transgender Anthology*, ed. Brett Beemyn and Mickey Eliason (New York: New York University Press, 1996), 282.

5. Morgan, "Pages of Whiteness," 286.

6. Morgan, "Pages of Whiteness," 288.

7. Edwards, *Erotics & Politics*, 96–97.

8. John Champagne, *The Ethics of Marginality: A New Approach to Gay Studies* (Minneapolis: University of Minnesota Press, 1995), 30. Systematizing is the key here. It does not mean that there is no heterogeneity, but it is organized in a way that it does not challenge the normalized gaze (e.g., as a fetish, specialty, exoticization, etc.).

9. See Healy, *Gay Skin*, 143–144:

> After the clone look in which gay men adopted very "straight" signifiers of masculinity . . . there developed a stylistic flirtation with S&M imagery, leather-gear, quasi-military uniforms and skinhead styles. Politically, these elements project highly ambivalent meanings and messages but it seemed that the racist and fascist connotations of these new "macho" styles escaped gay consciousness as those who embraced the "threatening" symbolism of the tough-guy look were really only interested in the eroticisation of masculinity.

Healy quotes Isaac Julien and Kobena Mercer: "While some feminists have begun to take on issues of race and racism in the women's movement, white gay men retain a deafening silence on race. Maybe this is not surprising, given the relative apathy and depoliticised culture of the mainstream gay 'scene,' " and "If the frisson of eroticism conveyed by these styles depends on their connotations of masculine power then this concerns the kind of power traditionally associated with *white* masculinity." Julien and Mercer, "True Confessions," in *Male Order: Unwrapping Masculinity*, ed. Rowena Chapman and Jonathan Rutherford (London: Lawrence and Wishart, 1987), 132. (Originally published in *Ten*, 8 [Summer 1986].) Though created by whites for whites, as the only images available, they are consumed by gay men of other races as well. See Healy, *Gay Skin*, 200: "Even if hard masculinity is not attainable by all gay men, it is expected that all gay men will desire it. Such is the strength of the ideal that any gay man who professes otherwise is treated with suspicion." However, one must be careful not to deny the political power inherent (though maybe hidden) in the so-called consumerist and depoliticized gay community, as John D'Emilio demonstrated with his study of San Francisco in the 1970s. See D'Emilio, 1983.

10. Healy, *Gay Skin*, 102.

11. Marita Sturken, *Tangled Memories: The Vietnam War, the AIDS Epidemic, and the Politics of Remembering* (Berkeley: University of California, Press, 1997), 90.

12. Sturken, *Tangled Memories*, 232.
13. Morgan, "Pages of Whiteness," 287.
14. Morgan, "Pages of Whiteness," 290.
15. See Champagne, *The Ethics of Marginality*, 77:

> There then occur three separate shots of images of Black men, presumably from gay "pornography." The first is a photograph of a naked muscular man shackled around his neck. One white hand reaches into the frame to hold his head down. Another, its wrist wrapped in a leather band, squeezes his left pectoral muscle. Across the top of the photograph appears, in red letters, "Slaves for sale." The second image, a drawing, depicts a naked, muscled white man wearing only black boots, who is whipping a muscular Black man hanging from a tree. The third image is a caroon of a Black man with exaggerated muscles, penis and nipples. The camera slowly pans up this figure.

16. Paul EeNam Park Hagland, " 'Undressing the Oriental Boy': The Gay Asian in the Social Imaginary of the Gay White Male," in *Looking Queer: Body Image and Identity in Lesbian, Bisexual, Gay and Transgender Communities*, ed. Dawn Atkins (New York: Haworth Press, 1998), 290. Hagland writes, "What is yet more marginalizing is the general exclusion of APIs from gay publications outside of the specialized confines of the RQ genre, whether pornographic or nonpornographic. The general invisibility of Asians from the social imaginary of gay culture consigns gay Asian men to the margins of the subculture."

17. Hagland, "Undressing the Oriental Boy," 283.

18. Although there has been much emphasis on emasculation, it is important to note that Asian men were not always portrayed as feminine. The stereotype of Asian men being a sexual threat (to white women) was prevalent in the early part of the century when nativist sentiment was on the rise. When immigrants were scapegoated for a depressing economy, this stereotype justified anti-Asian legislation, such as anti-miscegenation and exclusionary immigration laws.

19. Yen Le Espiritu, *Asian American Women and Men: Labor, Laws and Love* (Thousand Oaks, Calif.: Sage Publications, 1997), 90–91.

20. Espiritu, *Asian American Women and Men*, 111.

21. Espiritu, *Asian American Women and Men*, 91–92.

22. Sturken, *Tangled Memories*, 42.

3

A Fascism of Desire

ASIANS NEVER LIKE OTHER ASIANS

No one remembers exactly when the River Club became a "gay Asian bar." Located on Riverside Drive just at the mouth of Griffith Park, it had catered to a mostly Latino clientele before the mid-1970s, with some black, Asian, and white customers. Because it did have a strong presence of people of color, Asians knew that they wouldn't be hassled at the door or feel unwelcome inside, like some of them did in more prevalently white establishments. By the mid-1970s, word began to spread that the River Club was where many Asians would go, thereby attracting even more gay Asians and their "admirers." "There was no discrimination," recalls Roy Kawasaki. "People who went there knew there was a mixture of different groups. So there was no problem about that." André Ting says, "I would go there on Saturday. Because of the large number of Asians there, I did not see Latinos and whites anymore. They were there, but I did not notice them. I would bypass the Latino area without even knowing they were there. I would go straight to the Asian area. It got all my attention. It was so unusual for me that I would go there right away."

Yet, inside the bar, there were borders and barriers. "You would have the Asians all in different groups," says Roy. "You had the Japanese in one, the Chinese in one, the Filipino in one, and the foreign-born in another. All staring at each other [Laughs]. Give each other dirty looks, like competitors. We never came together." Sometimes there was even competition within one's own ethnic group. Stanley Rebultan was reticent in his association with his "fellow Filipinos" in the River Club, where he used to go every weekend. He recalls, "There were two occasions I had a good-looking guy I was going out with. Before I knew it, they were almost snatched or stolen by Filipinos. So I said, I'm not going to associate with them anymore. It's much better for me to be with a different kind. I felt more safe. I'm not putting them down, but that's a bad experience I had. Even if you're with your own kind, there's always some problem that might occur." Until the early 1980s when first Mugi's and then Faces came along, the River Club was the only bar in town where one would find a significant concentration of gay Asian men. And unlike these later "rice" bars, which were predominantly Asians and whites, the River Club retained what some narrators describe as its "cosmopolitan" or "international" demographics until it closed in the early 1980s. (The number of blacks remained small probably because black gay bars like Catch One had already been part of the black neighborhood and there was less of a need on the part of gay black men for something like the River Club outside of their community.)

Despite the ethnic segregation, or because of it, certain racial dynamics and contradictions were highlighted. With both its positives and negatives, many narrators believe that the River Club is the precursor to the formation of the first gay Asian organization in the city, the Asian/Pacific Lesbians and Gays, and eventually a gay Asian community in Los Angeles.

Steve Lew

I'm trying to remember the River Club now. It was dark [Laughs]. I know it had a U-shape type of bar. There was a fairly large dance area. It was almost always busy in the evenings. The clientele was fairly mixed. I remembered always running into other Asians or Latinos there. At the same time, the Asians really didn't socialize with each other. It was all to connect with non-Asians.

The music was generally decent dance music, like the best of the disco years: Evelyn Champagne King, the Whispers, all the stuff that they're playing at the Box [a gay bar in San Francisco] now. It was music that I liked. I liked to dance. It was hard, but I would still ask people to dance. During that period, there was this real feeling among Asians—and I would share this feeling, too—that it was harder to approach another Asian. At the same time, you kind of viewed them as competition, competition for primarily white men, although I was actually interested in dating other men of color.

I knew this one Asian guy there who was about two years ahead of me in high school. He would always come to the bar also. And we consciously avoided each other because of that connection. I've talked to him more recently, in the last few years, and I don't think we ever talked about that period. I do remember sometimes I felt like saying "hi" to him, but it seemed so taboo and scary to connect to somebody whom you knew from suburban Asian America. Certainly there was some fear that he might tell other people back home. I'm sure that's why he avoided me. Secondly, you know, I think there were a lot more things that would reinforce low self-esteem and internalized homophobia during that period. Not having any sense that there were groups for gay Asian men, positive types of organizations, it was like . . . how do I say . . . I felt more fear in confronting my own feelings about being Asian and gay, and the fact that you were dealing with a gay man who was also Asian [would force me to confront those feelings].

I separated things so much at the time. On the one hand, I was very political and very much into Asian American identity and how I looked at race critically. But I couldn't put the two [gay and Asian] together. During that time, I did date some Asian men, but we really never talked that much about our backgrounds. I would think I was even avoiding the topic. That wasn't our connection.

Paul Chen

[Paul's partner, Chris Gaynor joined us in parts of this interview.]

I'd drive up to L.A. for the River Club Friday, Saturday nights when I was still living in Fullerton. God, it was packed in those days. Sometimes you couldn't move. It was another Asian who told me about the River Club. I didn't quite understand what he said, but I was curious. I never knew the concept of rice queens. Unless you've been to an Asian bar, you really don't . . . of course, you have.

By then, I really did find out what it was like to be Asian in America. In high school, I got a job at a place called Japanese Deer Park, which was actually an amusement park based on Japanese culture, right near Knott's Berry Farm. And that was the first time I've been with a whole bunch of Asians besides my family. I actually found out the difference between being Asian American versus being Chinese and part of my family. The next summer, I got a job in Disneyland and worked at a restaurant called Tahitian Terrace, where they put most of the Asians to give it some sort of flavor and atmosphere. That was the start of the Asian American movement. We had our own dances. We had our own music. Have you heard of the band Hiroshima? They were still in college then. I used to drive all the way up to East L.A. to go to Asian dances where Hiroshima would play. I think I have most of their albums. Listening to *Cruisin' J-Town*, it was fun. I actually was somebody finally. I wasn't different or strange. I was part of the movement.

But I knew I was gay then and still felt I didn't have a place. So when I finally went to the River Club, I felt like this is the first time that all of me, all different parts of me, fit in some place. I was Asian and gay.

Not everyone in the bar was Asian.

No, because there were different sections. There was the main body of the bar. And since I didn't drink, I didn't really go there very much. And then there was an area where there were pool tables off in this other room. So we [the Asians] had the area from the main bar through the pool tables. Hispanics had the main area of the bar. And the blacks were on the side. So you didn't really go to other people's areas unless you were walking through to get a drink or go to the bathroom. I think the largest number was Asians. There were probably three or four hundred of us. So there were probably a couple hundred of Asians. It was a fairly large bar. Really packed every Friday and Saturday night.

There wasn't much interaction among the different groups, except for Carlo [Laughs]. I knew him from Cal State Fullerton. He was actually Hispanic, but he didn't want to be Hispanic. So he hung out in the Asian section. That was the only person I knew who would cross the room.

We each had our own area and our own circle of admirers. Rice queens stuck with us. The guys who really liked Hispanics stuck there. Most of us, whether non-white or our white counterparts, didn't switch areas, as far as I know. Most of the rice queens that I dated were simply not interested in practically anybody else [besides Asians].

Of course, I understood, either unconsciously or consciously (probably was unconscious for the longest time), that, when a man is only attracted to me because I'm Asian and he's not attracted to other people because they're not Asian, that gives me some sort of power. And I could use that power. Going outside of rice bars and finding that I did not match those people's sexual fantasies, more or less, that caused me to think I did have power in those situations with the rice queens. But that limited me to this one group of men. You know—positive reinforcement/negative reinforcement—you go to places where you get picked up. I think the limits were what bothered some of us.

Rob was an example. Rob really, really, really wanted to be accepted in non-Asian bars. I think that was partly why he didn't want to be seen as Asian. [He believed] that Asians are quiet, passive, have less power. And then there was your chiropractor, Chris.

[*Chris:* Mike. He wanted to be Latino.]

He didn't want to be Japanese. So he thought if he permed his hair and wore dark glasses, he could look Hispanic. He just looked like a Japanese guy with a perm and dark glasses on. And the artist that we met at the Garden Show, Stan. Stan was a West Hollywood clone, you know—short crew cut, big muscles, work out in gym. He had this absolutely gorgeous house above Griffith Park Boulevard. He only socialized with West Hollywood clones. They would not go to rice bars or join A/PLG.

Terry Gock

I remember an interesting experience meeting this Caucasian guy at Rendezvous in the early 1970s in San Francisco. Rendezvous was the equivalent of Faces in L.A., which was a place where there was quite a number of Asians and mostly Caucasians who were interested in Asians. I dated this guy several times, and he introduced me to a friend of his, a Chinese guy, in Rendezvous. The two of us hit it off very well, and he got really upset. He actually left the two of us. The next day, he gave me a line that I would always remember. He said, "Asians never like other Asians." That wasn't my experience. It made me feel like something was wrong with me, although I didn't buy it. It sounded quite ludicrous to me. In fact, we never dated after that.

At the same time, it seemed like at that place, the Asians all saw each other more as competitors for the attention of these white guys than as friends. I found that in the River Club as well. There were cliques. Like most bars, there was a lot of posturing and positioning and trying to attract. It was competitive to begin with; we have to acknowledge that. But I think at Rendezvous and at the River Club, there was more of that competition along racial, ethnic lines, too, in those days. So I think he was quite accurate in terms of assessing how things were, true to a certain extent. That was his experience. But it doesn't have to be.

Dean Goishi

I used to go to River Club and see gay Asians there, but I never talked to them as gay Asians, only because I think the thinking that you don't talk to gay Asians was true. You always talk to other people, but don't talk to gay Asians because they're family. [Laughs] Many first generation [immigrants] didn't speak English very well, and they would only stay and congregate within their ethnic groups. On the other hand, I did have a lot of bar friends who were Asians at that time. The American-born tended to mix much better; my group was Chinese, Japanese, Malay, and Asians from Hawaii. The first six or seven that I met have become a core group of close friends for me today. We stood around and talked and chatted, but not from a sexual standpoint, from more of a social standpoint. I think Asians had fewer opportunities for sexual encounters than whites, African Americans, or Latinos. The environment in the [rice] bars was very, very competitive. Asians were always looking for non-Asians as partners, and then non-Asians were competing for any Asian friends that you had, unless they were already coupled.

Now that I look back on it, I think it was very racist in a sense. Asians were not attractive to me. My models were primarily Caucasian models. Everything up to that time that I read or saw within gay publications and things was all white. Therefore, to me, white became the object of my sexual fantasies, you might say. It wasn't until later when I started working in AIDS and these kinds of social issues that I even became aware that I was totally wrong, that everything was not white.

Besides the bars, we would go to restaurants, primarily Chinese restaurants. None of the ones we went to we would announce that we were gay. I think in Chinese restaurants it was acceptable for a group of men to gather and have dinner and not really be looked at real funny. But they were also cheap and you'd get more food. They were also open late at night. So at eleven or twelve, when we were getting ready to leave the bars and go home, we'd decide to get a bowl of noodles or something. It seemed like it was always cheaper to go to a Chinese restaurant than an American restaurant.

Doug Chin

Roy Kawasaki is my longest friend that I've known here in L.A. I met him the summer of 1974 when he came back to Hawaii for a visit. A mutual friend of ours, Dr. Momyer, was hosting a dinner party at this restaurant out in Makaha, and Roy was there. That's where I met Roy.

Well, in December of that year, after Jim and I had moved back to L.A., we decided we wanted to go to a bar. He found out the name of a gay Asian bar called the River Club, which was up in the Los Feliz area. And we walked into this bar. I was ordering drinks for both Jim and me. Then this person right next to me turned around, and it was Roy! I recognized him. So we started chatting. We've been fast friends ever since then.

I also met a number of people at the River Club, people that I've maintained long-term friendships with. I made a lot of other friends, and some of them were single. We would also go to some of the West Hollywood bars. Jim particularly wasn't interested in going to those bars because he was more into Asians. He really liked Asian men. For instance, when Bob and Clark were together, Clark and Jim would go off to the River Club or to Asian bars, and Bob and I and Erwin would go out to some of the West Hollywood bars to dance. Jim wasn't a dancer. He enjoyed watching people.

The West Hollywood bars were different from the River Club?

Oh, very much so. People were not as friendly there [at the West Hollywood bars]. You had white men there that were not into Asians, and that's okay. I went there just to have fun with my friends, not to seek attention or anything of that sort.

Jim and I actually went to the River Club practically almost every Saturday night. If not Saturday night, maybe on a Friday night, depending if we were entertaining or not. When Jim and I, being very outgoing, bought our first home, we threw a party almost once a month. I would try to prepare these lavish parties, hors d'oeuvre and meals for anywhere from twenty-five to fifty, to a hundred people. We enjoyed meeting people and entertaining them. And during that time, I thought Jim and I were somewhat in a closed relationship because when I made a commitment, it was a commitment for life. Over the years, I guess from what people were telling me, he'd been flirting with a number of Asians. Being as naive as I was, I didn't realize that.

At some point, my studies became very important to me. I was finishing up my accounting degree at Cal State Dominguez Hills, and my position with CBT Financial Services had already started increasing. I needed my study time, which was my weekend. And Jim would go off by himself, with my blessings. I just figured he'd be as faithful as I was to him. But anyway . . .

Paul Bautista

I was seventeen, the first time I was at the River Club. It was before [high school] graduation. I remember the bouncer looking at me. He must have known I was underage, you know. Because I was very good at art, I came up with this phony Filipino driver's license. I took like little seals from Philippine stamps and all this stuff and made it look really official and laminated it and gave it to him. I came up with my best Filipino accent, pretending I was a tourist. There I was. I had to memorize the number, the address, the age. I was like sweating. He looked at me and said, "You haven't been here before?"

I said, "No." On my way to New York, you know.

"Okay, come on in. Have a good time. Thanks for coming."

But I'm sure he knew. I'm sure he knew.

I walked into the bar. Up to that point, it was all me looking at the world, looking at gay life. It was I who was on expedition, discovering a new world, me looking at things, looking at people: what they were doing, how they reacted. When I walked into the River Club, it was the first time where every eye in the place all of a sudden turned to me. It was like someone had turned on a spotlight.

Then I suddenly found out about this group of guys called "rice queens" who were attracted to Asians, which I thought, first of all, was a joke. How could you be just attracted to Asians? I'm attracted to guys who are cute. Having been growing up in the Philippines, there were a lot of cute Asians there, so I was attracted to them as well. In high school here, it was all white kids, so I was attracted to cute white kids. This idea that all they were attracted to were Asians was really bizarre. I had a sudden surge of self-worth that I had never felt before. The idea that there was this special attraction was . . . great.

I must have taken two, three steps and I started to get off of drinks. Back then, the only thing I knew how to drink was Tequila Sunrise because I think one of the girls I went out with ordered one once. I was drunk after half a glass.

After that first time, I went back to the Philippines that summer. It wasn't until coming back that fall that I met Bill in the River Club. That was it. He was everything I wanted. He was so manly. It was so weird to have someone to be so masculine and yet so proud to be gay and yet so responsible and so family oriented. What was so striking about him was that he knew exactly what he wanted. He had been out for fifteen years before I met him. He was at that point looking for someone to spend the rest of his life with, and I was just this kid, barely eighteen. He was twenty years older than me.

When I met Bill, I was dating this guy Kent for a couple of months. Kent was a little older than me and he was treating me like a kid. And of course, I was student body president, and nobody was going to treat me like a kid. Every weekend with Kent was like war and peace, war and peace. It was horrible. We were in the River Club when I met Bill. He was slipping a note in my hand when Kent was standing right there. Bill was so different from Kent. Kent was more a free-spirit. He was talking about opening up the relationship. I mean, we didn't have a relationship! [Laughs]

At that time, it was very rare for me to be introduced to an Asian in River Club that Bill hadn't been to bed with before. Almost every Asian I was introduced to was Bill's ex-boyfriend, which was unnerving. But Bill was so much in love with me. Little bit of jealousy and insecurity that came up was outweighed by everything else.

Bill and I met in 1978. I was still in school at that time, USC. On the weekend, like Saturday nights, we would have an early dinner, take a nap and then go out discoing until two. That was the thing then. Disco was the social life. I'd say seventy-five percent of the time we went to the River Club. It *was* the social focal point. There wasn't much else to do. There were no organizations.

We went out to West Hollywood, Studio One, maybe every other time. If you saw an Asian in Studio One, the only reason that person was there was because he didn't know there was a River Club. Within a few years, Mugi's opened up. It wasn't a dance bar. An older clientele would go there, people who didn't like to dance. That's kind of historically how it's been. There weren't that many places to go, outside of discoing.

My friendships all came out of the River Club. From there, we had dinners and little parties. We'd meet people that way. We were so happy to find that community. Everybody knew each other. It was like a small town. There was something very intimate about those times.

It's hard to believe now, but back then that was a lot for us. That was a lot more than a lot of us ever dreamt was possible: the fact that we could hang out together, have our own bars, have our own places, have love and relationships. It was still in the early days of Anita Bryant. We were still shaking from that incredible war. We weren't sure she was going to be defeated. And after her was Jerry Falwell, and then on and on. It was never like, we won the battle and it's over. Back then, it really was, okay, I'm here, you saw me at the bar, but don't tell my secretary, or don't tell our friends that you saw me here. Before somebody would have a normal conversation with you, you would already have this little conversation [with yourself] about who to tell and who not to tell. That was just very normal.

André Ting

Mugi's was a restaurant. It was not very popular. I've never gone to have dinner there once. Not even once. In fact, it was so bad that in 1980 or 1981, Roy [Z.], the lover of Morris Kight, went there for dinner with his friends, and after the dinner, he said to me, "Their food was so bad that I don't think they had a cook in there. We had to wash down the food with wine." And it was not in good conditions. We kind of felt like only the older people would go there. So it was not a very popular meeting place. There was no dancing. That was a minus. Basically it was a restaurant with a bar. It was smaller, narrower before. They took over one storefront, if I remember correctly. Because of the location, no parking space, and so on, I did not frequent Mugi's very much.

Reggie Bogan

The out and up purpose of Mugi's was a gay meeting place for Caucasians to meet Asians, and ninety-nine percent of them were ex-service people that were over in Asia, which I was. I was in Japan for several years. The Caucasians usually addressed the Asians a lot differently than they did with Caucasian lovers. The Asians had much more respect. For instance, if you were in your forties and you met an Asian who was in his twenties, age didn't seem to make a difference. But if you take two Caucasians, one in his fifties, one in his twenties, the latter is what we'd call a kept boy. You know, the kid didn't work and the guy was paying him money. But in the Asian community, the Asian had more respect for an older person. So most of the lovers that I found and had gotten together, there was quite a bit of age difference. Sometimes between ten, fifteen, twenty years. I met Kenya when he was in his twenties and I was just in my mid-forties. Like double his age. I didn't get along too well with some of the white men in their forties. With a younger Caucasian, I had to dip into the pocketbook every time—movies, dinner. I found that to be different with Asians. Asians usually liked to pay for their own way or even take you out now and then. I like a younger lover, frankly. Most Caucasians usually go with their own age.

I first went to Mugi's for dinner usually at five, five-thirty, or six. There was a bar when you came in the door, but when you turned left, it was like another doorway to the dining room, where you couldn't see the bar because it was totally enclosed. One night I went in there later than usual, around eight or nine. So I finished my dinner around ten and I decided that I'd go around the corner to the bar and get a drink. And it was like the whole atmosphere totally changed. It went from straight to gay. The restaurant was closed and there were maybe fifteen people at the bar, give or take. And as the evening grew, it really started getting crowded. And I noticed there were a lot of Asians and they had Caucasian lovers.

As the years went on, Yoshi, the owner, his restaurant business didn't pan out. So finally he just turned the restaurant into a total bar. He just took the walls down and made the bar circular so you could see on both sides. And the word got around, of course, from white people who liked Asians that, if you wanted to meet an Asian, Mugi's would be the bar to go to. So Mugi's became really popular in the 1980s. I met and dated several people from there. But after I met Kenya, we became lovers. He was a student and didn't have a car; he was living in a dormitory with some Asian students and he was taking the bus. So after a while, he moved in with me while he was still going to school.

We kept going to Mugi's on the weekends. What would happen if I walked into Mugi's was I would sneak off to my Caucasian friends, and Kenya would probably go play the pinball machine, whereas the other Asians [who came with their Caucasian lovers] would get into their own [ethnic] groups. A Filipino would go to a Filipino group, and a Chinese to a Chinese group. In this case, the Japanese would probably stay at the bar and talk to Yoshi. He had his little clique there. But when we left, we left with our lovers. So it was a cliquish bar.

At that time, Mugi's, to be blunt, became a very good pick-up bar for Asians. Now if you were going to go into Hollywood, you'd find a smidgen of Asians. Maybe out of three hundred in a bar, you'd be lucky to count five Asians. It was totally different from the 1990s. If you were single, you make friends very fast with Yoshi because Yoshi had gotten me a couple of dates.

For instance, there were a couple of Japanese kids here on vacation and they were talking to Yoshi. Now they were looking to meet a Caucasian. So Yoshi picked up on this, and he got an inkling what they were looking for.

Or let's say, somebody saw me and liked me. Yoshi would talk to me and say, "Hey, I want you to meet this person." Most of the tourists, particularly Japanese, usually spoke a fair amount of English to get by. And you would pick up on it and go home together. As you got to be a regular customer, you mingled with other regulars, too. It's called cruising.

Same thing with the River Club. Usually I went there and I'd see a Caucasian I knew. Maybe he had an Asian lover and there'd be another Asian that came in on his own that knew the lover. And the next thing you know, you'd have three or four people in a group. And somewhere along the line, somebody would click. That's how you would meet people, an introduction from a friend of a friend.

So in that environment, you felt pretty free . . .

Because first of all, everybody in there was gay. You knew the Asians were looking for Caucasians and the Caucasians were looking for Asians. So that's the atmosphere that you'd already built up. It wouldn't be like going into a disco bar cold turkey, where you didn't know anybody. You might be in there all night and still go home alone. When you went to Mugi's, you were pretty sure that you would meet some people.

Did Asians usually approach Caucasians in the bar?

Rarely. You got to remember a lot of them were foreigners. I'm talking about the ones that weren't born here, that came here to go to school or on vacation. They were very shy basically. Before Mugi's, they either went out to a gay [theater] or an openly gay bar, which was full of Caucasians. Now you can imagine how uncomfortable they'd be walking into . . . well, it'd be just like me walking into a black bar. I mean, I'd be very nervous. But the ones that were born here and had been out in the gay community, they would not hesitate to come and approach me, no.

I ended up bartending at Mugi's on and off between 1983 and 1988. I was talking to Yoshi one night with some friends and he overheard that I used to own the bar down the street called the Stop Over. So he got me at a corner at the end of the bar when it was real slow and asked me if I wanted to be a bartender there. I said I could only do it on weekends because I still had a full-time job, working at *Pasadena Star News*. So I started on Friday and Saturday nights. And then Sunday, and Monday, which was the slowest night, when he wanted to take Monday night off. It got too much, so I quit. But when I left the *Star News*, I hit him up again for a part-time job. My last night was October, 1988, when Yoshi decided that he wanted to have all Asian bartenders.

Since I had been a steady every weekend, I knew pretty much everybody. Most of the people I knew were already paired up or they were dating. Once in a while, I would introduce somebody. Or if I knew there was a bad dude there, I'd do the same thing as Yoshi. When you bring a trick home, you stand a good chance of getting ripped off if you don't know who the person is. But if Yoshi knew somebody had ripped somebody off, he would tell you. That's the advantage of going to Mugi's or what I call a neighborhood bar. But Yoshi had his own Japanese crowd, which a lot of other customers resented in a way. He had his clique and would get them preferences. I told him a few times. I said, "You ought to speak English more."

Virgil Vang

This is what I would do. I'd put on my Levi's and a shirt and go to the River Club. There were a lot of Asians and Latinos there, and white guys who liked Asians. It's interesting because at that period most Asians didn't go with Asians, but I never had any trouble. I just figured, "Okay, don't be a flaming queen. Just be kind of macho and you'll get what you want usually." For a lot of the Asians I went with, it was their first time with an Asian, and they would tell me that. Basically for them, it was sort of experimental. Maybe because I was American-born. Maybe they felt I wasn't quite as Oriental. I wasn't an *Asian* Asian, so maybe I wasn't that close to home and they'd feel less uncomfortable.

It's also interesting that I think ninety-nine percent of the Asian guys I went with were from Asia, not here. Many of them were tourists or students. I was in an airplane back to Los Angeles. There was this good-looking Japanese guy at the ticket counter, buying a ticket. We happened to have the same row. He was an advertising executive. He said he wanted to draw me. So okay. We got off and I invited him to my place. After we had sex, he took a $50 bill and said, "Well, here's some money."

I said I wasn't a hustler.

He said, "No, it's too cold here. Why don't you buy a heater?" He said he had to get married. His parents were going to make him get married. Maybe in a couple years, he couldn't see me anymore. But maybe in the next couple of years, he'd call me when he was in town.

And I remember this beautiful Vietnamese guy that I met at the River Club. We had a few drinks, danced, talked, came home, messed around. I think he stayed. Maybe he didn't stay. He was kind of glassy-eyed. Then I realized he was on drugs. He was kind of beautiful and messed up. Well, I was messed up, too. Just not beautiful.

I think just living in Asia for a couple of years and raised in the Asian community, I was not afraid to deal with people from Asia, whereas a lot of Asian Americans who grew up just with whites or in the suburbs, they just didn't know how to deal with somebody from Asia. But for me, it was no problem.

Are you different in terms of having relationships or encounters with gay Asian men versus having them with other minorities?

Well, with Asians, a lot of time, they'd like to eat. So maybe after the bars, we would go and eat something. If they didn't like me, they could at least like the food. No, eating was a preparation for sex. We'd go to an Asian restaurant, in Hollywood or Chinatown. A lot of them were open after one o'clock. You know Asian restaurants; they're open pretty late, they're pretty down home. The other thing is, it had a leveling effect because whether you are Thai, Chinese, Taiwanese, Japanese, you could basically eat anything. The food was palatable. You'd get to know the other person. It was a nice transition between a bar and driving somebody home. It was less threatening. It gave you a chance to unwind. Food always reminds you of who you are, about home. So it has a positive effect on your psyche. Maybe that's putting too much on food.

I'd run into people [in the restaurants]. Sometimes we could go as a group. So I think community could be formed at the dinner table. Whereas for Americans, a lot of it was through alcohol. Or maybe the gym. I think in the 1970s, Asians were not that much into gyms, but they were still into food. That seemed to be something that bound us socially.

Did you feel comfortable in that space? Do you think the waiters knew you were gay?

They didn't say anything. I mean, customers are customers. And besides, if you are a waiter, you've seen it all. It shouldn't really faze you, you know. You're concentrating on giving good service, getting a tip. It doesn't really matter who's sitting at the table. And also, you might be a gay waiter yourself. You have to remember also that a restaurant like that erased class lines. For one thing, they were inexpensive. Everybody could afford to pay. In a restaurant, you might see gay men. But you might also see singers from clubs, Asian singers. Or you might even see some call girls, different types of street people, or women working in hostess bars. After they finished, they might go to the restaurant or come to pick up something. So in that sense, people weren't going to get uptight about who was there. It was sort of democratic, not like American restaurants where people might look at you. Nobody gave a shit.

A VICIOUS CIRCLE

According to *Gay Histories and Cultures: An Encyclopedia*, "Gay bars diversified as L.A. grew. Bars where blacks and whites could cruise each other . . . were popular until the 1965 Watts riots, which caused a temporary rift among black and white gays. But by the seventies they were back, along with salsa bars for the Latino crowd and bars catering to Asians of all nationalities."[1]

The rise of these rice bars, though, also came on the heels of a significant moment in American history that might constitute a crisis in American masculinity—the Vietnam War. Lillian Faderman suggests that it is during this time that the butch/femme dichotomy in the gay men's community began to loosen up. She writes, "Gay men were often seduced by this need [for a butch/femme binary] as well [as lesbians], and it took times more open to complexity, such as the Vietnam era, to devalorize heterogenderality for them and to encourage both members of a male couple to wear mustaches or otherwise manifest masculinity."[2] Indeed, the popularity of the white masculine ideal became even more popular during the post-Vietnam era. Tim Edwards concurs that these "masculinists" began to dominate not only pages in gay periodicals but the gay scene as well in the 1970s.[3] Like Faderman, Sturken asserts that the Vietnam War and its outcome shattered the image of America as the epitome of universal masculinity. The Vietnam War, according to Sturken, "follows on the historic upheaval of the civil rights movement and intersects with the rise of the feminist movement. It has refigured the image not only of American technology and global power but also of American manhood and its relation to the feminine."[4] This was a time when white men found their previously unquestioned privileges under attack. The defeat in Vietnam further undermined patriarchal authority. Susan Jeffords writes, "The male Vietnam veteran—primarily a white male—was used as an emblem for a fallen and emasculated American male, one who had been falsely scorned by society and unjustly victimized by his own government. . . . No longer the oppressor, men came to be seen, primarily through the imagery of the Vietnam veteran, as themselves oppressed."[5] Marita Sturken further develops this point by citing writer Peter Marin on the unique bond that American servicemen in Vietnam shared as victims of "betrayals" by the American government. She writes, "Marin writes of the potential for the Vietnam veteran to produce a new kind of masculinity, one based on comradeship yet also caring and compassion."[6] This bond is taken to its homosexual extreme in the novel *Anywhere, Anywhere*, by Tim Barrus. The novel revolves around two Vietnam veterans who became lovers during the war because the experience they shared in Vietnam was so horrible and surreal that they could not find comfort and empathy in anyone—not even their sisters, mothers, girlfriends—but each other. Although the characters still exude masculinity, they suggest that the war experience has refigured men's relationships to each other and that their gayness is of a new and different breed.[7] Faderman is correct in suggesting that gay appropriation of masculinity did not escalate by coincidence, but rather it took advantage of this crisis of American manhood to offer a new definition of masculinity that does not exclude the possibility of same-sex eroticism. This liberated gay men from "heterogenderality." It was not inevitable anymore for gay men to conform to a butch/femme binary when one side of the equation was no longer a constant. Instead, they could explore the many possibilities being a butch could have.

But such "complexity" or the acceptability of "*homo*genderality" seems only to have been extended to "butches" but denied to "femmes" and, by extension, to Asians. In the 1970s, because the prevailing stereotype of Asian men, straight or gay, was one that is feminized, the only naturalized relationship that gay Asian men could have was with white men, the standard-bearers of American masculinity. Narrator Leo Joslin, who was involved in what may well have been one of the few Asian–Asian relationships in Los Angeles in the early 1980s, says, "They called us [me and my partner who was also Asian] lesbians because they were saying the appropriate relationship was a white guy and an Asian. Two Asians who like each other were lesbians." Any Asian man, regardless of his sexual predilection, was automatically assumed to be a femme, and the derision that Leo encountered implies that a sexual relationship between two Asians (read: femmes) was naturally inferior. According to Faderman, John D'Emilio has a theory to explain what she calls "homogenderal social arrangement" where lesbians and gay men who take on the same gender role (i.e., butch or femme) would be discouraged from considering each other as anything but platonic friends. She writes, "He [D'Emilio] sees its function as being analogous to the incest taboo, which guarantees that parental and sibling relationships remain stable though erotic relationships may fluctuate: lovers might come and go, but friends would always remain the same as long as they were off-limits as lovers. Butches would thus always have other butches as friends, and femmes would have other femmes."[8] Indeed, some narrators refer to each other as "sisters" and have characterized Asian–Asian relationships as "incestuous." However, D'Emilio's theory cannot encompass all the factors in the dearth of Asian–Asian relationships when race is involved. Most of the narrators have had sexual relations or attractions to other Asian men during the 1970s, even though they might have viewed these encounters as exceptions to the rule. Many of them also grew up in segregated neighborhoods where the only outlet for their early sexual desire was toward members of their own ethnic groups. D'Emilio's explanation is compelling, but it has left certain questions unanswered (which is understandable, since it is probably not designed to be applicable in this particular case): Why was it that the fluidity of butch/femme roles was operative in other racial communities, but Asians—as a whole race—were categorically confined to only the femme role? As narrator David Hong has so incisively pointed out to some white gay men who belittled his sexual preference for other Asians, "How come when I was at Studio One [a mainstream gay bar], I'd see other whites with other whites. What do you call that?" Is the femme personality something "essential" in all gay Asian men or did they feel they had to conform to it in order to partake in the gay scene? The perception of "incest" is more of a byproduct of the racialization of desire, rather than an explanation of it.

I argue that it has everything to do with the Vietnam War, not only because America, as the preeminent superpower of the West, lost. But what is also important is to whom it lost. In this case, I'm using Vietnam as a metonym for all of Asia. Asian American studies scholars, like Jinqi Ling, have suggested that passive and subservient images of Asians are tightly associated with the history of American imperialism in Asia. Ling writes, "In such contexts, the traditional Western concept of masculinity—which values men as embodiments of civilization, rationality, and aggressiveness and devalues women as embodiments of primitiveness, emotion, and passivity—was extended to account for the West's sense of economic and political superiority over Asia by projecting the latter as a diametrically opposed feminine Other."[9] As Ann Laura Stoller suggests, "a profusion of literary and historical studies have catalogued the wide range of sexual and gendered metaphors in which the feminized colonies, and the women in it, were to be penetrated, raped, silenced, and (dis)possessed. . . . Colonialism itself has been constructed as the sublimated sexual outlet of virile and homoerotic energies in the West."[10] Stoller's point is ironically illustrated in David Henry Hwang's *M. Butterfly*, a reverse *Madame Butterfly* or *Miss Saigon*, the later derivative Broadway play. In Hwang's play, Gallimard, a French diplomat, is tricked by Song Liling, a Communist Chinese spy who pretends to be a woman and who wins the love of Gallimard by manipulating his colonial fantasies. In the end, it is Gallimard who commits suicide. The connection between imperialism and colonial desire is made perfectly clear through the character of Renee, a younger Danish woman with whom Gallimard has an affair. She says regarding the white male penis,

> And there's so much fuss that we make about it. Like, I think the reason we fight wars is because we wear clothes. Because no one knows—between the men, I mean—who has the bigger . . . weenie. So, if I'm a guy with a small one, I'm going to build a really big building or take over a really big piece of land or write a really long book so the other men don't know, right? But, see, it never really works, that's the problem. I mean, you conquer the country, or whatever, but you're still wearing clothes, so there's no way to prove absolutely whose is bigger or smaller. And that's what we call a civilized society. The whole world run by a bunch of men with pricks the size of pins.[11]

The portrayals of Asians as "childlike" and "subservient," needing and *wanting* the protection of the superior and more democratic America not only justified American foreign policies,[12] but more interestingly, this stereotype also became indoctrinated into the American imagination to win the consent of both military personnel and civilians for American military involvement in Asia. And the Vietnam War as the first televised American conflict not only perpetuated, but also compounded, this indoctrination like no other war had before.[13] Despite the rapid changes in gay men's relations to masculinity in the 1970s, the Vietnam War informed how gay Asian men continued to be marginalized as feminine, passive, and dependent. While a gay white man now had the option to be a bodybuilder and still had his chiseled body worshipped and his gay credentials intact, the gay Asian clone in Paul Chen's narrative worked up a sweat as a way to turn his muscular back on his racial community. Race relations in the gay community cannot be divorced from this context.

Asian American cultural critics and researchers have commented, sometimes using statistics of outmarriages, on the effects of these images in discouraging Asian women from perceiving Asian men as potential sexual partners. I suspect the same element is at work here with gay Asian men.[14] However, unlike their heterosexual female counterparts who could look at their parents for the possible model of heterosexual Asian–Asian attraction and love, gay Asian men had no such models. In addition, as men, they could also internalize these images and perceive themselves as not masculine, and therefore not desirable.

Because Asians were categorically excluded from the white model of masculinity, the white/masculine and Asian/feminine binary became naturalized. The archetypal white–Asian relationship excluded other possibilities, constituting a sort of fascism of desire that was predicated on a heterosexist ideology that normalizes only sexual unions between "males" and "females." As Viet Thanh Nguyen writes, "This [masculine/feminine] binary model serves, as Judith Butler has argued, to affirm a continuity between sex, gender and desire which naturalizes heterosexuality. This naturalization arised [*sic*] from an analogy in which sex is to gender as nature is to culture, with desire and sexual practice consequent to the strict correlation of sex/gender."[15] However, it is not only this dominant heterosexist ideology at the time that dictated the sexual incompatibility of two femmes, and in effect, two Asians, since, as David Hong retorts, sexual encounters between two white men were perfectly acceptable. But the dismissal of Asian–Asian sexuality also stemmed from the sexist notion—even among gay men—that somehow "lesbian" relationships, or relationships between two women, are inferior and less authentic. Narrator Leo Joslin, for example, received a hostile reaction when he told a white bartender in a gay Asian bar that he preferred Asians. He says, "On one level, it was my preference. On another, it was an act of defiance. Some people didn't like it that I would come out and say it, that I would rather be with an Asian than with a white guy. Then at Mugi's, I remember telling the bartender that, and he just really treated me badly afterward."

Some narrators offer different theories on why Asian–Asian relationships were discouraged. Invisibility has often been used to explain the difficulty in organizing gay Asian men. One recurring complaint was, "We couldn't find each other." There was a lack of gay Asian role models in leadership positions. Gay Asian men were isolated because they did not find representations of themselves in either the mainstream (read: white) gay community or the mainstream (read: straight) Asian American community. Not only were they invisible to each other, but they themselves felt invisible to the rest of the world. In such an environment, should anyone be surprised that an Asian–Asian relationship was such an odd phenomenon?

But numbers cannot explain everything. It might be true before the 1970s that gay Asians were few and scattered, but certain dynamics persisted even with River Club or Mugi's, sites where one to two hundred gay Asians congregated every weekend. The experiences of the narrators in rice bars prove that it was not only the alienating environment of being a minority in a mainstream gay establishment that kept most gay Asians apart. Instead, I argue that the white/masculine and Asian/feminine binary reinforces the dependency of gay Asian men on their white counterparts. Not only were gay Asian men led to believe that other gay Asian men were not desirable, but feeling unworthy themselves, they could only find validation from white gay men, and not each other. Even when one gay Asian man met another, there were already sets of expectations that informed how they were going to relate to each other. As long as those expectations were left unchallenged, no matter what kind of space gay Asians occupied, or how many of them occupied it, those expectations would inevitably be inscribed in the spaces around them.

While I do not wish to deny the importance of this theme of invisibility in the narrators' lives, a closer examination of gay bars in Los Angeles—the focal point of social and sexual life for many gay men at that time—reveals a much more complex and strategic geography of both absences and presences. This spatialization of desire is another layer of the power dynamics between white and Asian gay men. In other words, gay Asian men were simultaneously invisible *and* conspicuous in their marginalization and necessarily so, since you cannot marginalize someone who is not there. Michel Foucault argues that "discipline proceeds from the distribution of individuals in space."[16] And one of the techniques of this distribution is what he calls "enclosure":

> Its aim was to establish presences and absences, to know where and how to locate individuals, to set up useful communications, to interrupt others, to be able at each

> moment to supervise the conduct of each individual, to assess it, to judge it, to calculate its qualities or merits. It was a procedure, therefore, aimed at knowing, mastering and using.[17]

The gay bars constituted various "sites of assembly" with their own rules and manners, which in turn enforced a self-identity for those populating them. Because power was already inscribed in how these spaces were arranged, authority was not visible and the people within it were therefore internally disciplined.[18] By looking at where gay Asian men were invisible and where they were conspicuous, we gain a deeper insight into the nature of the power relationship.

Though a gay Mecca in one of the largest metropolitan cities in the United States, West Hollywood, as we have seen in the previous chapter, was not particularly inviting to people of color in the 1970s and early 1980s. Recent immigrants and tourists who did not have American driver's licenses faced yet another hurdle. Even when gay Asian men made it into the bars, they often felt invisible because the clientele in mainstream gay bars were generally not interested in Asians at the time. Sometimes they could be downright hostile. To avoid disappointment or negative reinforcement, many gay Asian men lowered their expectations and resolved that outings to these places would not be romantic or sexual in nature. As David Hong says,

> Going to Studio One was more like partying around, dancing with your friends and things like that. It was not an outlet for me to find and to have sexual encounters. I hung around with other friends. It was like a group thing. I would not go to Studio One on my own because I didn't find it to be entertaining going alone. I didn't want to stand there like a model. . . . It wasn't that I didn't feel welcome. Feeling welcome is based on what you're looking for. If you're out there for sexual encounters, then you can easily say that it's not a place for you.

The spaces of mainstream gay bars and gay Asian bars were clearly delineated for many gay Asians. If an Asian man wanted to find a sexual partner, he would go to the gay Asian bars, where he could be sure the men there would be interested in Asians sexually or romantically. As narrator Roy Kawasaki suggests, "I enjoy the gay Asian bars, like Mugi's, although it was like a cesspool. . . . The Caucasians that went there, you know they were interested in Asians, so you didn't have to guess or play mind games."

While gay Asian men found themselves exiled in gay Asian bars, creating in effect instant enforced "colonies," these spaces constituted for white gay men "ghettos" to which they could go "slumming" and find Asian men. Here I have found the concept of "ethnic tourism" to be useful in analyzing these spaces. As Pierre L. Van Den Berghe suggests, tourism is the ultimate form of ethnic relations. It is the active quest for the exotic Other that characterizes "ethnic tourism" from other forms of tourism or cultural encounters. Van Den Berghe explains, "Modernity produces homogenization, instability, and inauthenticity, and thus generates in the most modernized among us a quest for the opposite of these things. The tourist searches for the authentic encounters with the other. The greater the otherness of the other, the more satisfying the tourist experience."[19] The very word "clone" that describes gay men striking a masculine pose exhibits the very homogenization and inauthenticity that Van Den Berghe writes about, against which men of color become perfect "exotic" foils.

Using the concept of "ethnic tourism" to characterize the behavior pattern in such a relationship is not new. Lillian Faderman describes Harlem in its heyday during the 1920s as also a tourist site for white gay men and lesbians. She writes, "White fascination with Harlem seems to have smacked of a 'sexual colonialism,' in which many whites *used* Harlem as a commodity, a stimulant to sexuality. And as in many colonized countries, Harlem itself, needing to encourage tourism for economic reasons, seemed to welcome the party atmosphere."[20] Likewise, rice bars have also been characterized as tourist spots. In an article in the gay magazine *Stallion.* its author, an "Occidental" named Blade, writes,

> Gay travelers, whether they're civilians on business or vacation, or members of our own armed forces, have been hooked on Asians ever since Butterfly met Pinkerton, but those of us who aren't free to travel must try to satisfy our cravings here at home. It isn't all that difficult. Practically every large American city has its "in" place (a meeting ground for East and West), usually a bar or restaurant where yellow-or-tan-skinned fellows, young, willing, and exotic may contact Occidental men who (perhaps recognizing their self-imposed stereotype) have dubbed themselves "rice queens," men who seem to prefer submissive, effeminate little "geisha guys" or "sing-song boys." The stereotype of "old and white" plus "young and yellow" remains so strong that at first glance an outsider might easily be led to think he'd stumbled into a pedophile's club.[21]

Here we see the "specialty bars" as a sort of ersatz tourism for white men. *Pacific Bridge*, a magazine founded in 1982 and based in San Francisco, provides another example. The magazine is devoted almost entirely to personal ads between Asians and non-Asians. In the introductory letter of its first issue in May 1982, its editor asks, "How can gay Asians and non-Asians get together? Sure, there are 'specialty bars' in New York, San Francisco, and Los Angeles. And some of us are able to travel overseas. But for most of us, meeting new friends is a difficult, time-consuming process." In this case, for those rice queens who were too lazy to drive across town, these ads are even cheaper and less time-consuming alternatives, almost like being a tourist without leaving the comfort of your own home. Using the word "specialty" to characterize gay Asian bars also reinforces the primacy of whiteness in gay male desire. Who is the "specialty"? And for whom? Browsing through *Pacific Bridge*, it becomes obvious who the "us" is in the introductory letter with whom the editor identifies. It's always the non-Asian (overwhelmingly white) men who are the "tourists."

In his research on magazines that cater to rice queens, Paul Hagland finds that the white men's fantasies are often manifested in stories of international travel and they all share something in common. He writes, "In none of the 'traveler's tales' or fictional accounts in these publications does an API actually reject a Caucasian as sex partner. . . . The narrative constructed by the orientalist apparently does not grant the Asian such an option. In fact, the Caucasian partner or would be partner is rarely described at all . . . , but it does not matter in the universe of the rice queen: his physical profile is not at issue."[22] I would argue that it is not so much that their physical profile is not at issue. Rather, this lack of details allows the target audience of white readers to step into these erotic tales as the protagonists. Any physical description of the protagonist—aside from the fact that he is invariably white—would interfere with the mental re-enactment in the minds of the white readers. Whereas the exotic settings are variable, the young Asian men's pliancy is a constant. As mere props, they have no sexual autonomy.

Just like the traveler's tales or personal ads, the "specialty bars" privilege white men as the primary audience. And if they are the active tourists and these bars the tourist spots, the geography of these bars is significant. Both gay Asian bars in Los Angeles during the 1970s and early 1980s, Mugi's (East Hollywood) and the River Club (Los Feliz), were situated just far enough from the main West Hollywood scene, or the "outskirts of Hollywood," as Reggie Bogan describes it. This spatial arrangement delineated a border that made crossing it a more authentic "slumming" experience for the white men and in effect kept the majority of gay Asian men from going to other bars in the more actively gay part of the city.

The narrators found the same sexual hierarchy reinscribed in the gay Asian bars. All the narrators comment on the ethnic segregation in these bars as well as their competition for the same object of desire. Certainly, language and cultural barriers played a role in this ethnic segregation. But the hostility and suspicion could better be explained by the perceived notion of Asian–Asian sexual incompatibility, which made white gay men the prize they would compete against each other for. Gay white men were free to "tour" the different cliques. Often they would meet other Asians through fellow Caucasian friends and/or their partners or dates. Under each other's watchful eyes, though, the Asians were relatively immobile. Lack of access to each other prevented them from truly conceiving a panethnic sexual identity, let alone a community.

The gay Asian bars themselves manifested the different roles and relationships that Van Den Berghe classifies in his study of ethnic tourism: the tourist who consumes exoticism; the native or "touree" who puts himself on display for economic reasons (except in this case it might be economics of a sexual nature); and the middleman, the "tour guide," who brings the two together and facilitates the transaction. Narrator Reggie Bogan remembers Yoshi and him playing a matchmaking role between the Asian and non-Asian clientele. And like the middleman in Van Den Berghe's research, they would also try to minimize the potential for exploitations in these fleeting encounters by steering patrons away from regulars who had a bad reputation. To maximize profits and maintain its clientele, the "tour guides" had to fulfill a certain expectation of "a very good pick-up bar for Asians" and inadvertently reinforced the sexual hierarchy where whiteness was prized. This arrangement certainly gave the white men tremendous advantages.

The "tourees" were not always the stereotypical victim in this kind of relationships. While some resented being on display, others, like some of the natives in Van Den Berghe's research, "modify their behavior and their cultural artifacts in response to tourist demand, and seek to derive economic benefits from literally making a spectacle of themselves."[23] Narrator Paul Bautista, on learning about rice queens, felt a surge of self-worth and turned their gazes into spotlights. Similarly, narrator Paul Chen recognizes that Asians were not a commodity in mainstream bars. So the fact that their ethnicity was prized in the gay Asian bars conferred on them certain power when negotiating with white men. Even in the arena of personal ads, Asians seemed to have held a dubious advantage. Ted Hune remembers getting a lot of responses from rice queens through several ads he placed in the *Advocate* in the 1970s. "Each one that I would run," he says, "I would get maybe seventy to 150 responses. . . . Caucasian friends of mine would comment when I ran an ad that I would get three times the responses being Asian than they would as Caucasians, everything else we were looking for being the same." However, all of them are conscious of the fact that this is in no way to suggest that there was an equal power dynamics between whites and Asians. The kind of ethnic segregation that Roy Kawasaki and other narrators observed prevented any racial solidarity among the gay Asian men. Under this kind of sexual-economic arrangement, Asians viewed each other suspiciously, like competitors for the white men's attention, much like some tourees competed against each other to sell their artifacts to the tourists. This power to manipulate is a dangerous one. As bell hooks suggests, "Marginalized groups, deemed Other, who have been ignored, rendered invisible, can be seduced by the emphasis on Otherness, by its commodification, because it offers the promise of recognition and reconciliation."[24] Submitting ourselves to this seduction leaves a problematic racialized sexual ideology unchallenged and reinforces our Otherness.

But we should avoid making easy judgments. As narrator Virgil Vang says,

> I think it's easy to condemn the Asians to say that they buy into [racist stereotypes]. I didn't need to find another older white guy. My attitude might be because of my privileges, rather than anything else. My English is good. I have a job. Economically I'm independent. A lot of Asians I knew, from Japan or Taipei or other places of Asia, did have older white boyfriends who did have money and more security. I think they'd do it for pragmatic reasons. They might not even like it or know it. Okay, the guy wants a massage so I just give him a few chops on the shoulders. They want a flower arrangement? Okay, I'll figure it out. It's more strategic. If my English is lousy, I have no job, and I'm new in the country, yes, sure, I'd shack up with an old white guy. But you know, he'd better have some money. I don't really cast judgment on that.

Denied other sexual outlets, discouraged from seeing their Asian brothers as potential partners, and limited in numbers and supportive institutions and other resources, it should not surprise us that many gay Asian men did not regard rice bars as categorically something negative or debased, as later generations of gay Asian men, having inherited both a history and geography, might have. Michel Foucault suggests that the power of discipline does not solely reside in laws and regulations. Its genius often lies in the way the ideology of the ruling power is embedded in the spaces around us, so we must see each other through the eye of power, yet at the same time we know we are constantly being watched by each other in the same way. In other words, through specific spatial arrangement, we discipline ourselves. It is no different with the gay Asian bars.

For example, many narrators themselves describe Asians as passive and ascribe this trait to Asian culture in general, even though many of them are not the type that anyone could push around. According to them, this is why they would not approach each other or anyone for that matter. I believe that, rather than Asian culture, it is the culture within the gay Asian bars themselves that enforced "shyness" on gay Asian men. I agree with narrator Rummel Bautista when he says,

> It [the bars] promoted this thinking that we couldn't possibly be assertive. I mean, if you don't think you're marketable, why would you even dare to go out and even try to pick up someone? How could you? You'd probably think he's probably attracted to white guys, like the rest of them are. You'd think you're the only one who didn't get the formula.

Roy Kawasaki expresses a similar sentiment: "I think I just never pursued Asians because of the feedback. It's like, there was no sense trying because you were not going to get anywhere with an Asian. He probably wouldn't be interested." Even though a conventional cultural explanation is often used to account for "Asian passivity," it is more probable that a strict sexual code was already embedded into these spaces. In fact, this "Asian passivity" bears a remarkable resemblance to the timidity Frantz Fanon attributes to colonized Africans more than thirty years ago.[25] The circle is indeed fascist: a preexisting sexual hierarchy prevented Asians from relating to each other in a sexual and romantic way, and in turn, the visible lack of Asian–Asian relationships made this hierarchy a natural law. The edict, "Asians never like other Asians," was both evidence and cause.

These gay Asian bars in the 1970s and early 1980s were indeed ambivalent spaces. They presented sexual opportunities to gay Asian men, and they offered them a refuge from the sometimes hostile and racist mainstream gay community. However, they did not foster an openness and intimacy among gay Asian men. As narrator Harry Park points out,

> You have to take into consideration the time period and the fear of raids and the fear of giving out too much information about yourself. Because if there is a raid, subconsciously you don't know if the other person is going to fink on you. There is always that threat, that fear. So it was better to be anonymous. It was just like an unwritten law. Unless I give you permission, unless I want to tell you my last name, where I live and whatever, you never ask. And you never give out that kind of information freely.

André Ting agrees, "River Club was okay, but River Club was only for fun and sex. There's no bonding, no camaraderie. The Asians played at the River Club, but it's not for gay liberation, not for consciousness raising." Even among the circle of friends that eventually became the leadership of early A/PLG, there were barriers in the beginning. Tak Yamamoto, its first president, remembers this from his pre-A/PLG days,

> We never got deep because I think there was a certain reluctance to reveal yourself. You knew nothing of confidentiality. You didn't know any of this was going to go anywhere. You didn't know if it was worth even delving into. You didn't know if there was an interest in any heavy dialogue at all. . . . Not until the formation of A/PLG did we actually develop heart-to-heart.

In *The Making of the English Working Class*, E. P. Thompson states that people comprise a class when "some men, as a result of common experience . . . feel and *articulate* the identity of their interests as between themselves, and as against other men whose interests are different from (and usually opposed to) theirs" (emphasis mine).[26] To bring a group of people together under one identity, it is not enough for them to just share a common interest. That interest has to be articulated. It is clear that gay Asian men share many experiences in these bars, but these bars did not afford them a space to *articulate* an identity. They would need another space to complete this last step of group formation. Until then, the men could not yet begin to share a collective history. However, these spaces presented a powerful visualization of the contradictions they had felt all along. Why did they not find other Asians attractive anymore? Why did they have to look beyond themselves for validation? Why could they not talk to each other? For the first time, they found themselves congregating in the same space and they could not avoid these questions any longer. Roy Kawasaki remembers, "We got more exposure to more cultures at these venues. We noticed more groups than we otherwise would've been able to see." In effect, these gay Asian bars hastened the process of community formation. As Andy C. says, "[The bar dynamics] set a trend for A/PLG to really have to do something to make the Asians band together as a group. I think the River Club accelerated the formation of A/PLG." Articulation is a key component to group formation. As a group of gay Asian Pacific men and their supporters came together and founded A/PLG in 1980, they began to struggle—sometimes against each other—with these questions.

NOTES

1. George Haggerty, ed. *Gay Histories and Cultures: An Encyclopedia* (New York: Garland Publishing, 2000), 549.

2. Lillian Faderman, *Odd Girls and Twilight Lovers: A History of Lesbian Life in Twentieth Century America* (New York: Penguin Books, 1991), 173.

3. Tim Edwards, *Erotics & Politics: Gay Male Sexuality, Masculinity and Feminism* (New York: Routledge, 1994), 3.

4. Marita Sturken, *Tangled Memories: The Vietnam War, the AIDS Epidemic, and the Politics of Remembering* (Berkeley: University of California, Press, 1997), 15.

5. Susan Jeffords, *The Remasculinization of America* (Bloomington: Indiana University Press, 1989), 168–69.

6. Sturken, *Tangled Memories*, 119.

7. Tim Barrus, *Anywhere, Anywhere* (Stamford, Conn.: Knights Press, 1987).

8. Faderman, *Odd Girls and Twilight Lovers*, 174.

9. Jinqi Ling, "Identity Crisis and Gender Politics: Reappropriating Asian American Masculinity," in *An Interethnic Companion to Asian American Literature*, ed. King-Kok Cheung (New York: Cambridge University Press, 1997), 314.

10. Ann Laura Stoller, *Race and the Education of Desire: Foucault's* History of Sexuality *and the Colonial Order of Things* (Durham: Duke University Press, 1995), 174.

11. David Henry Hwang, *M. Butterfly* (New York: Plume Books, 1988), 55–56.

12. See John W. Dower, *War Without Mercy: Race and Power in the Pacific War* (New York: Pantheon Books, 1986).

13. See Sturken, *Tangled Memories*, 115. Sturken finds the feminization of Vietnam replicated by post-war films about the war, often made by veterans. She writes,

> There are no male Vietnamese protagonists in these films. . . . The absence of the male Vietnamese protagonist allows Vietnam to be represented in these films by women. In *Full Metal Jacket, Casualties of War,* and *Heaven and Earth*, women are emblems of the victimized Vietnam, not the victorious Vietnam but a feminized, passive, violated country. In all three films, women represent the country of Vietnam under the control of American GIs.

14. See also Richard Fung, "Seeing Yellow: Asian Identities in Film and Video," in *The State of Asian America: Activism and Resistance in the 1990s*, ed. Karin Aguilar-San Juan (Boston: South End Press, 1994), 169.

15. See Viet Thanh Nguyen, *Writing the Body Politic: Asian American Subjects and the American Nation* (Ph.D. diss., University of California, Berkeley, 1997), 167.

16. Michel Foucault, *Discipline and Punish: The Birth of the Prison* (New York: Pantheon Books, 1977), 141.

17. Foucault, *Discipline and Punish*, 143.

18. See also Peter Stallybrass and Allan White, "The Grotesque Body and the Smithfield Muse: Authorship in the Eighteenth Century," in *Politics and Poetics of Transgression* (Ithaca, N.Y.: Cornell University Press, 1986), 80–101.

19. Pierre L. Van Den Berghe, *The Quest for Other: Ethnic Tourism in San Cristobal, Mexico* (Seattle: University of Washington Press, 1994), 8.

20. Faderman, *Odd Girls and Twilight Lovers*, 68.

21. Blade, "Hard-Boiled Rice: Are the Days of 'Rice Queens' and 'Geisha Boys' Giving Way to a Tough New Breed of Oriental Men?" *Stallion: The Magazine of the Alternative Lifestyle* (May 1984): 48.

22. Paul EeNam Park Hagland, " 'Undressing the Oriental Boy': The Gay Asian in the Social Imaginary of the Gay White Male," in *Looking Queer: Body Image and Identity in Lesbian, Bisexual, Gay and Transgender Communities*, ed. Dawn Atkins (New York: Haworth Press, 1998), 282.

23. Van Den Berghe, *The Quest for Other*, 15. Again, I extrapolate "economic benefits" in this case not in the monetary sense.

24. bell hooks, *Black Looks: Race and Representations* (New York: Routledge, 1992), 3.

25. Frantz Fanon, *Black Skin, White Masks* (New York: Grove Press, Inc., 1967).

26. E. P. Thompson, *The Making of the English Working Class* (New York: Pantheon Books, 1963), 8–9.

4

The Call from Morris Kight

STRUGGLE WITH MY GAYNESS

It is erroneous to assume that one racial community is more homophobic than another or that the white community is more enlightened about sexual matters. The forms that homophobia takes simply cannot be removed from their contexts and quantified to be measured against each other. Perhaps a more useful examination is to analyze qualitatively how racism complicates homophobia in communities of color. For many minorities, including gay men and lesbians, their home community is not only a safe, supportive space, but they also draw strength from it to survive and resist the prejudice and discrimination in the larger society. But the conflation of homosexuality and effeminacy in men connotes a weakness to some that makes gay men not positive models in their community. For Asian men especially, who have suffered a long history of emasculation, their gay brothers become accomplices, even if unwitting ones, in the purveying of negative stereotypes. Further, as some narrators will attest in this chapter, the rise of the Asian American movement in the late 1960s and early 1970s owed much of its origins to Marxist-Leninist-Maoist thoughts that devalued homosexuality as a product of bourgeois decadence that would be eliminated with the eventual demise of capitalism.[1] Many gay Asian men active in the movement also learned to adopt the same radical personalities as ideological role models. Virgil Vang, for example, is a writer heavily influenced by Mao Tse-Tung's teaching. "We were reading a lot of his stuff at the time," he recalls. " 'Serving the People.' 'Who is Art For?' A lot of socialist realist art. Looked like everybody in China was pretty healthy. Rosy cheeks. There was one famous poster where people of all different colors are holding rifles or something, and they are all supporting the revolution. So those kinds of icons were pretty prominent." Caught up in the ideological fervor, many of them had to either ignore their sexuality or reconcile it with their commitment to the movement on their own.

That was not an easy task. Many of their peers saw the re-masculinization of Asian men as a key project in the recovery of the history of Asians in America. Gay Asian men could scarcely turn to "Asian American history" to find examples of their "ancestry." As Sylvia Yanagisako notes, most of the Asian American history taught in colleges focuses on conventionally masculine men. She writes,

> The emphasis on the active agency of men in Asian American history is likewise a conscious attempt to challenge the metonymic equation of Asian with the feminine. To celebrate male ancestors characterized by an "indomitable spirit, fiercely hopeful and resilient" is to undermine the symbolic equation that East is to West as female is to male. This celebration of fierce resistance is taken the farthest in Carlos Bulosan's book [*America Is In the Heart*], which recounts several instances in which he had to be forcibly restrained from killing his White humiliators.[2]

This, of course, does not mean that gay Asian men must be feminine by nature, and not "fiercely hopeful and resilient." But the re-inscription of masculinity is often at the expense of someone else (and in Yanagisako's case, it is Asian American women who are devalued). For example, in the introduction to *The Big Aiiieeeee!* (a follow-up to their pioneer anthology in Asian American literature, *Aiiieeeee!*, in 1974), its all-male editors write, "It is an article of white liberal American faith today that Chinese men, at their best, are effeminate closet queens like Charlie Chan and, at their worst, are homosexual menaces like Fu Manchu. No wonder David Henry Hwang's derivative *M. Butterfly* won the Tony for best new play in 1988. The good Chinese man, at his best, is the fulfillment of white male homosexual fantasy, literally kissing white ass. Now Hwang and the stereotype are inextricably one."[3] Whether intended or not, this kind of rhetoric has an alienating effect on their queer brothers. As David Eng writes, "The *Aiiieeeee!* group's 'solution' to the mainstream racist and (homo)sexualized stereotype of 'Asian and anus'—their recipe for political resistance—is a simple and inadequate movement of reversal: locating homosexuality outside the Asian American community and back within the aegis of a white male homosexual fantasy."[4] In addition, it reproduces a logic of gender hierarchy that assumes and naturalizes only heterosexuality and suppresses "deviant forms of sexuality." The questioning of exclusive or normalized heterosexuality in such an ultimately homosocial environment as the bachelor society is only beginning to be explored recently.[5]

Underestimated for its revolutionary potential, homosexuality, in the many ways that it was conceived and perceived in the Asian American communities, was incompatible with the anti-racist strategies of the community. I have often found it both ironic and tragic that some of the more closeted individuals that I have come across for the research of this project—a few of whom declined to participate—were the ones who were more active in progressive politics in the community that has given them the strength, pride, and the political analysis to combat racism in their lives.

To be fair, there were always gay Asian men—especially since the 1990s but long before that as well—who had no qualms being out in the community and working side by side with heterosexual Asian men and women to make sure the community was accountable to gay men and lesbians. As early as 1972, *Bridge*, a community publication organized by a group of Asian leftists on the West Coast, received and published a letter to an editor from an openly gay Asian man calling for the end of homophobia in the movement. Hung Nung, the letter-writer, proclaims,

> I am Asian, a male and gay. For the past year since I've gotten involved with the Asian Movement, or at least tried—I have been scorned, ridiculed and rejected by many so-called sincere Asian Movement people, especially the males. The females have been much kinder and understanding. But the males somehow feel that I'm undermining their fragile male egos. I strongly believe in honesty, I won't pretend that I'm not gay, just as I'm proud to be Asian. And the two are not mutually exclusive. Unlike a number of gay Asian males—I for one prefer Asian partners. White men do not appeal to me![6]

Hung Nung underscores the prejudice in the Asian American movement that many narrators echo in this chapter. He also expresses dissatisfaction of an interracial dynamics between white and gay Asian men that must have been pervasive enough to warrant mention in a brief letter that is supposed to be about homophobia in the Asian American movement. This could be an interesting rhetorical strategy: Nung's preference for other Asians is evidence for his credential in the movement. It is as if, without this explanation, he could be dismissed as just another gay Asian man who is only interested in white men, a race traitor. Maybe because of the anti-establishment ideology of the movement that predicates itself on a sense of racial pride, many gay Asian participants of the movement did look upon other Asian men or men of color as potential sexual and romantic partners. I have to wonder what impact the Asian American movement would have on the prevailing white–Asian dynamics in the gay community, had the movement embraced their lesbian and gay comrades wholeheartedly. Though not lacking straight allies, gay Asian men who worked on the Asian left organized their work life and social life a little differently from their counterparts who had no such affiliation with the Asian American movement.

Virgil Vang

Homosexuality was sort of like spousal abuse, sexual abuse, or drugs. Those things were no-no. Nobody ever talked about those things in the Asian American community. They were just under the carpet. So I never really looked to the Asian American community for that kind of support. During my [Asian American] movement days, I knew some gays and lesbians, but they had to figure out how to reconcile it.

How did you yourself reconcile it?

You do your thing in the daytime. You go to a community meeting from seven until ten P.M. Then afterward, maybe you go home and change. Then you go to a bar or something. You just schedule it so you don't mix them together. Later on, of course, you have these gay Asian groups, and that's different.

But back then when I came down to L.A. [from San Francisco] in 1977, just the nature of my job, I had to deal with Asian American community organizations, a lot of different people. So I'd see the same people at certain kinds of community functions. I brought some of my boyfriends to these events, only the Asian guys, because they would blend in [since these were events in the Asian American community]. So my co-workers would just think they were just friends. I wouldn't bring a black guy or a white guy or a non-Asian. But I never got the sexuality involved in my work. . . . Although in the 1980s, when people gave speeches, they'd say they are anti-homophobic, I don't know what they meant. Did they really believe it or were they just saying it? That's what you were supposed to say: I'm anti-racist, anti-homophobic, anti-whatever.

I wasn't so much afraid of losing my job if they found out. I think I was more afraid of the stereotypes people in the community had of being gay—basically, you know, that gay men are disloyal to their family. There was such a big stress on family. Of course, gay couples are adopting nowadays, but in the 1970s, I don't think that was happening. I was more afraid of their value systems or expectations.

Also, it was so much trouble to educate people around you. So what am I going to do? If some Asian Americans go, "Oh, are you gay?", I am not going to be talking about Stonewall, you know, and how that was the beginning of gay liberation. That'll just flow over their heads like water. I don't think I came out at work maybe until the last ten years. I was then able to integrate my being gay into my work, into my writing. A lot of people have read different things I've written. So they sort of knew anyway. So there was less of a separation. Also by my late thirties, early forties, I think I have accomplished enough so that people have to judge me or evaluate me on my work, rather than my sexual orientation. That makes a difference. By that time, I have done a few things. Even if they don't personally agree with my sexual orientation, they have to at least look at the work.

Stan Yogi

In 1981, my freshman year at UCLA, I was rooming with one of my best friends from [Gardena High School]. We had an apartment on Brockton. He came out to me first. By that time, he was starting to go out to bars and meeting different men, dah, dah, dah, but he wasn't telling me about it. I don't think I came out to him right at that time. I didn't reciprocate right away, but I did eventually. It was the safety of knowing that he was gay, too, and he was okay with coming out to me. So I think that was really good for me because he was one of the few people during my undergraduate years I could just talk openly and honestly with about being gay. I wasn't doing anything in terms of seeing people or even putting myself in situations where I would date people. He was the first person I was out to. At least I could talk [to him] about that kind of attraction.

Instead, I channeled my energy into being a student and then I was involved in a lot of activities, both on campus and off, mostly on campus. I tutored for AAP [Academic Advancement Program for low-income and first-generation college students] and was involved in the Asian American Studies Center. I wrote for *Pacific Ties* [UCLA's Asian Pacific Islander student newsmagazine] and was one of its associate editors for several years. At that time, we shared an office with *Ten Percent*, the gay student paper. So I had a lot of interaction with gay men who were involved in *Ten Percent*. But it was always in the context of my identity as a *Pac Ties* staff person, as opposed to a gay person. If they knew I was gay, they didn't say anything.

The Asian American Studies Center once organized a forum for Asian American men to basically talk about how they felt about depictions of Asian American men in the media, in the sense that we were depicted as being sort of asexual and emasculated. I remember that striking a chord with me. Even at that time, I recognized there was a broad spectrum of what masculinity meant and it wasn't just one rigid definition. But I think there was a little bit of homophobia that I internalized because I, too, associated those depictions of Asian men as being feminine as negative.

I was also involved in community groups like NCRR [National Coalition for Redress/Reparations]. Homosexuality didn't come up a whole lot as a subject. But I remember being in different meetings and having conversations with different progressive activists at that time, and people were just talking anecdotally about having interaction with gay people. I remember this woman talking about going to a women's bar, which wasn't necessarily a lesbian bar, but just a bar for women to go to and not have to worry about being hounded by men. I guess there was this woman at the bar who was interested in this activist narrating the story. Just the sense of disgust that she conveyed in narrating the story led me to believe that she was not open to gay sexuality. And the reaction of her audience was one of general support—like they understood what she was going through—if not implicit agreement. Little things like that would happen off and on. On my part, I just avoided talking about intimate relationships. If the subject came up, I'd try to change the subject. And nobody really pressed me. Once in a while, there were people who would basically set me up with a woman. I don't remember how I deflected that, but I did. A lot of the progressive Asian Americans in the 1970s and 1980s were involved in these larger Communist groups from my understanding. I guess the party line for these groups was that homosexuality was not good. I was still too afraid to be public about being gay, even though I think more and more people were wondering whether I was because I never had a girlfriend for four, four and a half years of college. There were some of those tell-tale signs [laughs] of telling whether someone was gay. And actually Steve Lew told me years after we were both living in L.A., one of our mutual friends was telling him that, "Oh, I'm glad you're hooking up with Stan because he was questioning his sexuality." So obviously people were wondering, if not speculating aloud, about that.

I [first] met Steve Lew through my involvement with progressive Asian American organizations [in Los Angeles] at that time. We weren't necessarily in a group together. I was volunteering for KPFK, the Pacifica radio station here [in L.A.]. There was this Asian American program called *East Wind*. Steve came on the program for some reason I don't remember. We didn't see each other often, maybe once in a while at Asian American organizational parties and events. I didn't know that he was gay at that time. It wasn't until we were both living in the Bay Area that I found out he was gay. I remember him telling me once that people in the organization that he was involved in basically asked him to quote-and-unquote "struggle" with his homosexuality: AKA, don't be that way anymore. We knew a lot of the same people. So I knew that was the kind of attitude that was taken. I think after the fall of the Soviet Union, these groups tended to lose some of their rigid rhetoric.

What were your political influences?

Gosh, I can't identify any particular individual or thing. I guess recognizing I was gay from an early point in my life, whether I had a language for it or not. And knowing that I was different and knowing that difference could result in serious injury or death to me. When I was in tenth grade, there was an initiative to ban gay people from being teachers. Fortunately, that didn't pass. That was one moment where there was sort of a crystallization of my recognition of how reviled, at least in certain circles, gay people were. I didn't know about Stonewall definitely. I didn't know about the gay and lesbian movement as an organized movement, *per se*. But I knew that gay men were organizing. There were these marches that I knew of. I was vaguely aware of the Harvey Milk assassination and the gay community's response afterward. I was vaguely aware of organizing going on, but not a movement, *per se*.

Given the community in which I grew up, having a very early identification of being Japanese American contributed to my political perspectives and beliefs. You know, the redress movement was what I got involved in initially in high school. I wasn't terribly enthusiastic about it until I learned more about what happened during the internment and tapped into this sense of injustice. I was looking through books that my parents had that were, in part, about the internment, and there were pictures of the internment and all these things that led to the internment, banners and things that were expressing hatred toward Japanese Americans. I really took that in at a deep level and identified with the feeling of persecution, knowing that I'm Japanese American and this could be me.

Steve Lew

My dad was always fairly liberal/progressive. He kind of instilled that in my oldest sister and I (the sister that had died [in 1977 in a car accident]). She and I were both involved in stuff, and we encouraged each other to get involved in alternative politics. For myself, what I ended up doing in junior high was working with a group called People's Lobby, which was the first group to start getting legislative work on the ballot through the initiative process. Then I tried to work on things like the McGovern campaign and all the failed progressive Democratic candidates [chuckles]. By high school, I've gone through my reformist stage [chuckles] and ended up in more like Saul Alinsky and Marxist types of study. And my sister moved to the Santa Cruz area and started forming a Third World women's group. She influenced me a lot, more around sort of feminist politics within Marxism, particularly around Third World identities. By high school, probably by my junior year, which was about 1975, I came out to my oldest sister. And then the next year, I came out to my other sister. Yes, I'd say that I was pretty conscious that I was gay in high school. I wanted to seek out a gay community, but I also wanted it to be a radical gay community.

It's interesting because at that time in Sacramento I was more in touch with or had access to Asian American publications. So as I was becoming immersed in that, I came across a magazine called *Bridge*. There was this [column] that was written by Dan Tsang [who was already out and active in the Asian American movement then].[7] He was talking about being gay in the Asian American movement and how there was homophobia. It really just struck me, and when you are that age, anything sort of causes big emotional reaction. I sent a letter to the editor and tried to have him forward it to Dan, which got to him. He called me and we started corresponding. I know I wrote a lot of letters about what it was like coming out at the time, or feeling like I needed to deal with my sexual feelings. So by the time I graduated from high school, I was determined to move out of Sacramento because I wasn't out to my parents and because I wanted to find a gay men's community that was progressive.

I'd been in contact with this Asian American group at the time called I Wor Kuen [IWK][8]; they had some people down in L.A. I also wanted to work with a gay Marxist group, and I found one that was called the Lavender Union. Once I got down there, I realized neither was going to work for me.

The Lavender Union was almost all white, and it was a Trotskyite organization. They were just very, very dogmatic. The first meeting I went to, they were just arguing back and forth about Soviet history. They didn't have much to do with what I thought was day-to-day struggles that I or other people in this country were facing. I felt pretty invisible from that experience as a gay person. Here were all these white folks who were supposedly interested in involving people, but at the same time, I don't think any of them really engaged me at all in getting involved. I felt a lot like not only the politics weren't right for me, but they also didn't see me as part of the gay community. I ran into them several other times when they were out flyering or doing recruitment at events like the gay festivals. They didn't even think that you would be a gay person to hand a flyer to. It was like their conception of people who were gay was a stereotyped one. So if you were a person of color, you probably weren't a gay person.

How about the IWK?

Some of the older Asian activists that I had gotten to know in Sacramento eventually joined IWK. I was in their study group in Sacramento for about a year before I left. So they hooked me up with people in L.A. Before I moved to L.A., I came out to some of them up in Sacramento. I told them I wanted to be involved with IWK and I was going to be out, and I wanted to talk about how they dealt with gay people.

Well, they didn't really deal with gay people because they didn't have "out" gay people in the organization. No, they told me that they didn't see gay people as being truly revolutionary. [To them, homosexuality] was sort of like symptoms of bourgeois capitalism, like prostitution, drug use or wife-beating was. It was sexuality deformed because of capitalism. While that was offensive to me at the time, I still wanted to be a part of them. I really respected a lot of their community work. They were doing a lot of struggle around redevelopment in Chinese and Japanese communities, some union stuff, and a lot of Asian American studies organizing. So I stayed involved with them for several years as a supporter, but not as a member. Mostly I was involved in student organizing. I'd been going to East Los Angeles College at the time. There was the beginning of a network at the time that eventually became the West Coast Asian Pacific Student Union [APSU]. So I worked with the network of people that were organizing APSU at the community colleges.

With IWK, I tried to live up to be a good Marxist and be out to people about my sexual orientation at the same time. It was fairly understood that if I had wanted to be a member, I would need to struggle with my gayness and try to develop a relationship with a woman and not be sexually active with other men. That was partly why I never joined. I would be in a study group discussing women's oppression. That was the way that they thought they could deal with gay people—to get them to understand how that tied to women's oppression.

How about personally with people in the organization, did you change any minds?

It wasn't just myself. There were other people affiliated with the group who were gay, lesbian, or bisexual. Maybe we didn't change their minds, but questioned their assumptions about gay people and sexual orientation. Most of the people that were in the organization were young like myself. So they were very impressionable. Some of them didn't get the reason why I couldn't join. Others were like that's the group mentality. I run into some of them now and I ask them, "What was up with you? Why did you think that way?" And they'd say, "I don't know. Everyone else did." People might have struggled with the group position internally, but it was hardly shared with one another. There were only a very few Marxist-Leninist organizations that had ever been open to gay people. So it was pretty typical in a way.

I was involved with I Wor Kuen until they became the League of Revolutionary Struggle about 1980. Around 1981, I had decided that I wasn't going to join the organization ever, even though I wanted to be supportive of their work. I started going to Long Beach State. That was also when I became more serious about being in school, more like a student than a student organizer.

Terry Gock

I remember my friend Sally telling me about this one time in the early days when we started going to APPCON [Asian Pacific Planning Council] because we were both on this HIV/AIDS committee or task force within APPCON. She was working for APLA [AIDS Project Los Angeles]. So she told this story about going to the APPCON meeting early one time. She was sitting there, and people were talking about what to do on the weekend. And she said, "I went to this Fantasia [a fundraiser] of A/PLG, Asian/Pacific Lesbians and Gays." She talked about how wonderful the event was, and people were little puzzled and silent at first. They expected it to be a small event. Sally said, "Oh, no, there were two, three hundred people there." So the next question was, "There must not be many Asians there?" Sally said, "About half of them were gay Asians there." People were totally surprised, number one, that Sally—who's not a lesbian—was there, and two, that there were so many gay Asians. That tells you how much people didn't know even within APPCON. And these were the social service providers across the county. Well, more than that, they were mostly the *leaders* of agencies across the county. One hundred and fifty gay men is nothing . . . to us, right? But for the people in APPCON in those days, they thought 150 was a lot because they had not encountered that many. I think they cannot say that now.

THE RIGHT THING TO DO

Gay Asian men in the Asian American movement in the 1970s and early 1980s were often confronted with what activist Gil Mangaoang calls a "schizophrenia" in their personal and political lives. In his autobiographical essay, Mangaoang writes,

> While my primary political identity and organizing efforts was [sic] directed toward issues confronting non-white minorities, specifically the Filipino community, my gay identity took on a different character in other situations.
>
> My main social links were through places patronized by gay white males in San Francisco where minorities could be found. . . . Often I was the only Asian or Pacific Islander in these places and usually was tagged the "Asian Doll." . . . I knew of no minority gay organizations where I could go for support to deal with being Filipino and gay.[9]

The feeling of isolation was not only a psychological burden on Steve Lew, Virgil Vang, Stan Yogi, Gil Mangaoang, and others like them, but it also prevented them from utilizing the racial analysis—one of the more fruitful legacies of the Asian American movement—to organize around their sexual identity at the time. For example, like many in his generation of Japanese Americans, Stan was able to reclaim a sense of ethnic pride by working on the redress movement, even though he was born after the internment.[10] His activism in the Asian American community imbued even his academic work.[11]

Yet it wasn't until later in his life after he had found a gay Asian community that he could resolve this feeling of "schizophrenia."

This does not mean that gay Asian men at that time were not politically active outside of the Asian American movement. Some, like Paul Chen, see themselves as "enthusiastic observers" of the movement, but not necessarily participants. Nevertheless, Paul, Terry Gock, and Tak Yamamoto, for example, were active in the more politically mainstream Asian American community in various ways. Along with other early A/PLG leaders, they were also involved in many political campaigns in the gay and lesbian community at the time. Their rising political consciousness allowed them to ask tough questions and to begin to articulate common interests shared by gay Asian men. There is a conscious strategy on my part to put this chapter in between the previous one on rice bars and the following on A/PLG formation. The bars had provided gay Asian men a place to share common experiences, but it is a handful of individuals who translated these political experiences into a viable political and cultural identity. When Asian/Pacific Lesbians and Gays (A/PLG) came into existence in 1980, they already had a wealth of experience and a network in and out of the community. This proved instrumental not only in forming and institutionalizing A/PLG, but also in forging a confident presence of the organization in the Asian American community.

Terry Gock, for example, credits the passage of a resolution by the Japanese American Citizens League to support same-sex marriage in 1994 partly to Tak Yamamoto's long history of involvement with the organization. "Our presence could not but affect the agenda of many a group, but I don't think you could see it [immediately]," he says. "Take a long-term point of view. One of the earliest groups that came out in support of gay and lesbian marriage was what? The Japanese American Citizens League. How did that happen? From last fifteen, twenty years, starting with A/PLG getting involved because Tak was the president of the San Fernando Valley chapter [of JACL] and he got us into San Fernando to talk about being gay. And getting the chapter to support our many, many efforts that went on from there." Before any collective organizing, however, the gay Asian community, denied a powerful tool of racial analysis of the Asian American movement, had to emerge under a different framework.

June Lagmay

Both my brother and I were educated in Catholic grammar and Catholic high school because that's the religion of my family. I went to Our Lady of Loretta Grammar, which still exists up on Union, not two miles from here [Little Tokyo, where the interview took place]. It was reflective of the immediate community: mixed, a lot of Hispanics, some Asians, some blacks. And I also went to Catholic girls high school, Our Lady of Loretta High School, which is also about two miles from here, but the Archdiocese has since closed it. I have a lot of fond memories of grammar and high school. And it was actually at the high school that I met my current partner, at age thirteen. So we kind of joke to each other that we've known each other longer than not known each other because we've been together for almost thirty years. And I only have thirteen years that I didn't know her.

So you came to terms with your sexuality rather early.

Yes, I think a lot of it had to do with being so young and finding out about sexuality at the same time as homosexuality. In other words, it wasn't that Rita [her partner] and I had dated men first, and then we found, *oh my God, there's this whole other thing.* It was like sexuality just happened as a natural thing and it just happened with another woman. A lot of contexts took place in the decade that it happened in, which was, say, 1971, 1972, end of the flower power era. Even in the school context, it was a very affectionate school, anyway, being an all-girl school. It was not uncommon for best friends to walk hand in hand around. Rita and I knew that what we had was extraordinary and it went beyond just holding hands. But it happened in a very comfortable context. We never felt like what we did had a name necessarily or had a stigma attached to it. It was just a very natural kind of blossoming thing.

The whole Catholic religion during that decade was being questioned, anyway. The nuns were leaving the order all the time. So you figured, you were already in the mix of dynamic change of the Catholic Church, questioning bishops, questioning religion, questioning the Bible. So it wasn't as though there was one horrible rule that we were breaking. The whole nature of the Catholic religion was being questioned, anyway.

It was like a complete bonding, and we [Rita and I] didn't need anything or anyone outside the two of us. But that doesn't mean we were blind to the world around us. As we grew a little older, I did go away to college. I went to UCLA. I went to Pepperdine [University] for the first year, ran out of money, dropped out to work for a year to get my funds again, and then I put myself through UCLA the last three years, got my B.A., did one year of graduate study under scholarship. And I do remember some things about college. This would've been the years 1973 through 1976. Because the nature of school is sifting through popular culture and the world and making sense of it, I probably became more cognizant and militarized in school than anything. I like to tell people that actually I gained an Asian identity while at UCLA. Because growing up, like I said, in such a mixed neighborhood [Echo Park], and I'm of mixed ancestry myself, I didn't take on like a militant Asian attitude until college. I started doing things like, I started writing articles for the *Pacific Ties*, which [first] came out the year that I was there. Wrote some poetry and some articles for them, which I was real proud of. So I became an Asian American in college. And then I was a sociology major. In sociology, I find it incredible now, but at the time, 1973 through 1976, homosexuality was considered deviant behavior. They had a class entitled "Deviant Behavior." It started to ride on me because what Rita and I had was so natural and so good that I put on my lesbian militant hat at that time and I asked the professor if I could address the class. I remember that. I remember addressing the class in Deviant Behavior and telling them that I was a lesbian and that it wasn't wrong and these were the reasons why. And in philosophy class, my papers were on . . . why it is unreasonable philosophically to say that homosexuality is wrong. And born-again Christians would pester me at lunch and tried to convert me and I would tell them immediately that I am a Catholic and I am an Asian, and I am a lesbian. *Oh, God, you know, God's going to* . . . I would get into these voracious philosophic arguments with them. I was so fired up then that if I got people that came up and said I was a sinner and going to hell, I liked it. It was like, oh, I got a reaction out of you. Mostly, I think people honestly came up and said, *You've given me something to think about or thank you for having the courage to be open as you were*. At that time. And I appreciated that. It was a really weird time.

And probably from there, because I would bring home articles and I would tell Rita what happened, maybe both our consciousness started to lift at that time and we understood our place in the larger world. It wasn't just housekeeping. And it wasn't just a self-contained unit, you and I. But we owe something to change people's attitudes outside our unit. And we would do things like, find out about a protest march at CBS or NBC [because they were showing negative images of gays and lesbians], and we'd join the march just because it was the right thing to do.

Tak Yamamoto

I think I came into my own realization [as an out gay man] in the late 1960s in a short-lived group called PRIDE. The acronym PRIDE means Personal Rights in Defense and Education. Morris Kight was one of the founders. Back in the 1960s, there was this incident called the Black Cat raid, where the police raided this night club that gays attended. They beat the bartender, hurt him badly. I think they ruptured his spleen. And the owner who was a female was also accosted. Back then, it was just a given. Of course, the Black Cat incident did come to a head after that. There was some police investigation on that. They said the police were provoked to do some of these things, which was too harsh to be viable anyway. It's like the beating of Rodney

King, you know. The guy's already down. You don't have to keep beating him.

I don't know what got me started. I felt righteous in that we had to do something. So I attended these meetings. We were supposed to do this: When we got a call of an incident of police harassment, we were to go to whatever location it was, take down the names of the people who were there, who saw the incident, and take a brief report and document that. So should the case get to court—and if people were willing to—we would have witnesses. A lot of people were nervous about coming out at that time, but some people felt vindicated by saying what they saw. All of us could be hurt. We needed to do something. So some of them were willing to come forward.

At the time I was working in the federal government. I was thinking, "Gosh, am I really stupid enough to do this? I could lose my good job." But I said, "Maybe I'll get another job if I lose this one. I just have to do this." It kind of liberated me from having to think about all the little intricacies [about being out]. I became more comfortable with that.

Did you join an Asian American organization?

I was a member of the Japanese American Citizens League (JACL) since 1976. I was the president of the San Fernando chapter in 1981–1982, after I'd been involved with A/PLG. It was great. During that first year, with A/PLG in my background, I said I wanted to do a lesbian and gay coming out to the chapter. They said, "Gee, okay." So I had June [Lagmay], Dean [Goishi], and Roy [Kawasaki] come to our meeting. There was always dinner before the meeting. So what we did initially was I had the three of them dispersed within the place, having dinner with all these people. So the JACL members didn't know they were gay, that they were the gay panelists. Before we started the dialogue, I told them they were exposed to some gay people and hopefully, I joked, there weren't any germs there. And of course, they asked the very kinds of questions that Parents and Friends [of Lesbians and Gays] had all answered at this point, but at the time, it was still not in our community. Like what made you gay? Was it in the genes? Were you raped by your uncle? I mean, who cares? But we had to work from there.

We did this with a Methodist group in Monterey Park, too. I took about five people there with us: Roy, Dean, myself . . . same old staff people that would always go. [Laughs] And the same kind of things kept coming up. What made you gay, you know. We had that whole number. I had to ask Terry [Gock] for what it was that the American Psychological Association had that we could use. Of course, by the 1980s, they had already determined that it was not a mental illness, and that there was no one factor that you could point to and say this was it. I thought to myself, "I don't know if we're reaching these people at all." Because at the time, Methodist was quite conservative.

I also joined the Manzanar Committee in 1975. I met Sue [Kunitomi] Embrey [the Committee's founding chair]. She knew where I was coming from. All of the members of the Manzanar Committee and I talked about it, and they got to meet Carl [Tak's partner]. By 1975, I was finding some acceptance by straights, Asian Pacific straights. That was important to me. I didn't want to worry about the whites too much because if I was going to make an impact, it had to be on an Asian Pacific group. I mean, even gay white organizations didn't know about us. If we were one percent, we were lucky. So if we were that scarce, there was no issue. At the time, I was trying to indicate to people that it was okay, I was okay, that I wasn't going to infect them, that we needed to acknowledge the fact that there was another possibility out there, that I didn't choose necessarily to be gay. I had a family who had accepted me. They hadn't turned gay. Maybe we could at least come to some understanding.

Were there any instances where they weren't accepting?

Maybe, but not in my face. You know, as Asian Pacifics, they wouldn't do that. They don't say, "We don't want you here." They might say it in other subtle ways, but I never received that. At least I never got the message. Maybe I was too dense. Besides, they were always looking for people to do stuff.

JACL has kind of a conservative history.

Yes, but the thing about it was that in 1994, I went to the [JACL] National Convention in Salt Lake City. I mean, of all the crazy places to have a conference, in Mormon country! [There was a resolution to support same-sex marriages.] I was able to talk to [different members all over the country]. There was a tendency of some of the members to say it was going to divide the organization because they thought we were definitely way outside somewhere. Listening to some of the more conservative members . . . well, the Salt Lake City people anyway—you can't imagine Japanese Mormons, but there are some . . . to hear them say, "Gee, you know, we'll take you but you got to deny your gayness." Give me a break! We'd gone that route before. Why should we continue doing that? The thing I enjoyed was the fact that we didn't do a whole lot of heavy lobbying, but we did do some to see who would vote in our direction. It passed; close, but it passed. So that was really nice. We were convinced that we needed to start a gay and lesbian JACL chapter. So we started Lambda. I felt pretty good about that, too.

Stanley Rebultan

I was very active in the campaign to defeat Proposition 6. Are you aware of that? Yes, I was. That's where I started meeting people who were active in the gay community, advocates of different kinds of causes. And I said, this is fun.

You must understand, in the beginning, I was talking about my training as a teacher in the Philippines. I'm passionate about teaching, although I didn't practice it here. Because of my upbringing, I value education. Half the people who would be saying kids are the future of the nation wouldn't give a shit about the kids, especially politicians. Then came Proposition 6. It was a very hard issue. The proposition was sponsored by Senator John Briggs, one of the right-wing legislators in Sacramento. Proposition 6 stipulated that any overtly or out gay teachers would be dismissed from the public schools. Plain and simple. That's it.

When I found out about this initiative, I said, "What? What is the big deal about being a gay person? The best educators in the world have been gay. Are we going to deny children nowadays to learn from gay people?" I was going to get involved in the campaign. That's when I started knowing Morris Kight because his house was like the center for the campaign against Proposition 6. That's where I picked up materials to distribute. You know where I used to go? I used to leaflet all the different Catholic churches here. I was chased by cops. I was chased by parish priests. I was chased by parishioners.

One time I even got into an encounter at a restaurant. Around that period it was a fad to take slogans and iron them on your shirts. (As a matter of fact, I used to do that to meet people. I had a red T-shirt that was really fitting on me. I was notorious for things like that. It says in silver letters in the front, "Latin-Oriental. Hot and Loyal." And when people cruised me and asked if that was true, I would turn around and walk away to expose what was on the back, which said, "Try me." In my peak, I was not bad-looking. I had my good fun.)

Anyway, I used to wear a T-shirt that says, "Vote No on 6. The Briggs Initiative." And my estimation was about seventy-five, eighty percent of all voters, because of the heated campaign on that proposition, knew what that proposition was. One day I went to a Norm's Restaurant. And there was this real ignorant, stupid guy, straight, maybe a redneck, who came and sat beside me. I was reading the papers. And the T-shirt got his attention, with all these slogans in the back and front of me. He asked, "Excuse me. What does that mean?" "Oh, this is a campaign against Proposition 6," I explained.

"What the hell is that?" He said, in a redneck way. The counter was loaded with people, mostly guys. At that time I was really versed in my political philosophy. I explained what it was about.

"Oh, that thing about those queers being kicked out of the schools."

And I said, "Excuse me? Please watch your mouth because you would not like me to call you a honky either." I said that to him.

He said, "Oh, I'm sitting with a queer."

"I beg your pardon," I said. "I might be a queer, my dear." I said *My Dear.*

"But have a look at yourself in the mirror." See, I have a sharp tongue. "If you would be standing on Santa Monica Boulevard, peddling your ass, you are not even worth ten cents." I picked up my plate and moved to a table. And these guys, they were like, *Good for you. You told that creep off.* This guy walked out and he was challenging me to come outside. Where would I go? I mean, he's an idiot. So I've gotten into encounters like that.

Proposition 6 eventually went to the ballot, and thank God it was defeated. And that was the end of it. But my connection within the gay community, Morris Kight, and all these activists, flourished. That's how A/PLG was developed. Morris knew a lot of people who were in the Asian community who were about my age level, who had been out. He was like the godfather of the gay movement at that time. I had said to him, "Please get all of us in touch and let's form an organization." Every one of us probably had advocated to him. One day, in 1980, I got a call from him. He said, "Stanley, you're invited. We're going to have a meeting with . . ." He started mentioning names.

Ted Hune

The job that I had [in Los Angeles] sent me to Denver for a year. Then I came back. Probably that was about 1974 or 1975. That's when I decided to become more active in the gay community. I ran some ads in the *Advocate* at the time. I did meet one person; his name was Larry. There was no physical attraction, but we liked each other. We became really close friends. So we went out a lot together. He told me about this gay club that was just starting; it was the Gay Rights Chapter of the ACLU [American Civil Liberties Union]. They were just starting their gay rights chapter. So we went to a couple of meetings. I saw this one guy there, who was one of the co-chairs of the Ways and Means Committee in the Chapter. I decided I wanted to get to know him better. So I joined his committee. It turns out that they had a committee meeting at his house. While we were in his house, in came this hot-looking Latino guy, who was his boyfriend. So I said, well, that takes care of that. But I still stayed on his committee, and I became active. Within a couple of months, he ran for president of the Chapter. When he was running for that position, he asked if I would run for a board office, too, so that I would serve on his board. I did; I ran for secretary. My friend Larry ran for treasurer. And Peter became president. So we had sort of a clique. Once a month we had a board meeting, and one a month we had another committee meeting. And then usually we had two or three socials or fundraising events during the month. So every week there was something going on. They became my closest gay friends. I was the only Asian in the group. Once in a while I'd see another Asian and they would come to one of the meetings. But they would only come once or twice, and they would never show up again. So, yes, all my friends were Caucasians.

[The GRC] was two things. It was a social outlet because I was with these friends so much, doing these activities, that we became very close. I hung around with them all the time. At the same time, there were two big issues that were going on. One was a California issue. It was the Briggs [Initiative]. Briggs was a state senator for Orange County. His [initiative] has something to do with the banning or the not allowing of gays to teach in public schools. That was a big issue that we were fighting against. So that's one reason why I became active in GRC. The other was Anita Bryant. She was becoming very vocal, mainly in Florida. She was very anti-gay at the time. She was fighting some of the gay rights ordinances there. Because she was a known entity, she took it nationwide. So we were fighting Anita Bryant as well. That increased the interest of a lot of gays to become more politically involved in gay causes. When I joined the Gay Rights Chapter, it was just beginning. We had maybe about thirty-five members. And in a very short period, we became the fastest growing chapter of ACLU. We probably had over three hundred members within less than a year. And then our group and our president Peter sort of became the spokespersons whenever the media wanted the gays' viewpoints of what was happening over the Briggs [Initiative] or with Anita Bryant. So we got a lot of publicity.

We had the biggest gay rights fundraiser that was known at the time. What we did was, we held it at the Hollywood Palladium. I can't think of what the award was, but we honored Willie Brown. At the time, he was the Speaker of the [California] Assembly. He pushed through some legislation. I think it was so that you can't discriminate against state employees if they were gay. Because Brown supported that, he was honored. He was given that award. We had five hundred people at the banquet. Rev. Troy Perry of MCC [Metropolitan Community Church] was our keynote speaker. He was very good. It also became a fundraiser for our chapter and raised money to fight the Briggs [Initiative] and Anita Bryant or any anti-gay legislation. It became quite a media event because we had a lot of the local politicians and judges there. It was one of the first times that any political figures came out and supported a gay organization that openly.

Every time [Morris Kight] came to a Gay Rights Chapter event, he was delighted to see me. I didn't know him personally, though. He was always very friendly because he loved Asians. Of course, he was considered one of the founders of A/PLG. So whenever I see him anywhere, he greets me like I was a long lost friend. He doesn't know my name. Whether he recognizes me or not, I don't know.

When I first started voting, when I became twenty-one, I was a Republican.

It was not so much about gay rights. I was more in thinking the way the Republicans were thinking. It wasn't until I became politically involved with GRC, and seeing that the Republican Party wasn't very strong on gay rights, or human rights, that I started voting Democratic. GRC changed the way I looked at things, the way I voted. I'm still a registered Republican because I like to vote in the primaries, and I think I could do more with the primaries by voting against the right-wing candidates and trying to put the more moderate Republican on the ballot. Then when it comes to the general election, I would vote Democratic. I still consider myself moderate, but I'm probably leaning toward more liberal beliefs than conservative beliefs now.

Paul Chen

By sophomore year in college, I thought, Paul, you should do something about this. I knew there was a gay student union on campus [California State University, Fullerton]. So I went to it. They used to hold their meetings at the bottom of the Student Union, which was actually a really large room with a whole bunch of couches and chairs hanging out. For the meeting, we used to pull a bunch of couches together and sort of have a meeting in the middle of this giant room. So you could actually be in the room without being in the meeting. There were other people around you, standing or playing pool. You got to remember, at that time, it was an unofficial group on campus. Because it was unofficial, we couldn't have a meeting room.

My first meeting, I remember sitting near the meeting, wondering what these people were like. Sort of watching them. I don't remember exactly when I joined the group. Probably the next meeting. I have never been shy. Actually, the very next year I became the secretary of GSU.

In the beginning, we just gathered and did things. Later on we developed programs. One of them was Christopher Isherwood who came down to campus to speak. I actually had to drive out to Santa Monica to pick him up. We had quite a few people speak. And because of all of our programs, because of all the things we did, we became the second largest gay student union in the state of California. The first was UCLA. The second was us. The third was USC. We were even bigger than Berkeley and Stanford.

We eventually had a big conference. We had held it yearly for two or three years, and we called it Gay Think. As far as we knew, it was the first sort of gay student union conference. I remember Leonard Matlovich was our first keynote speaker. He had just come out and was on the cover of *Time*. He was really innocent, he was really sweet. Later, he turned into a Republican. But we knew him before that.

That year both Chris [Gaynor, Paul's partner] and I got voted onto the student council. And the president of the board was Jerry Deeds, a Mormon. He was really homophobic and they tried running some stuff against us. [*Chris:* They tried to defeat the funding for the Gay Student Union. We were supposed to draw up the budget. It was about $900. By then, the Gay Student Union had an allocation for a couple of years. And they decided that year that we weren't going to have any. We would not vote to close on the budget hearing, so they couldn't present the budget. So Morris came out and spoke to the council, very eloquently, about why this was wrong and homophobic.]

Chris and I were already a couple by then. We were the only couple in the GSU. We rented a house that was about three blocks away from school. Leonard Matlovich stayed at our place when he did Gay Think.

[*Chris:* So did Vito Russo. He presented *The Celluloid Closet* to the GSU, with his unedited film clips. His commentary was wonderful, much more interesting and more hard-hitting than the film that was made.]

The film was horrible.

And then in 1978 came the Briggs Initiative. Morris organized an organization called the Orange County Against the Briggs Initiative (OCABI). Chris was president, and I was vice-president of OCABI. Our house was sort of the central place, as it turned out to be, where we had a lot of meetings. Morris was offended by the official No on 6 Campaign, which was elitist. They were pretty closeted. They wanted to do a pure television/radio media campaign against it. They were afraid that drag queens and leather queens, those kinds of people, would participate. They wanted to show nothing but clean-cut West Hollywood clones.

[*Chris:* The leader of No on 6 was David Mixner, who later became famous as an advisor to Bill Clinton.]

He was real closeted then. He said that he was straight and that he was doing that as a favor to all of us.

So what did OCABI do?

A guy named Frank Valle was going to walk from the Mexican border to the Oregon border, shaking hands and telling whoever would listen about the Briggs Initiative. So we organized a rally in a park across the street from Briggs' office in Fullerton to welcome Frank when he walked through Fullerton. We had fundraisers. And one of them was actually organized by the Quakers [American Friends Services Committee]. They were doing a soup-and-bread fundraiser at our house. Every time I looked outside of our house—we lived on a dead-end street—there was a cop driving by. I had a big mouth then. So I walked out to the cop and waved him down. I said, "Excuse me, excuse me! Why are you driving past our house all the time?" And he said that they had gotten word that the American Nazi Party, which had their headquarters in Placentia, were going to do bad things to us, like fire-bomb us or something.

[*Chris:* They had threatened to bomb us. At that time, they were called the National Socialist White People's Party. After (Lincoln) Rockwell died, they changed their name.]

The police were actually coming to protect us. And I confronted them. [Laughs] We were doing fundraising. Unfortunately, the money that we were raising eventually went to the state organization. Toward the end of the campaign they just flew in and swallowed us.

[*Chris:* We just backed out, and they just took over and blended all the little organizations in one because it made more sense.]

So after that, we moved out to L.A. and I applied for graduate school. I took a year off, and I worked at the Gay and Lesbian Community Services Center when it was still on Highland. (It was actually before they added the "Lesbian" to its name.) I was head of the Speakers Bureau because I did that for GSU. Anyway, they hired me mainly because I was not white.

That's where I met June Lagmay. I remember sitting on the stairs, saying to June [who is Filipina and Japanese], "You know, we should do something." I've been going out to River Club for years and met all these Asians, but none of us knew each other outside of River Club. And actually, the following week, I got a call from Morris.

NOTES

1. See William Wei, *The Asian American Movement* (Philadelphia: Temple University Press, 1993), 31.

2. Sylvia Yanagisako, "Transforming Orientalism: Gender, Nationality, and Class in Asian American Studies," in *Naturalizing Power: Essays in Feminist Cultural Analysis*, ed. Sylvia Yanagisako and Carol Delaney (New York: Routledge, 1995), 287.

3. Jeffrey Paul Chan, Frank Chin, Lawson Fusao Inada, and Shawn Wong, eds., *The Big Aiiieeeee: An Anthology of Chinese American and Japanese American Literature* (New York: Meridian, 1990), xiii.

4. David Lin Eng, "Managing Masculinity: Race and Psychoanalysis in Asian-American Literature" (Ph.D. diss., University of California, Berkeley, 1995), 5.

5. See, for example, Jennifer Ting, "Bachelor Society: Deviant Heterosexuality and Asian American Historiography," in *Privileging Positions: The Sites of Asian American Studies*, ed. Gary Okihiro et al. (Pullman: Washington State University Press, 1995), 271–79.

6. Hung Nung, "Letter to the Editor," *Bridge* 1, No. 5 (May/June 1972), 51.

7. Daniel Tsang Chun-tuen, "Gay Awareness," *Bridge* 3, No. 4 (January/February, 1975), 44–45.

8. For a history of I Wor Kuen (1969–1978), see Fred Ho, "Fists for Revolution," in *Legacy to Liberation: Politics and Culture of Revolutionary Asian Pacific America*, ed. Fred Ho with

Carolyn Antonio, Diane Fujino, and Steve Yip (Brooklyn, N.Y.: Big Red Media, 2000), 3–13.

9. Gil Mangaoang, "From the 1970s to the 1990s: Perspective of a Gay Filipino American Activist," in *Asian American Sexualities: Dimensions of the Gay and Lesbian Experience*, ed. Russell Leong (New York: Routledge, 1996), 108.

10. See Yasuko I. Takezawa, *Breaking the Silence: Redress and Japanese American Ethnicity* (New York: Cornell University Press, 1995), specifically pp. 172, 200–208.

11. See, for example, Stan Yogi, "Ladies Revealed: Uncovering Buried Plots in the Stories of Hisaye Yamamoto and Wakako Yamauchi" (M.A. thesis, University of California, Berkeley, 1988) (both Yamamoto and Yamauchi wrote extensively about the internment in their work); and "Yearning for the Past: The Dynamics of Memory in Sansei Internment Poetry," in *Memory and Cultural Politics: New Approaches to American Ethnic Literatures*, ed. Amritjit Singh, Joseph T. Skerrett Jr., and Robert E. Hogan (Boston: Northeastern University Press, 1996), 245–65.

A/PLG members gather for a picture after a retreat. Photo courtesy of David Hong.

An A/PLG contingent marches in the Christopher Street West parade in Los Angeles, early 1980s. Photo courtesy of David Hong.

A/PLG members performed Chinese opera at Fantasia, an A/PLG fund-raiser, in 1983. Photo courtesy of Tak Yamamoto.

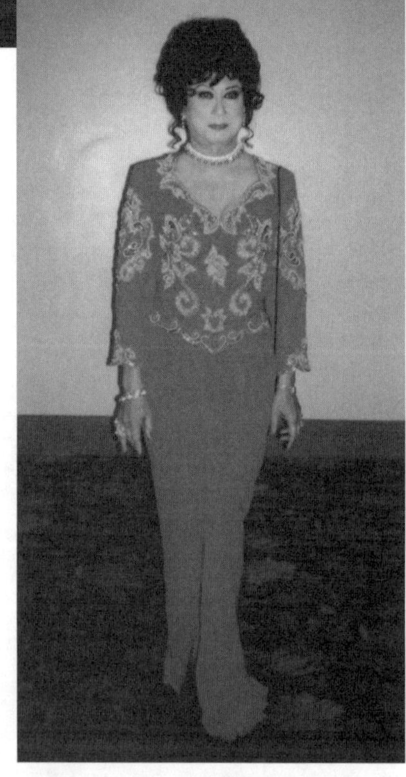

Andy C. attends an A/PLG Fantasia fund-raiser in the 1990s. Photo courtesy of Andy C.

Andy C. gets ready for the preliminary round of a drag ball in the early 1970s. Photo courtesy of Andy C.

André Ting in the early eighties. Like many others at that time, André put his own personal messages on the back of his T-shirt. This one indicates that even in that time period, many gay Asian men were exhibiting their pride in being both gay and Asian. Photo courtesy of André Ting.

Three unidentified narrators ham it up at a gay bar in Mar Vista. Photo courtesy of Tak Yamamoto.

Morris Kight with Roy Z., his partner at the time A/PLG was founded, at an A/PLG event at Ken's River Club. Morris Kight was instrumental in bringing together a group of his gay and lesbian Asian friends, which eventually led to the founding and organizing of A/PLG. Photo courtesy of Tak Yamamoto.

David Hong, with his partner, Nid, in 1994 in front of their house in West Hollywood. They met in 1984. Photo courtesy of David Hong.

Harry Park, his partner Herb, and their adopted son Chase, photographed in May 2001. The adoption was finalized in 2000. Photo courtesy of Harry Park.

5

Old Scars on a New Body

TAKING CHARGE . . .

The idea of an organization to support gay Asians occurred to quite a few people before Morris Kight called a meeting at his home. They recognized the limits of the bars in advancing the formation of a gay Asian community and in addressing the diverse needs of its members. Even with the existence of the River Club and the informal network that developed out of that, "the feeling that we were alone was very, very common among all of us," says Dean Goishi. "We were competing for the same object, the non-Asians, that we never did talk to each other. We had to put a stop to it."

With his extensive experience and network in the gay liberation movement, Morris Kight was instrumental in setting the process in motion. But Morris the shrewd political strategist had his own personal reasons as well. As Roy Kawasaki says, "Morris' main concern was Roy Z. [Morris' lover at the time]. He was anxious about Roy's welfare because Roy didn't have any Asian friends. He would always say, 'When I pass on, make sure you don't forget Roy.' Morris was so much older than Roy and he wanted Roy to have us as a support group for him." His motivation, be it personal or political—and it was probably both—should not be grounds for minimizing his contributions to the history of A/PLG and the gay Asian community in Los Angeles. At the same time, it is important to recognize that, having been kept from leadership positions in both the Asian American movement and gay liberation movement, most gay Asian men at the time simply were not in the position or had the resources to initiate such an enterprise as A/PLG. Morris Kight was an important ally, but, as Dean Goishi notes, "If it didn't happen with A/PLG, [the community] would've happened in another way." But once the opportunity presented itself, a group of gay Asian men took charge to define and shape a community. Though not without struggles, their accomplishments demonstrate tremendous insights and vision on their part.

Paul Bautista

Boy, who told us about the first A/PLG meeting? It must have been through a phone call from one of the guys. It was at Morris Kight's place, him and his lover Roy [Z.]. The only reason Bill and I were there was to find other couples to hang out with because there just weren't many. There were at the meeting these Asian-Caucasian couples, lesbian couples—it was so neat. There were Morris and Roy, Dennis Akazawa, who passed away. Let's see. Stan [not Rebultan] was there, but he wasn't with his lover Anthony yet. There was a Philippine senator who was exiled during the Marcos era. From what I hear, he was quite fine living his gay life here because he was in different company. He came from a very huge political family back in the Philippines; [he] was there with his then boyfriend. I'm getting this picture. It's so vivid. Morris' place was a huge room, like a hall. Then there was a loft upstairs where Roy and Morris' bedroom was. So it was perfect for political gatherings. I could see what people were wearing, the LaCrosse shirt and jeans. That's what gays wore. You'd have this really tight pair of jeans, and the shirts, all the colors of the rainbow. It was such a uniform. [Laughs]

There wasn't really a direction yet. Is it going to be social? Is it going to be political? What is this going to be about? The meeting was attended by no more than two dozen people. They had some exercises and separated us into discussion groups. I remember talking about very academic things, very political things. There were a lot of opinions. There were these two forces: the political versus the social. Back then, a few people, like Morris Kight and the guys, really had to fight and be so vocal because there weren't many of them. It was so much easier to be a social organization because there was no risk. The organization [in the early years] was very tense. I really didn't expect the organization to last more than a couple years. We thought that the organization would fill a certain void, bring the community together, meaning the separate Asian groups together—you know, the Japanese, Chinese, Korean communities. And once that's done, okay, we'd go on to the next thing. We'd join a mainstream gay organization, like the Human Rights Campaign Fund or something. But it didn't. Eighteen years later and here it is. It's pretty amazing.

You mentioned before that you and Bill went to the first meeting because you wanted to meet other couples. Were there other needs, too?

No, because there was no political need. I just didn't want to get involved politically then. Bill and I decided that even though I had this incredible political ambition, it was going to be tabled until my forties or my fifties when I'd grown up quite a bit and could say things and back them up with some experience. A/PLG was purely to meet people because [up until then] we could only go to the bars every weekend. We could only go to the River Club and sit there for so long. After a while, I was telling myself, "Wow, that was a really short weekend. We didn't do anything."

In the late 1970s and early 1980s, before AIDS, it was just a battleground between promiscuity and monogamy. We had plenty of single friends, but we really had nothing in common. Our social calendars were filled by very, very different things. Now there's more balance between couples and singles because there were so many things to choose from. Back then, for singles, there were bars, bars, pick-ups, pick-ups, whatever. Couples were staying home, going to dinner. The bar scene was a different collection of people at any given night. People come and go, come and go. People had to behave in a certain way, or misbehave in a certain way. With A/PLG, without the smoking and cruising, you could actually talk to people. They had lives that they could share with you. Because it was such a small group then, there was a family character to it. People were better behaved in the meetings because other people's homes were opened up for them. So it was real.

June Lagmay

The best memory I have . . . a couple of scenes in my mind. One is talking to Paul Chen about it. He said he has a very strong memory of him and me sitting on the stairs of GLCSC [Gay and Lesbian Community Service Center], having found each other. Mine is a little more foggy, but I do remember sometime around that time Morris Kight—bless his heart, he's still alive—who knew of me and Paul and Tak and Roy Kawasaki and a number of other people, asked us to come to his house, which to me was like going to the house of God because Morris Kight has such a wonderful reputation and deservedly still does so for being such a patriotic father of the [gay and lesbian] movement. The way he would say, "You got to have a way of expressing yourselves and don't depend on the European community to do that." I thought that was so charming. I never forgot that. So we all came to his house. I remember that mostly because I was in such awe of being in Morris' house. And the next [scene] I have in mind is Paul Chen's apartment. . . . They [the two meetings] had to have been within the same few months because it was before the organization was actually gelled. And it came together very fast. That's my memory. It came together very fast. It had to have happened within weeks, or two months of each other.

And the next memory I have are some of the actual A/PLG events: Nisei

Week booth, meetings. You know, I don't know how or why I did this, but I remember bringing my mom and dad to a meeting. I must've been just like, what the f—, you know, and I just grabbed them by their hands. I just said, "Come on, there're some nice people here." Everything went fine. My parents were just grateful for my company in any context. Actually, as I look back, I think that was really ballsy of me. But at the time, you don't think about courage. You don't think what you're doing is brave. You said, "Oh, my mom and dad have been pressing me to see them. I have a meeting coming up. Okay, I'll take them with me."

Paul Chen

The meeting at Morris' was in 1980. June and I thought it was really funny because it was the very next week after she and I sat down on the stairs and talked about starting such an organization. At that time, Morris had a lover named Roy. I don't think Roy wanted to be known, and Morris wanted to turn him into a political animal also. So he wanted Roy to have his own group. So he called all of us together. He sort of pushed Roy into it, and Roy went in reluctantly.

There was this collection of people I had never seen before. There were only like twenty of us. Morris knew me the best, and of course he wanted to have gender equities. So he thought that June and I should lead. And we didn't do it until the very first meeting at our [Paul's and Chris'] apartment. That was the next month after the meeting at Morris'. There was a pre-meeting where several of us made up a poster announcing that meeting, and we tacked them up all over the River Club. That was about the only place we put it, huh? We were really scared that we wouldn't have anybody come. But there were scads and scads and scads of people that day.

[*Chris:* We had a one-bedroom apartment upstairs in a four-plex . . .]

But we had a dining room that was quite large. All four apartments were gay, including the owner.

[*Chris:* But he was a closet case. When the apartment filled up, people were out on the landing and down the steps and all the way out on the sidewalk, lining up and listening through the window.]

We had put speakers next to the window. The owner came up and complained that we were flushing the toilet too much. I said, "Walter, we have all these people. Of course, we're flushing the toilet a lot. Okay, I'll pay for the water." He was real upset. We were just amazed that we had that many people. Just amazed.

At first we decided that we would try not to have hierarchy, so there were just co-chairs and a board of directors, more or less. June and I were the first two co-chairs. I was already in graduate school [at UCLA] when it first happened. After the first couple of meetings I felt really overwhelmed. So I bowed out of being co-chair after about two months. Maybe three months at the most.

Doug Chin

Roy [Kawasaki] was encouraging me to go to A/PLG. At the time, Jim was living in Hawaii. His old company called him up and said they had this job they wanted him to do in Hawaii. So Jim opted to move back for a couple of years, 1979 and 1980. I remained here in California, and for two years we had a commuting relationship. Roy was my buddy buddy. On weekends, we'd go out to dinners and to the bars and have a few drinks. Or we'd go to the theaters. Roy, of course, over the years had been a good friend. During the formation of A/PLG, since I was pretty much alone, Roy decided to get me involved. . . . I'm not a good politician. In that sense, I call it as I see it. I'm very black and white, very honest to a fault. Sometimes people don't like to hear what I have to say. I guess he felt I had a strong enough personality that would help the organization out. [Laughs] So I went to the first meeting at Paul Chen's home.

There were about seventy-five to eighty people there. We were falling out the front door. I remember that because I was by the door. I would say forty percent were Asian. A lot of them were Asian–white couples. I remember about three or four women. I don't remember a lot of them. We talked about the formation of a group, if there was a need for an Asian support group. There were a few people there who didn't think there was a need. I remember a white attorney who loved Asian men. He didn't want it because I think he saw an organization would be a threat. I guess he wanted more control over his relationship. People responded to him very negatively. They booed him out actually.

Did you think there was a need?

Yes. I think I was pretty able to take care of myself. But in having seen a lot of Asian and non-Asian relationships, the Asian male has always played a very subservient role. One friend in particular was so controlled, and he was an educated Asian man. He went to one of the best schools in Hawaii, Punahou, and he taught for the public school system there. His lover was a white man, originally from Ohio. He was teaching at a private school, so they were both educators. But my friend could not even go out of the house without his lover's permission. I mean, it was to that extent! I thought this was ridiculous. Anyway, their relationship obviously ended after several years of marriage.

I knew of another Asian guy who was a doctor, who was in a relationship for two, three years with this white man who didn't have much of a career. The relationship ended because the guy ended up cheating on the Asian fellow. Well, the Asian guy decided that he didn't need this relationship, and he didn't. But, within six months, he met another white guy. The white guy would not let him socialize with any of his old friends. It was really sad because this Asian doctor and I were very, very close friends. It was sad that we had to give up our friendship of four or five years. And I thought A/PLG could help educate them, other Asians, to become exposed to a number of different things, and to help support them to be less dependent on their lovers, so they could take whatever action they needed to become self-sufficient. I thought we could do that by getting people active into doing things, volunteering, or even assuming a leadership position within the organization.

My relationship with Jim had already dissolved in 1981. After he moved back to California, he wanted to have an open relationship, and I did not want that. I decided if he really needed to go out and play at this point of our relationship, then we needed to call it an end. So we did that. We continued to live in this house together for four, five months, being roommates. That didn't quite work out. We had made an arrangement that he wouldn't bring anybody here. But when I went to the guest cottage, I would catch him in bed with people. The guest cottage is now my office.

Tak Yamamoto

My membership number is one. I wanted to be the first person to join A/PLG, even though I wasn't at the first meeting at Morris'. I went to the next meeting at Paul Chen's house. Scarce furniture, which was a good thing, because there were seventy people in the apartment. There wasn't quite all the space for everybody. [Laughs] It was a mixed group, so there were Caucasians there, too. The ratio was probably sixty-forty because a lot of the Anglos were kind of inhibited. There were a lot more Asians than they'd ever seen. All the people I could think of went to that meeting, and people I had never met before were there, too. We were like, I'm here and I want to be counted. And in the middle of this thing . . . this really got me and I got really adamant about this . . . in the middle of these Asian Pacific people trying to come together and feeling we could do things with seventy people in the meeting, some white person came up and said, "Why do we need another organization? Why don't we just join all these other organizations?"

And I said, "Because it doesn't meet our Asian Pacific needs." See, if we join a white organization, it would be a white thing, and we would be the tokens again. We wanted an organization that was going to address our issues. I got very adamant and said, "If you don't think you need this, then you need to get out, because there are seventy of us here. We are here because we feel there is a need." I kept him quiet. I was so vocal and upset that he wouldn't suggest why we didn't need it. Maybe for his own personal needs, there was no need for it. But as an Asian Pacific person, we felt there was a certain power that we were now bringing together. There we were: we never had seventy of anybody speaking on the same subject coming from the same location and feeling a certain power that we never would've otherwise been able to generate, going into a white organization with our Asian faces. What would we be? Nothing, you know.

So what were the needs and issues that were specific to gay Asian Pacific men at that time?

One of the things that we felt was, of course, validation. We didn't say that in so many words, but the idea was: Why do we hate each other? Why is it necessary that we have to look for validation outside of ourselves? Many people asked that. And with the realization that we could do this, we could say we're okay, that was really the beginning of something. Before that, we were always asking someone else to tell us we were okay. That seems ludicrous now, I know, but back then, I mean, who was going to tell us that it was okay to say that we were okay?

After that meeting at Paul's, we really got into high gear. We decided to have raps because we got to find out where we were coming from. The raps were integrated, but there were other issues that could not be resolved in an all-encompassing rap. As Asian Pacific men, there was a certain amount of perceived suppression and we always put it on our white friends and lovers. They were our oppressors. While we needed to get past that, we couldn't dialogue with each other with them there. We couldn't call them motherfuckers or any number of things because we could only do that within the context of safe Asian Pacific group, not out of secrecy, but certainly confidentiality. We needed a space where it was okay to talk about them. For our own development, we needed to put those things back to where it really was.

Before A/PLG, we socialized, we had dinners, we hung out. We could talk to another Asian person, but we still didn't reveal ourselves heart-to-heart. You might have a common area of interest, but not until the formation of A/PLG did we actually develop heart-to-heart. With A/PLG, we were then able to focus on specific things that put us down and that we had no one to talk about with. You know, in bars and other functions, you don't want to hear all kinds of gripes that go on in the real world. You want to be light and airy and you want to feel good. But we weren't making a real impact, and until a group like A/PLG formed, there was no one to discuss these issues with.

One of the persons who brought that about was Dr. Terry Gock. We had an extensive weekend in Big Bear, the twelve of us, all the Asian Pacific board members and a few others. It was wonderful because we got down the barriers. One person I met at the retreat is a friend of mine now. I had to get on his case because he talked about cultural things on a "we" basis. I said, "Andy, I don't want to hear that. I don't care what the other people in Malaysia think. I want to know what *you* feel." Now he says everything "I". I'd like to hear some "we" once in a while. [Laughs] Now Andy can't stand anybody who says "we" or who skirts the issues. He gets on their case now.

Terry Gock

When I came out to Los Angeles in 1980, I hooked up with Paul Chen. He said that there was this meeting of a new Asian group that was going to start. That was the first meeting at his place. I was new in town. I thought it was wonderful to have a space that was both gay and Asian. It was about that period of time that I was looking much more at not the separate identities, but the integration of identities, both race and sexuality. Well, I had been doing that all along. But I think A/PLG provided a space that could help the process. It's sort of a similar thing that you can worship a god outside of church. Yes, but the church does give you something, a space to do that, in a much more concentrated way. The timing was good. This guy in 1973 or 1974 who told me Asians never liked other Asians, I thought it was about time to prove him wrong, in a major way.

In 1977, I participated in a weekend retreat organized by Don Clark, who wrote *Loving Someone Gay*. He had some of the earliest writings on this whole thing about self-acceptance and integration of one's sexuality into one's life. He wasn't talking about ethnicity. So another psychologist friend of mine in San Francisco, Dr. Bart A., and I designed a similar retreat to look at what it meant to be gay and Asian in a supportive and accepting environment that we could create. I offered to do it for A/PLG. Tak was wonderful as usual, came up with the space. So I pulled in Bart because I liked working with him. We met while I was at one of the professional conferences, and we found out that each other was gay and Asian, and we were having a good time with each other. I said, "C'mon down. We could plan this thing out. We could do this, and we'll have a good time." [Laughs] We put a lot of work into it and had a weekend of different exercises and sharing to look at what it meant to be Asian and gay.

I think primarily the retreat would be the beginning of a process. I wanted them to walk away with a better space about who they were as Asian and gay. More integrated. Perhaps it's something that they could appreciate and be proud of, especially since they talked about what they had gone through in the bars, the experiences of being so few and so segregated. When you really cannot be friends with others who are like you, what you are unconsciously saying is that somehow there is something wrong with some parts of you. That's the part you cannot be friends with. It's like looking into a mirror and not liking part of yourself. That's the byproduct of the competitiveness. I mean, we already didn't get enough validation for who we were, as being gay. We didn't get enough validation for who we were, as being Asian. The competitiveness continued to reinforce that somehow these white guys were better, that we all had to compete against each other for them, that we had to blind ourselves to certain parts of ourselves and not like certain parts of ourselves in order to be okay. What we were hoping to do was to stop that process. But I was realistic even in my early naive clinical days that a weekend was not going to change a person or the world, but it would hopefully start the process of an evolution for oneself, if you will.

There were lots of stuff that we did in two and a half days. We did some journal writing, too. There were a few exercises that dealt with sexuality, few that dealt with getting in touch with the coming out process and their relationship with each other. Really, the exercises were not as important as many of the discussions that followed. It provoked a lot of ideas of who they were. Remember, we were in the early 1980s. We had very few models of, at least overtly, Asian men who were interested in or attracted to other Asian men. I think, at least for some of them, there were certain barriers that came from self-image issues. For me, one of the tell-tale signs was that this participant, who after the retreat was beginning to be able to verbalize more positively about himself and started getting more interested in other gay Asian men, which he thought would never happen in his life. So that tells me something.

Andy C.

I had read about A/PLG in a magazine, but I was hesitant. I did call the phone number given. Someone was volunteering their phone numbers out. I did talk with someone who gave me more information about the club. You know, when you [are gay] and come from Asia, you are more likely not to mix with Asians because you're afraid of being exposed. It's a small circle, and words get back to whoever you don't want to know. You would rather keep hush-hush. Finally, one of my friends said, "We really need someone to do some chow-down. Would you like to help cook something? Just come. If you don't like it, you don't have to go back." It was a small group then. So I said okay. I dragged my feet there. I was kind of nervous about it.

I stopped going after that, and then I went back on my own. I was curious. I didn't get a chance to know them because of my fear. I said I shouldn't allow that to hold me back. I said to myself, "You have to give yourself a chance to understand what's going on. You can't really judge anything without getting involved." That's how I met Tak. It's funny that Tak and I have gotten real close. I would avoid him in the beginning because he was so loud and that scared me. He would usually pick on me, making me think I was crucified. And I used to stay away or run away from him at times.

Were you at the retreat in Big Bear?

I was there. At first, I was a little bit hesitant because I was very shy, and I didn't like to share a room [with people]. But Tak twisted my arm and he wouldn't let go. He said they needed help. So I was assigned to do the kitchen thing again. I said I would cook but I wouldn't wash. By putting myself through that retreat, I learned that I shouldn't shy away but keep an open mind. I thought one of the greatest things was opening up and learning from other people. It was a great experience. (From there, I've facilitated several myself. I did one for Asian Pacific AIDS Intervention Team last year.)

At the retreat, we had different workshops. People were assigned to different tasks and they would be working together, like we had a kitchen crew. We had a bonfire and we sang songs. The night before the last day of the retreat, we had a stage event just to lighten things up. It was like a contest; everybody did sketches or dances or whatever. We got to know each other. I had become friends with people at the retreat. I remember I didn't use the first person reference, like I, I, I. I used to say things like "we." Tak could not understand that. He would say, "Well, say I." And I got aggravated with him a lot. "Well, it's not my experience. Why would I say I?" By the end of the retreat, we understood each other better. Now I can tell him, "Get off my back."

. . . BUT WHO'S THE BOSS?

After Paul Chen resigned as co-chair, the group adopted a more traditional and hierarchical structure, with a steering committee consisting of elected officers and delegates-at-large. Elections were quickly held and the elected board were the first to sign on as members. Tak Yamamoto became the first secretary of the organization (the position was renamed president later); his membership number was one. Dean Goishi was the membership chair; his was four. Doug Chin remembers he was the last on the board to join. "All the officers at that point signed up. That's why I was number twelve. I was the last one. Roy Kawasaki was the one who spoke up because the treasurer spot was still open. It was between me and another guy. And Roy said, 'I vouched for Doug.' " The board had a majority of Asian members. As a co-founder, Morris Kight was not one of the them, and the board acknowledged his contributions by giving him a complimentary membership later on.

Immediately, the official group began to meet, a monthly meeting for the general membership and a separate meeting for the steering committee to prepare for the general meeting. The general meeting consisted of a potluck where members could socialize and a cultural program. Organization business or decisions made by the steering committee would be presented and discussed at the general meeting as well. In an attempt to inculcate a panethnic identity, each month a spotlight was given to a specific Asian culture. Roy Kawasaki says, "In the beginning, we made it very cultural. What we were trying to do was bring about understanding of each other. Although the leadership basically came out of the American-born, the membership was drawn from a lot of different Asian ethnic backgrounds. We showed films. People brought all these different ethnic foods. We had fashion shows or cultural talks. We were trying to bring together this fragmented Asian community. It worked out pretty well." These meetings were held at various homes of A/PLG members, particularly the Caucasians, like Morris Kight and Jack F. Roy remembers, "The Asians really weren't established at that time. We didn't have large homes like some of those more established white men. We had to depend on them to get ourselves started. As a matter of fact, we depended a great deal on them to give us the support. So we really could not exclude them in the establishment of A/PLG."

At around the same time, a group of members, including Doug Chin, Terry Gock, and Jack F., began drafting a mission statement. This process turned out to be quite contentious. The founders had wanted to break down the barriers among the different ethnic groups. Many of them also wanted to use A/PLG as a vehicle to develop gay Asian leadership. But how was this to be carried out? What would the role of non-Asian members be? Could they be full-fledged members and run for offices or sit on board and committees that shaped the policies of the organization? Or were they to be supporters working behind the scene and contributing their resources that eluded most gay Asians at that time? Should they have equal access to functions, like the monthly raps, that were supposed to be safe spaces for Asians only? These questions might take a new form within the context of a nascent organization, but they really spoke to an old dynamics that had never been addressed before in the gay community. The body was new, but the scars were already familiar. By tackling these issues, as Terry Gock points out, "we were carving out what our identities could be. We were not really discussing an organization in the abstract. We were discussing who we were. And for the group of people who were willing to engage in that process and journey into uncharted territories, at least it gave us a lot of confidence in terms of understanding who we are [now as gay Asians]."

André Ting

One man demonstrated the Chinese *pipa*, a traditional Chinese [musical] instrument, at an A/PLG meeting. He was a professional *pipa* player. People were awed. It was just one instrument. Many people came and we were just awed. And at that time, I volunteered to do a Chinese painting, Oriental brush painting demonstration. They liked it very much.

[In August, 1981,] I conducted a workshop during the A/PLG first [membership] retreat at the San Gabriel mountains. It was a weekend retreat. I was not one of the organizers. I was one of the presenters. There were several workshops. It was well attended. I would say about fifty people. At that time, it was supposed to be a consciousness raising event, to un-learn our baggage, like self-loathing, inferiority complex as a gay person, internal homophobia, things like that, to learn to be proud of who we are. I did the workshop called "The Foods of China." And I knew that a lot of people were into Chinese foods. So I thought it was a vehicle that I could use to introduce Chinese culture to the people. I didn't do the actual cooking because it was a camping place. They did not have all the facilities. At that time, I was teaching Chinese cooking in two different school districts. One of them was Saddleback College. I was leading a college class called "Chinese Gourmet Cooking." I had my recipes. I was already an instructor in Chinese cooking. So I took some of my notes, recipes and we kind of vicariously, you know, have cooking class there. But mostly I tried to use cooking as a vehicle to introduce Chinese culture to the people. So when they eat something, not only do they know the dishes, the names of dishes, but also why the dishes are prepared that way. So they can appreciate the food that they eat more. They would know the ingredients. They would know why Kung Pao chicken is so special, the history of the recipe.

There was another workshop about Japanese language. They tried to make the workshops a cultural thing so they were more purposeful. I don't remember much of the other workshops because at that time I was concerned with preparing a good workshop. I think that it was good. They said that my workshop was well organized, with handouts. I think one of the reasons is because I was already an instructor.

I imagine that it would be so nice to have more workshops. Mostly I really appreciated the self-actualization [aspect] of it by learning different Asian cultures as well as gay culture. For example, I think I was becoming more interested in Asians sexually not so much as a result of a sexual experience [with another Asian], but rather as a result of understanding Asian culture. In the 1970s and 1980s, I started teaching Oriental brush painting and Chinese cooking. I did research on Chinese culture and Asian culture. I started to appreciate Asian culture or Asian people in general. I think that's the reason. I realized then that every culture has its own standard of beauty, that you cannot judge beauty by the Western or the white culture alone. That, more or less, opened my eyes to the world to appreciate people of different races in their own terms. That intellectual awakening truly influenced my sexual preference.

Dean Goishi

I think A/PLG had two allies. One was the rice queens, those who wanted to take care of Asians. I had to call them allies because they helped organize A/PLG. The other side of it was non-Asians who felt that Asians needed a place to feel safe and build leadership. There was a group of non-Asians that belonged to that category and not necessarily felt that they had to take care of us. Of course, there was a faction of the first group who wanted to run A/PLG. They wanted to take the top leadership and everything else. That was stemmed, with the help of the non-Asians who felt they could help but needed to be in the background. They were very helpful. They gave advice, financial support, whatever else they could.

I think the non-Asians who felt they should be secondary partners or stayed in the background probably had more skills in other organizations. I would say the rice queens that were part of A/PLG had no other place to go to. That's why they stayed at A/PLG. They felt they could be in a dominant position, a leadership position that they otherwise could not attain in white organizations.

Andy C.

When we first formed A/PLG, it was not just the Asians alone. We did have our American friends in there. So the controversy was like, are we going to have this as just any club, or are we going to have this as an Asian club? We Asians fought for an Asian club. I'd say, "You Americans have all kinds of clubs. We Asians don't have a club." There would be members that were non-Asians. Then the question became, would we allow them to vote, etc.? In the beginning, we decided that the President, Vice President, and [Treasurer]—the three major offices—had to be Asians. And the rest—the committee chairs and the delegates—could be a mixture of nationalities. But I personally felt that all the positions had to be Asians. I was even against the non-Asian members being able to vote. This was an Asian club. It should be conducted in the interest of Asian Americans, and other nationalities could join, but they should be supporting members. They could contribute, but they could not be there to tell us what to do. If they had something to say, we'd be all ears. This was an Asian thing, so it had to be done solely by Asians. That's my feeling. But I guess it didn't happen. It was put to a vote.

The presence of non-Asian members in A/PLG was both good and bad. I can't say we shouldn't have any non-Asian members because we benefited from them, too. We shared ideas. They gave input in forming projects and support and everything. The bad part was the "domination," which I didn't care for.

Even though they didn't hold the top positions?

Yes, they ganged up and showed power play. I always felt some of the Asians didn't know much of anything. If they had a Caucasian lover, the majority would do whatever the Caucasian lover encouraged and they remained dormant. To me, one should participate as an Asian and give feedback. They shouldn't be controlled. I'm not saying non-Asians shouldn't join, but they should see the Asians' point of view and build this as an Asian club. Of course, there were the few Caucasians that understood our needs and supported us throughout without trying to dominate us.

Tak Yamamoto

When we wrote the by-laws, one of the things we stipulated was that, yes, we like to have people other than Asian Pacifics in the organization, but they were not to take leadership roles. That wasn't spelled out, but it said that they would be helping. The reason we put that clause in was that most of our leadership was English-speaking, mostly non-immigrant types. But there were still some people who were born here, who were hesitant to take on leadership roles because they never had the opportunity. What we were hoping to do with A/PLG was to develop that leadership capability through actually serving on a position and making changes. If not as president, then at least one of the other positions, delegate-at-large or secretary. Any number of offices or committees where they would be able to assert themselves. So at the beginning, we would always have a token non-Asian Pacific on the board. Let's say he would be a delegate-at-large or maybe a treasurer. But I would say nine-tenths of the positions were filled by Asian Pacifics, which we felt was really important.

So we put some people together to work on the by-laws. The board voted on it and then we had to have the whole organization vote on it, too. We dialogued lots of times about the fact that while we didn't want to make Anglos second-class, we didn't want to—this sounds like a terrible thing—give them equal representation. After all, this was supposedly an Asian Pacific–focused organization, maybe not by membership, but by design. The focus was to develop Asian Pacific consciousness throughout the communities and we didn't want to do that with whites leading the organization. We had the impact at some point in the early 1980s by going to different Asian organizations and expressing who we were with their leadership. If, for instance, we had a white president, that would not have worked at all.

An example of that: I'm in another group called the Manzanar Committee. One year we had interacted with Native Americans in Poston, Arizona. The Committee at that time was probably five whites and ten Asian Pacifics, primarily Japanese. We had this little booth at the Indian Festival in Poston. At the time, I had to leave the table to take care of something. When I came back, I saw the governor of Arizona then talking to the person sitting at our booth, Don, who happened to be white. The governor objected to a white person representing the Japanese. I had to come back and correct him right away that Don was a member of the Committee but he was not the person who made decisions for the organization. He was . . . again, I don't want to call it second-class, but it was the same thing how I felt about A/PLG, that white people were there as part of the numbers and they would be supportive, but they would not take on leadership. Don wasn't trying to do that. He was there to answer questions because I had to leave the table for a while. The governor's response was, "All of these organizations always have some white person in them directing them." I think that would've also have happened early on if we had left that possibility of a white person running A/PLG.

So in the by-laws, it said they would assist or all that kind of craziness. The whole basis of the organization was to enhance the qualities for Asian Pacifics to take on leadership roles, which to me indicates that you might have all the qualities we need, but if you were white, I'd rather we didn't do that. Everybody who joined the organization back then knew that we were looking to develop leadership for Asian Pacifics because we didn't have any other organization for that. If you were white and you wanted to lead an organization, then go down to the [Gay and Lesbian Community Service] Center or go down to one of the other places and become their president. We didn't want you to become this president. We were careful about not putting that [explicitly] in our by-laws because we were going for a non-profit status. And you couldn't do that. What we did instead—within our ability to dialogue with people who thought when they came into the organization, they were going to run it—was we wanted them to assure us that that was not their intent. If someone said they wanted to run for president, then we would go through that whole dialogue again to discourage them. We would ask them to consider a delegate-at-large position because they could still help and support the organization that way, or maybe the AIDS chair or something like that. I think they got the message. We didn't have to beat them over the head with it. I think we had someone as high up as a treasurer. The numbers of non-Asians in the Steering Committee was never greater than that of Asian Pacifics. We were very vehement about that.

Paul Chen

I remember further down the line in the first year, we were having a lot of troubles with non-Asians. They kept on . . . how should I say this? It seems that we would snap into this sort of group consensus type of decision-making. It wasn't a style that we planned on. Yes, we would take a vote at the end [of each discussion], but it wasn't until after everybody had agreed to the central decision. The question would bounce around enough, and everybody would put in their two cents. And only then would a vote be taken, with everybody making a compromise. It would take us hours, hours, and hours to make one decision. But by the time we made the decision, everybody had a part in it. Of course, everybody agreed on it and so it would pass. That drove the non-Asians absolutely bananas. They just wanted us to vote on it and get a majority and get done. We kept on trying to say to them, "No, no, this is how we make decisions, so everybody has a part in it. Nobody feels left out. Nobody feels outvoted. There is no minority." It drove them absolutely nuts.

Terry Gock

The major challenge certainly was, Who's in charge here? The goals of A/PLG, the mission of A/PLG, included one part about developing gay Asian leadership. And how were we going to start developing gay Asian leadership if non-Asians held positions on the steering committee? And yet, on the other hand, we were also struggling with the fact that there weren't many gay Asians who were stepping forward to do things. And yet when Asians and non-Asians tried to come together in the steering committee, there were some cultural issues about how things ought to be done. I think the gay Asians were very sensitive to—and perhaps some of us were overly sensitive—the roles that non-Asians played. On the other hand, some of the non-Asian members were not sensitive enough on how intrusive they could be. Asians tend to go for consensus and consensus takes much more time. Caucasians members would say, "We could do this much faster." It really came to a point where I actually brought in a straight couple—the woman is Asian and her husband is non-Asian—to come in and do a workshop on Asian/non-Asian communication. The woman was Gladys Lee, the director of Asian Pacific Family Center. Gladys and I started working ever since 1980 in different capacities. We had organized a whole bunch of stuff in the Asian communities. It was clear that, yes, we would take more time. And yet we generally came up ahead, and partly I think it was because we tried to build consensus instead of disenfranchising a bunch of people with just a majority vote. And her husband Hal was one of those people who could see that and was able to talk about their own struggles in their communication and how they would come to appreciate the strength of each other. Certainly, in those days, too, the Asians tended to be younger than the non-Asians. It was like some of them thought, "Why don't you listen to us? We have more experience and we can do it better and faster. We can show you the way." At the same time, my position and some of the other people's position was, "If you don't leave us alone, we will never develop Asian leadership."

AN AMBASSADOR'S JOB

The narrators who are early A/PLG leaders divide the white membership into two camps. First, there are those who were willing to put in the work for the organization and shared the belief of the Asian leadership that A/PLG was first and foremost an organization for gay and lesbian Asians. Then there are the rice queens who attended A/PLG functions with the same objectives as they would have in gay bars like the River Club and Mugi's. The Asian leadership could not accept one camp and ostracize the other, at least not officially or overtly. And the two were not mutually exclusive sometimes. As a new organization, and as the only gay Asian organization in town, they tried to be as inclusive as possible. Besides, whether or not their intentions were benevolent, they helped A/PLG recruit and retain Asian members. (The founders might as well take advantage of the rice queens' predatory skills.) If white men were to be a force to be reckoned with within the organization, conflicts were unavoidable, but not necessarily a bad thing.

Sociologist William A. Gamson argues that "construction of a collective identity is one step in challenging cultural domination. The content must necessarily be adversarial in some way to smoke out the invisible and arbitrary elements of the dominant cultural codes."[1] An identity is a consciousness that is as much about what you are as it is about what you are not. That consciousness can be obtained by disidentifying from the dominant culture and developing a politics of difference. Or, as Tak Yamamoto colorfully says later in this chapter, "We need to be able to have a safe space where we can call you [white friends at A/PLG] motherfuckers." In looking at the growth of feminist consciousness in the United States and Western Europe during the 1960s and the 1970s, Ethel Klein supports this point. She "describes how the dramatic changes in the division of labor between the sexes provided women with a new social identity: the self-image of 'women as workers' replaced that of 'women as mothers.' This new identity did not automatically lead to political activism, but it created new standards for social comparison; comparison generated the belief that the category 'women' was treated unjustly; and this belief was an impetus to political activism."[2] Similarly, the conflicts between whites and Asians as described by the narrators actually furthered the process of identity formation. Their dissatisfaction with the lack of leadership opportunities for Asians stemmed from an analysis of inequality in the division of labor. By consolidating behind a strict policy of self-determination, the Asian leadership was drawing boundaries on what was acceptable behavior in the relationship between whites and Asians and articulating for the first time a common, collective interest. This is what Terry Gock means when he says, "We were not really discussing an organization in the abstract. We were discussing who we were." More importantly, they forced the other side to react to their interpretation of injustice. By having to be on the defensive, what had been assumed to be the natural order of things were "smoked out" and made contestable.[3] Though the old hegemony was far from being eradicated, it could no longer thrive on the consent of gay Asian men.

Determining whether non-Asians could serve on the board was just the beginning of a war. What complicated the conflict is that the "adversary" is a legitimate part of the organization. They were not some external threats or targets around which the leadership could mobilize their membership. In most cases, they were at once friends and enemies. Even a first-rate army has room to retreat and regroup. A/PLG, on the other hand, fought each and every skirmish in the public. Everything it was doing became a battleground. For example, one of its missions was to build solidarity between Asian lesbians and gay men and between immigrants and American-born Asians. Some of the energy that could have been devoted to this kind of solidarity work was siphoned to negotiating and normalizing race relations. The interest was there, and some work was done. But when issues like white domination or cruising took center stage in the organization, they left little room for anything else. Lesbians and immigrants became easy casualties.

June Lagmay

I think Rita [who is Latina] and I were the only women in the very, very beginning, but eventually there was a woman named Kathy S. And what was ironic about Kathy was that she grew up when her parents still lived like two houses in the back of Rita's parents in City Terrace in East L.A., which kind of tickled us because we liked meeting Asian people who lived under Hispanic East side and had that kind of culture and history. And then Amy Y.

didn't join [A/PLG] until later. And I'm ashamed to say that I don't remember the other women. I think there must have been at least seven or ten. . . . Well, later we had our women's only rap group in our house and I remember there were at least eight or ten women there. It couldn't have been more than eight or ten.

I keep emphasizing this: the men, at least the men that I was friends with—I can't say I knew every single man in A/PLG—but the leadership that I hung out with were so genuinely interested in cultivating women's membership, were honestly interested in being sensitive. I remember a lot, a lot of good times laughing at dinner with Tak and Paul and the guys. I remember the men asked if the women could come and talk to them about what it was like from the women's point of view. They were fascinated with lesbian sexuality. They were. They were. As well as a lot of mainstream gay men's groups. For some reason, they just found that really fascinating. Not that they were being voyeuristic or getting off on it. But they were just honestly, genuinely curious because who else is going to tell them? [Laughs]

If there was acrimony, I didn't see it in front of my own eyes. And if it happened like behind my back or something, then it might have been some of the guys with really wretched consciousness. It could've been some of the women who were maybe a little self-conscious. I mean, we were all discovering things at the same time. Not only that, but the years, the decade, was a time of discovery. Think about it. In the real world, the Hispanics were starting to organize. And women. We [Rita and I] probably stuck around [A/PLG] for three, four years, and then we had other things going on in our lives. I don't know what happened after we stopped going. I can't vouch for what happened in the organization. But the thing I remember that was so genuine is people like Tak and Paul and Terry and Dean and some of the others never had a separation between men and women. We really were sisters and brothers.

I think the only thing that may have been more like divided by gender was when the guys decided to have a night out at the bars. Rita and I weren't that interested. We got invited to go. Sometimes we went and sometimes we didn't. In the beginning at least, [A/PLG] was to provide an alternative to the bars for the guys.

Was it an alternative to the bars for the women, too?

There were, as far as I could remember, maybe only two or three women-only bars. If you wanted to party, you would go to a mixed place where they had disco music. And even more than that, some places were straight like five nights out of the week and they had a gay night. So not only if you were a lesbian, you only had a place to go once a week, but the one night of the week that you got to go there, it wouldn't be just women. It would be men, too. I can't guess at the motivation why a woman would join A/PLG. The fact was it was just something. And if you wanted to come, you're welcome. And if you didn't you didn't have to. Maybe you can learn something. Maybe you can let down your guard and not feel so uptight. Maybe you can hook up with other women. Why not? You know. If there was cruising going on, that would be totally understandable and legitimate. But I think the women were not as interested in doing co-gender things. And it's perfectly understandable.

Tak Yamamoto

I don't think the white–Asian dynamic was an issue for the Asian lesbians because it seemed to me anyway that most of the women who came were either single or had an Asian Pacific lover. They were more secure than we were. I think that's one of the things that we saw differently. The women had a different attitude about where they wanted to get to. After the first eight or nine months, we were starting to see a schism anyway. The women were trying to get their own issues, their own agenda, on the table. There were fewer interactions with men, and they would not have interaction with white men because they didn't want to be dictated to either. But they thought they could at least dialogue with Asian Pacific men. There were all-Asian rap groups. We talked about who we were, what were lesbian issues, and how we could help resolve them for ourselves as well. It was all kind of Asian lesbians/male gays 101. It was an initial dialogue that we didn't have, that I couldn't talk to my sister about before. I was thinking, "Am I still doing those things [that oppressed women]? Am I being supportive? Am I doing something that my brothers did before?" At that time, we didn't even know that.

Even the socials were different [for the men and the women]. I think the most the women would do with the group most of the times was sports games—bowling, softball, you know, butch things. [Laughs] By the end of the first year, we still had a list of women that were paid members, but they were no longer active.

What other things did you talk about in the rap groups?

We were able to find out about similarities and differences between American-born and Asian-born. [Some of us American-born] thought if you were Asian-born, you had all these advantages. For instance, when you came here, you had to come with a certain reliance on yourself. You came here with the knowledge that you were going to succeed. We were like everybody else here. We got all these little prejudices to work out. We were just happy that we were planted in this ground. But they'd say, "I'm at a disadvantage. I don't have the language skills you got." Then we'd say, "But you're not looking for validation. You're not looking for someone to tell you you're okay because you came here with all your culture intact. We, however, are fragmented. We've got all the white knowledge and all the white prejudices. You came here with your whole culture. We're jealous of that." A lot of them initially had a difficult time with that. I mean, how could they possibly address that? If you came intact, how do you tell me how you are? But of course, we didn't understand that. We were very innocent at the time.

In doing the separate raps, sure, it created hard feelings for some non-Asians because they were excluded. Their whole point was, Why do you have to have an all-Asian rap group? We must be talking about them. But we said, "No, we need to be able to have a safe space where we can call you motherfuckers if we feel like it. We can't do that in a general rap. In a general rap, we have to mind our p's and q's and just sort of go along with the program. Whereas in an all-Asian group, we could say you're the ones who are holding us back. But we can't say that at the general meeting because then you would take offense. You would not necessarily understand the context." We tried to encourage the non-Asians to have their own rap, but nobody was really interested. They obviously had their own agenda. And of course, people in the Asian rap were getting a little antsy, too. They were saying, "God, we're creating this alienation. Maybe we ought not to do this any more." People started not showing up. We would get calls, "Oh, I have something else to do today." It was too much work to try to put it together. It just died a natural death. But [while it lasted,] we were able to talk about in-depth things. I really felt good about that because that gave us the opportunity to develop, to be able to express all kinds of things that we wanted to but didn't find a safe place for before that.

André Ting

I'm very happy with A/PLG in its first year. It was not very structured. We were all just finding our ways. It satisfied my needs at the time. Then I felt like it was becoming cliquish. There was some group, for some reason, they felt like they were doing a lot of work. They felt like they should be directing that organization more than anyone else. I was not one of them. They never called me back. They never asked me to do anything. I would go to a function and they would wear their tags as hosts, like they were an in-group. I was not an in-group, no matter how much I volunteered, as if they did not want my service for some reason. So I felt like I was an outsider for a while.

At the end of 1981, there was a formal election. I was nominated to be one of the two candidates for Vice Secretary [which would become the vice president position], and Tak was one of the candidates for the Secretary [which would, likewise, become the president position]. And I lost out to

Terry Gock. After that, I became not very active. It was not because I was bitter. I knew better than that. In university, I was already into organizations. I was president of the Press Club, I was the treasurer for Drama Society, I was the president of the Science Academy. I was already involved. I could take a loss easily. I'm not like that. No, I think it's because I felt that I wasn't being appreciated. There were some very nice people that were not political, not cliquish. Somehow I was kind of disillusioned, because I had such high hope for this organization, but it turned out to be quite different.

You know, when A/PLG was formed, it was dominated by American-born Asians with some non-Asians because the meetings were conducted in English. Being fluent in English, the native-born Asians had an advantage already. And being more outspoken than the traditional immigrants, they just became leaders. But there were a few non-native-born Asians who were fluent in English, who were outspoken, like Terry Gock, for example. They were elected, too. But at the time I already noticed, if not a schism, a separation between the two groups. If you do not reach out to the immigrants, they're just going to go away. When they are oppressed and rejected in the straight society, they want to feel accepted completely in a gay organization. If they did not find this complete acceptance and embrace, they are not going to last, they are not going to like it. And I kind of had that feeling already. But I think the native-born Asians did not make a conscious effort to reach out to the foreign-born Asians. I think it is their loss. One thing is like in the retreat, for example. After the workshops, they would sit around and sing songs and play games, but the songs they sang were American folk songs or what-not. A foreign-born Asian may not know the words to the songs, so they could not participate. Obviously they felt left out. In a way I cannot really blame these people. Many of the native-born Asians were monolingual. They only knew English. They did not really know Asian culture. But at that time, there was no such thing as diversity workshops or sensitivity trainings. Those terms were not around. Nobody knew about those things. They were just doing their own thing, I suppose. But I felt that they did not make an effort to welcome every person. I felt truly disappointed.

Andy C.

In the beginning, I always felt there was a barrier [between the American-born Asians and Asian immigrants]. I always bore this conflicting feeling about them putting us down, looking down on us, because we were foreign-born and we had lots to learn. There used to be a time I had to do some intermediary work. I was aware of the fact that both the local-born and the foreign-born Asians had to communicate and air out their differences and come to an amiable understanding. On the one hand, the foreign-born brought with them their family values and culture. Many local-born might not have full knowledge [of their own culture] or possibly felt threatened by us.

On the other hand—I can still see this—in most parts of Southeast Asia, a lot of us lived this American dream that we had learned from movies, magazines, and news media. You know, a lot of the foreign-born Asians, they were looking at all these movies and thought, "Oh, they [American men] are so caring." Back then, in Middletown America, gay life was not as out as it is now. So when the Americans left home for military and went overseas in Asia, they probably took the opportunity with the Asians there. It was like an escape. Sure, they'd take care of you then, but that was only temporary. They'd think, "Oh, he's so nice." But when [the Asians] came over here, the real life began. Most Asian men, I think, came with this idea of a fairy tale: I'll find somebody in America. It's going to be great because he will take care of me. That was not always the case. I'm sure a lot of them eventually learned that it's not as easy as they thought. Since by then I've lived here for a while, I could understand why my [American-born] counterparts here would say, "Why are Asians coming over here with this expectation? We are already labeled as 'geisha boys.' " I could see why they were fighting so hard not to have this happen. I could understand the difference. That's why in the beginning I did more of an ambassador's job, trying to analyze to them the differences between us and create a bond between the "two" Asian groups.

IT WAS ALL VOLUNTEERS

The rap for Asian men and women lasted about six months. The rap for Asian men was only slightly more successful. Even with the internal strife, the gay Asian leadership kept this space alive for about two years. Though its duration was limited, the Asian-only rap, along with other programming of A/PLG, was important in fostering a collective gay Asian identity. As Doug Chin says, "Part of the problem is if you have a non-Asian always dominating the Asian in a relationship, the Asian person is not going to speak up. And that's why it was important for us to get an Asian-only rap group going." All the narrators who were co-founders of the organization noticed a breakdown of ethnic barriers in gay Asian bars, like the River Club and Mugi's, and attributed this development to A/PLG. Paul Chen jokes that even though he had known some of the original members in the typically dark gay Asian bars before A/PLG, "it was interesting to meet them finally in the light and see what they looked like." Harry Park says, "After A/PLG was formed, if you saw someone in a bar or even in the public—it could be anywhere—as long as you knew they were with A/PLG or seen them at A/PLG meetings or functions, it was all right to go and speak to them. The barriers were down. Personally, A/PLG helped me get out of the closet among Asians. Rather than looking away when we saw another Asian, A/PLG gave us enough confidence in ourselves to try to be friendlier and more open."

Another way to foster a gay Asian identity was through its many community functions, like potlucks, chili contests, beer busts, and parties. Some of them were held in gay Asian bars, like Mugi's, the River Club, and later, Faces. Doing fundraisers at Mugi's was particularly memorable for the organizers. Not only was the food at Mugi's, the restaurant, "awful," but its kitchen was also dirty. They would find old bowls of soup that had not been thrown away. Doug Chin says, "We decided that Mugi's wasn't the place to do fundraising that involved food. I mean, we had to clean up the kitchen!" Nevertheless, these events attracted hundreds of participants, members and nonmembers both, and they were a significant factor in the exponential growth of A/PLG membership. Within the first year, the organization had gotten so large that they could no longer hold their general meetings at members' homes. Furthermore, these activities provided a concrete way for A/PLG members to work together, build leadership, and develop stronger bonds. Most of them were also fundraising events. The proceeds went not only to the day-to-day maintenance of the organization, such as the newsletters, but—demonstrating a pioneering sense of long-term vision—also to helping HIV-positive members and starting a "building fund."

Doug Chin

In the early years, we celebrated Chinese New Year. We'd prepare a Chinese meal. The first couple fundraisers we had were Luaus. We prepared the meals and fed the organization. I still have all these large [cooking utensils and instruments]. We only charged five dollars, but it probably only cost us two and a half. We also donated a great deal. When we first started out, my office paid for a lot of things.

Then, in 1983, I came up with an idea: Why not do a cultural extravaganza as a fundraiser? That's how Fantasia came about. We had a lot of talented members. It was like a Gong show, but, you know, that was part of it, getting the membership involved in providing a cultural demonstration of their background so that they showed it to everybody. We did that not only visually, but we also did it for food. We got groups of people cooking tempura. I remember making five-spice Chinese chicken. We had Indonesian salads. We must have had about nine different pockets of three or four people coming in and preparing all these exotic dishes. And we only charged fifteen dollars. Can you imagine? It was all volunteers. Our first Fantasia, we had over three hundred people attending. We must have had about a hundred and some people to help carry this out, dancing, performing, cooking, doing the decorations and everything else. It was wonderful. That's what we wanted the membership to get, so that we could help them pull together and do different things. And you know? That worked.

The first year we ended with a surplus of funds. It was some small amount, like three hundred and some dollars. So at the end of the year, I had a board resolution to start up a building fund to transfer the excess fund into this account. That was the start of the building fund. We also made a second part to that resolution. For any major fundraiser, fifty percent of the profit would go toward the building fund. That was in the hopes of someday setting up a retirement home for older Asian gays. At one point, the fund was up to $21,000. And that was after almost—when did I leave?—thirteen years, in 1993.

For me, being active in A/PLG strengthened my friendships with other A/PLG members. For instance, I knew Tak from the bars before, but I didn't really get to know him until the organization was formed. And the retreat [during the first year] helped, too, because we didn't know all the twelve members of the steering committee. We didn't know a lot about each other, especially in the early days, when we were not just making decisions about policies, but we were actually doing the work. I think anytime you get to see people more on a social level, you have a better inclination of where they're coming from when they make their decisions. And you'd respect that also. I've been around long enough to know that you can't have your way all the time. Making compromises, understanding where other people are coming from, that was very important for the organization.

I don't know if anybody has ever mentioned this. For a number of years, people in A/PLG used to refer to the six of us—me, Tak, Dean, Roy, Andy, and Ed G.—as the Gang of Six, not only because we served on the same boards, but because we were very supportive of each other. One of us would be organizing something, and the rest would help in the background supporting him to make sure the event got carried on. I could count my life on them. Some people called us cliquish, but that's how safe I was to them, how close I felt to them.

Do you feel you provided a space for other people to get involved?

Oh, yes. Sure. I've seen people blossom out of their shell, becoming more open. I can think of one now, a Japanese man from Japan, who was an extremely shy person and never said anything. His [white] lover always did the speaking. To his lover's credit, he's a wonderful and supportive person, very encouraging of his partner. But this guy has always been somewhat shy and closeted. Well, A/PLG has helped him come out. He always helped around on the fringes. And after being a member for a number of years, he finally decided to join the board as a delegate-at-large. During the board meetings, he would give great input. He wasn't afraid. He said what he needed to say.

Harry Park

The River Club was the nucleus at that time, and we would have a barbecue, chili contest, whatever, at the River Club. Everything that was there for sale was donated by the members. We would bear the cost. At that time, I was a credit manager for a liquor wholesaler. Herb and I donated almost two hundred dollars worth of wine to the club for sale to the members for an event. The profit strictly went to A/PLG. That's how it went on for a long time. If something needed to be done, the core leadership just automatically chipped in money. That's how we gradually built up our funds.

There were a lot of financial obstacles. We started meeting at the Metropolitan Community Church in the Valley. We would pay them for the meeting [space]. On too many occasions, though, they canceled out on us at the last minute because they had another function. So we had to move on. We met at so many different places. There was a church in Inglewood. As far as some churches were concerned, they were quite lenient to let us have the space, but it always cost us money. The newsletters cost a lot of money, too. In those days, people didn't have that much money to give away. We just needed funds to expand.

With A/PLG, I became more aware of and associated more with Asians than with Caucasians. It just brought a lot of us back to our own nucleus of Asians. On many occasions, a group of us would meet in a bar after a meeting to drink and relax, discuss how the meeting went, how we could improve, what we could do for the next meeting and so forth. People that were really involved did not care about titles. We had a job to do, and we did it. With A/PLG, I lost the fear of—shall I say—being gay. It gave me self-esteem. It was almost automatically done that we became public speakers. At work where I was a credit manager, I had to speak at a meeting in front of over a hundred and twenty people. I had to introduce myself, advise them as to what my goals were for the company and so forth. As far as I was concerned, if it was not for the experience I had with A/PLG, speaking to the general public like I did, I would've been terrible. A/PLG helped me with that, yes. It gave me enough self-esteem that being gay and being Asian weren't bad. I felt that if anyone had the guts to ask me if I was gay, I'd tell them the truth. There was a co-worker of mine once; we were both in management. He closed the door and said, [whispering] "I have to ask you something." I said, "What?" He said, "Are you gay?"

I looked at him and I said, "Of course, you damned fool." [Laughs]

In the mid-1980s, Herb and I became founders of Uptown Gay and Lesbian Alliance. It covers Highland Park, Eagle Rock, Pasadena, the [San Gabriel] Valley. Like A/PLG, it was formed to let the community, especially the police department, be aware that we do exist, that we are citizens and taxpayers, that we demanded equal rights and needed their help. The reason Uptown was formed was because a gay person was murdered in Highland Park, and we got together, with no real intention of having a club at the time, to protest the brutality of the murder and the lack of compassion and assistance from the LAPD. Herb and I, with A/PLG's permission, in fact, borrowed their bylaws to help form the Uptown Gay and Lesbian Alliance. My involvement in A/PLG definitely was helpful. Uptown's been in existence almost fourteen years. It's an extremely good group, too.

Reggie Bogan

I became a member at my second visit to A/PLG. If I recall right, we were still meeting at Morris Kight's. When you joined, they asked you what you would like to do. Would you like to help with fundraising? Outreach? Educational? Would you help set up the meetings? There were different [committees], and each one had a chairperson. I joined the fundraising committee. At that time, a Japanese was the fundraising chairperson. He did it for almost a year. And when he didn't want to run as chair anymore, I became the chair. I did it for almost three years. Basically my function was to organize garage sales and some auctions. We were raising money for newsletters and for different events. If we were going to have a dance, we got to have money up front. We'd make money from the dance, but we got to have the funds first. At the potluck, people brought food, but we provided the soft drinks. And we had activities and door prizes at the meetings. So basically [the money] was for the newsletters and different free functions that we did.

The fundraising chair was one of the positions that they let a non-Asian member take because it wasn't like the President, the Vice President or the Treasurer, who shaped the policies. They didn't want the Caucasians to be, nor did the Caucasians want to be, in that capacity. It was an Asian organization, number one. So they wanted Asians to run it and us Caucasians being supportive basically. In fact, I ran for Treasurer a couple of times against Doug and lost because they felt I was getting into a position where it should be an Asian. When you got into A/PLG, you either joined one of the activities, and then from there, you became active or worked into becoming a chair. I feel if you were going to be in a club, why not be active? But I always thought that policy was right, that we should be supportive and not play a key role.

The fundraiser was just a fundraiser. I would report to the [steering] committee how much money we made, what it cost, the expenses and stuff. That was my function. I was never into the politics of the organization, even though a lot of time the discussion got heated at the meetings. Well, a good example, we had a committee chair who was a Filipino. He was very much into politics, and many of us felt that we weren't ready for that. We were there for Asians and we wanted to form our own identity, and not to get involved in politics. Another example, if you wanted to be a member but they got a feeling that you were strictly looking out for tricks, that you wanted a different Asian every time you could, they kind of squelched you from being a member. I wasn't in the actual process of going through the applications. A few years into the organization, we started having name tags at the meetings. If you were a non-member, you got one of the stickers that you had to write your name on yourself. [That's how they would identify the non-members.] Out of a two-hundred membership, forty or fifty people could come. [So that was manageable.] But . . . talking about the fundraisers again, let's say the Thanksgiving dinner, which was totally funded through the fundraising money. If you were not a member and came just to meet a trick, you had to pay for your dinner. But with other functions like the [Fourth of July] picnics or dances, we'd have about three hundred people show up. When we did Fantasia, forget it, because we had families and non-gay friends attending. But you could see the different cliques. You could still tell who was cruising and who wasn't.

THAT HOSTILE ASIAN GROUP

At the same time when A/PLG was trying to strengthen the infrastructure, the leadership also made it a point to reach out to both the larger Asian American community and mainstream gay and lesbian community. Building gay Asian leadership and providing safe spaces so gay Asian men could develop on their own terms were all linked to a bigger picture. "It was to share our issues with the larger community," says Terry Gock. "Remember that A/PLG partly started out with the feeling that we were ignored in the larger gay and Asian American communities." Leadership development as a *raison d'être* for a gay Asian organization may not be such a revolutionary idea now. But at a time when resources were few and A/PLG was the first and only organization of its kind in Los Angeles, adherence to this principle with such vehemence took some conviction. Half the membership was non-Asian, and the nascent organization depended on membership dues to survive.

As it turned out, involving the larger Asian membership proved to be not so simple a task. Many members were not out. Stanley Rebultan remembers even before the organization formed, people were skittish about associating with an organization that has the words "gays" and "lesbians" in its name. "We had heated discussions about the choosing of the name," he says. "With the inclusion of 'Lesbians and Gays' in the name, people were really turned off because it really signified a gay and lesbian organization. I said, 'Look. What is the use of forming an organization if we are not coming out and telling the world what we are?' A lot of people, too, spoke in favor of that and we prevailed." That debate did little to alleviate the fear of less brazenly out gay Asians. In the beginning, A/PLG membership roster contained quite a few pseudonyms (of both Asian and non-Asian members), and a few more people only attended A/PLG functions but did not join the organization; sometimes because they were staying in the United States with either a student or a work visa and they didn't want to risk their status or prospect of permanent residence by belonging to a gay organization. As a result, A/PLG had a lot more members supporting behind the scene rather than in the forefront. Even those who were "out" generally might be reluctant in making presentations or otherwise representing A/PLG to their respective ethnic communities.

As Tak Yamamoto says, "If you look at the participation at the [Gay pride] parade in the first few years, that is the most telling. Out of two hundred people of our membership, I would say half of them were Asian Pacifics. You would find only ten or twelve of them but a lot more non-Asian members in our parade contingent. So if you saw A/PLG back then in the parade, you would've thought it was a composition of just a sprinkling of Asian Pacifics and mostly whites. The whites were willing to be out there, and the Asian Pacifics weren't. It they were, they wanted to be in costumes or masks, so they wouldn't be recognized. People we knew who were spectators on the streets were waving and yelling like crazy. We knew they were all part of the organization. Yelling and screaming was how they were supporting us, from the sidelines. And a lot of them did do that."

Tak Yamamoto

After A/PLG formed, there was a reason to have dialogue [among gay Asian men]. If we were to become a unified force, we had to know where we were coming from. We couldn't come from five thousand directions. Our ability as a group to come together, we felt that's where our power was. An example: In the early 1980s, there was a group that was forming with Mike Woo called

[Pacific Asian American Round Table]. A/PLG had just formed not too long before, maybe a year or so. We heard about this from Terry Gock, who was working in the Asian American community. He was the person who had all these entrees into these straight Asian groups. So he said, "Let's go to the meeting, and let's see if we can get on some of the committees."

So we went to this meeting in Chinatown. They were just about to start. I was the president of A/PLG at the time. I said, "Listen. Before we start, we as a group would like to announce who we are. You may not have heard of us, but we are Asian/Pacific Lesbians and Gays." I slowed down, so they could hear what I was saying exactly because there was no acknowledgment of A/PLG in any community at that point. I said, "We would like to be represented on this council."

They said, "Sure, we could probably have a gay/lesbian issue."

I said, "No, no, no, we want to be in each and every one of your committees."

So Terry Gock got into the one for Mental Health. Somebody else got into one for funding. If they had given us just the Asian Pacific gay/lesbian issue, we would have been this small minuscule group with no influence. We would not have any voice in any of the wider issues.

Later, we went to a group called APPCON [Asian Pacific Planning Council]. And the same kind of thing, they wanted to pigeon-hole us into just maybe mental health. Well, we got everybody getting into all these committees.

At the meeting, there was a Filipina women's group who would like us to come to their meeting, so that they could hear about our issues. Well, they were primarily looking for Filipinas, but we didn't have any Filipinas in the group at the time who wanted to speak in a Filipino group. So we said, if they set up the agenda, some of us would be there. It was interesting, because at that point, we were able to get into different organizations. There was a certain amount of apprehension, but I think most social agencies were willing to accept us. It was through them that we thought we could make in-roads into the community, to find wider bases to discuss our issues.

Also, after the formation of A/PLG, we became more strident in approaching bars that were trying to keep Asians and other minority people out. We went to one bar that used to be on Sunset Boulevard in Silverlake. I think it was called "The Jungle." We were going in different groups. First we sent two Anglos in. Then we sent in two Asians. Then we sent one Asian and one Anglo together. They were all accepted. Well, we found out what happened. One of the people from our group went to the bar earlier to tell the owner that we were going to do this, so they were willing to let everybody in that night. For a while, we really made ourselves known as "that hostile Asian group" and we would have started an action against the bar. People were not necessarily fearful of us, but they knew we would bring certain kinds of action against them if they discriminated.

There was another club in West Hollywood, too. It was very popular once. They would card you and make you show three picture I.D.s. If you only have one, they would say, "Sorry, but you can't come in because we don't know if you're really this person." And they kept women out for the fact that they had open-toe shoes. No, please, give me a break! That eventually died. I think it's with organizations that make a difference. That's the only way people would respond, not because they're nice people. They'd do it because they know the repercussions if they don't. As an Asian Pacific group, we felt that we were empowered because we could now do things as a group. Just individuals, there was no power in that.

Stanley Rebultan

When A/PLG was formed, I was very vocal about my political views. I even intimidated a few people, especially foreign-born Asians. When I became the president of A/PLG in 1983, we formed a task force to put surveillance on every bar and document Asians being discriminated against, so that we could go into a dialogue with the establishment. That was my initiative. Some people were saying, "Are you bent on creating troubles?"

I said, "Hey, look. We're an organization. What is the purpose of this organization if we cannot help our own brothers and sisters who are subject to discrimination? Is this organization only for cultural or social things or fucking, picking up a trick? If so, then I don't want to be a part of it!" I was proud to be a part of a group where we could at least express our views on things that were detrimental to our brothers and sisters. So a lot of people called me Mr. Political Activist of A/PLG.

I remember Mugi's as we knew it in the beginning. There was a raggedy lot in the back of that bar where people would get beaten up or robbed or accosted by outsiders. I think there was an incident where one of our members was robbed. So we put up a delegation and went to talk to Yoshi, who was the owner at the time. And Yoshi said, "Oh, yes, we'll take care of it." But he never took any security measure. He only advised his patrons, "Just be careful when you go over there." He gave a damn when he got your money, but he wouldn't give a damn if you were bleeding to death in the back. At least we brought it to his attention.

And then some establishments had reports of perceived or alleged discrimination. We had to write a letter or we put up a delegation usually headed by me to talk to these people. I think that's how A/PLG was perceived as a strong organization. We were neck in neck with other groups, like the Black and White Men Together and Gay and Lesbian Latinos Unidos. We were like a triumvirate of minority organizations that were blossoming in the gay community. I was even asked to sit on the Los Angeles Police Advisory Task Force representing A/PLG at that time.

But then I dropped out after my first term because I met my lover. That's him right there [pointing at photograph on the wall]. He was infected and he died in 1990. With him, I was willing to drop everything. He said, "If you continue to get involved with this organizational bullshit, I'm gone." I said, "No, no, no. Wait, you come first. I've done my part. There'll come a time when you understand and I'll go back again." So that's what I can tell you about A/PLG. It was a beautiful thing.

Terry Gock

The Pacific Asian American Round Table was the predecessor of LEAP [Leadership Education for Asian Pacifics]. Michael Woo, whom I knew, was involved in that in the beginning. He started it with Fred Fujioka and a few other people. We went and asked at the organizing meeting if the Roundtable was going to be inclusive. They said, "If you participate, it's inclusive." So a whole bunch of us became involved in it.

Did you think that these organizations eventually included gay Asian concerns as part of their agenda?

It took a lot of time. LEAP in the early years was certainly supportive in many of the gay civil rights issues. And we, on the other hand, supported Michael and his bid for the [Los Angeles City] Council, which he won.

More apparently, I think our involvement created a more open atmosphere within certain quarters of the Asian community. Some of the more moving experiences we had were more personal than organizational. We did presentations to different community groups. Primarily it wasn't so much conceptual but experiential, talking about our experiences of being gay Asians. At one of these presentations, I remember one who stood up and essentially told the larger group how she, when she was younger, rejected and abandoned a good friend who came out to her, and now understanding what was going on, she felt sorry for what she did. I mean, she was crying. You do make changes in people's approach and people's lives. It could not but affect the agenda of many a group. It's not like you could do it with just one presentation or two. Take a long-term look at it. One of the earliest groups that came out in support of gay and lesbian marriages was what? The Japanese American Citizens League. How did that happen? From last fifteen, twenty years, starting with A/PLG getting involved with JACL because Tak was the president of the San

Fernando Valley chapter, and he got us into JACL to talk about gay Asian issues and got the chapter to support many, many efforts that went on from there. It's all these connections and contacts that A/PLG started.

IF ONLY WE COULD HARNESS IT

Early A/PLG leadership was very vigilant about sharing their experience in the community with the membership by reporting it in the newsletters. After their first meeting with Pacific Asian American Round Table, Terry Gock recounts for the membership in the newsletter,

> Besides being a significant step in the network-building and outreach efforts of A/PLG, our involvement has also been a positive lesson. In these days of backlash against gay people, it is easy to feel pessimistic and skeptical. Our positive experience with PAART, however, is definitely a refreshing reminder that all is not hopeless. More important, our participation in a non-gay Asian group as openly gay persons is certainly a milestone in our communal effort to step out of our closet. Too many times we have told ourselves that it is not yet the time to come out openly in our own communities because they are not ready for us. Our own fears and anticipated rejection are certainly not validated at PAART.[4]

The newsletters were a venue for the leadership to raise consciousness among the membership as well as gain their support for the community involvement. They contained a calendar of events in both the Asian American and gay communities; reported news about gay-related legislation, protests against exclusion of gay immigrants from the United States, and even gay movement in Japan; and called for action. For example, members were asked in the November 1981 issue (no. 15) to write letters to then Governor Jerry Brown concerning the scrapping of a "Mental Wellness" television spot sponsored by the California Department of Mental Health. Furthermore, to build a tighter community, the newsletters profiled members, celebrated their coming-out to their families, and recorded their reflections on the organization. A letter from a "newcomer" illustrates both his self-transformation and the possibilities A/PLG offered to other members:

> My impression of [my first] meeting was startling. I had no idea that many other people of my own race were out there. To top that, they were gay. I have never been around so many gay Orientals. I learned later that the word "Asians" is used in lieu of "oriental."
>
> Weeks went by, and I was invited to attend a rap session. This gathering really helped me a lot. I began to identify myself among other gay Asians—an identity I

> was never exposed to. I learned that I am not the only one lost and that there are others like myself who need direction. I found that direction and it is A/PLG.
>
> I feel better now, both mentally and physically. My head is clear, and I can think once again. And to think all this took place in two months.[5]

Of course, not all the members were enthusiastic about A/PLG involvement in the community. Some couldn't participate because they were closeted. Others were simply indifferent because their motivation in joining the organization was more social in nature. And as long as A/PLG continued to organize events and meetings where they could socialize with each other, these members were not going to oppose vehemently the board's extracurricular activities. They weren't likely to run for offices or join the board. In fact, the 1983 election of Stanley Rebultan, one of the most politically vocal members of organization, as A/PLG's second president was an implicit endorsement of the direction that the leadership had been taking. After all, Stanley Rebultan had publicly declared as early as 1981 in a newsletter:

> Though I acknowledge that the formation of A/PLG has been a big political statement, I would very much like for A/PLG to get more politically involved. . . . I want to emphasize that we are a double minority; we are gays and we are Asians. It is for this reason that we need to provide input into the political process.[6]

So the leadership was relatively free to pursue a political agenda. And some members did become more politically conscious or active through working with the board.

That is not to say that the leadership did not have to be mindful of alienating the membership. For their part, they kept the membership informed of their activities. Time was apportioned in the general meetings where the leadership would report any new developments in their external affairs. They also provided detailed summaries in the monthly newsletters of community meetings they had attended. In the steering committee, board members would engage in heated discussion about how far they could go without turning off the membership. Paul Chen remembers,

> Everybody wanted to have some sort of an agenda. A lot of us wanted to be some sort of power, whether in the gay community or the Asian community. I think that all of us at least unconsciously understood that we first had to have numbers. June and I talked about it a lot. June and I were roommates for a long time, and she was an aide to Peggy Stevenson when she was a City Councilperson. We were both involved in politics. So we knew that this was the first time we had any numbers at all, that if only we could harness it. . . . But every time we tried to harness it, it would flow through our fingers because there were so many people that were closeted and afraid. We could get them in one place for a social event. But to get them to do something besides that was really hard. Only the same few people would show up.

Another concern that came up early in the organization's history was incorporation. While formalizing the organization would give it an advantage in fundraising, it would also inhibit the organization's political activities. "A lot of us founding members knew about the regulations regarding non-profits," explains Doug Chin.

> Therefore, we were careful about taking any hard-nose political stands. We were not a rich organization, you know. Most of the board members were supporting the organization out of our own pockets in the beginning to help the organization move along. We didn't carry any liability insurance. I built my personal wealth. I personally didn't want to lose that because of my involvement in non-profits. So I took more of a conservative stand. I also felt that we were a cultural and educational type of organization and A/PLG was founded for that reason. So hopefully if we got one Asian member to take a leadership position or to come out of his shell, we were helping and we were making a headway towards our goal. To me, that was sufficient in keeping me involved in the organization.

Most members, like Doug, felt that the 501(c)(3) status was important to the organization's growth and unfortunately A/PLG had to make some compromises.

Despite these limitations, the long-term vision of the leadership paid off when the AIDS crisis hit the Asian American communities. By the mid-1980s, Asian American social agencies had more than a decade of infrastructure-building and experience in delivering health services to the communities, and members of the gay community were beginning to gain access to information and resources to address the epidemic. But neither had the ability to reach the gay Asian populations. Around the same time, A/PLG established a committee to address the AIDS epidemic in the gay Asian community. Dean Goishi remembers the impetus for starting the HIV/AIDS committee,

> We started to see gay Asians die, and they were dying by themselves. They would keep it hidden until nothing could be done. When we found out about it, all we could do was hold their hands and watch them die, make it more comfortable for them to pass away. We were very reluctant to ask for help as well as offer help, unless we were asked, because we weren't sure if we were causing embarrassment to the person on the other end. At that point, a group of us decided that we had to organize to catch up with the rest of the gay community because we were so far behind.

Tak Yamamoto recounts,

> We were getting small funding from California Community Foundation to develop brochures. That's when we got our first bit of money. It was fun because we learned how to write up this proposal, which was not all that professionally done, but we

got $10,000. They re-funded the proposal the following year, so we were able to get some more money. It was a time when we felt a certain power as an Asian Pacific group that we could get out there and do these things.

Later on, the HIV/AIDS committee developed into a bona fide agency, Asian Pacific AIDS Intervention Team. Special Services for Groups, headed by Herb Hatanaka, became a fiscal sponsor for the nascent agency, as it was for other small health-related non-profits. Tak Yamamoto says, "He [Herb] wanted us because he was bidding on [the AIDS money], too, but they didn't have the experience. We did." With that, the Intervention Team secured more funding for equipment and staff development, including hiring Dean Goishi as its director. "Instead of just volunteers doing the street outreach, we were able to get a small staff," says Tak Yamamoto. "I think our first thing was going to different conferences. Before, it was like, Gee, can we afford it? Oh, sure, we could afford it then. We'd get a little funding here, and we could send staff to conferences." The timely expansion of the Asian Pacific AIDS Intervention could not have been possible without the years of involvement and networking A/PLG had been doing in the community since its inception.

The AIDS epidemic called for unprecedented political action, and A/PLG responded to the urgency. But it didn't mean the dividing line between social and political had disappeared. As the organization grew, it attracted more and more members who might not share the imperative of the early members. It didn't help that the first generation of organizers began to feel burnt-out. Some decided to take a lesser role and focused on other parts of their lives. Others took a hiatus or just left the organization. The shape of the community was continually shifting, as new organizations began to sprout out to fill needs yet unfulfilled. The next generation was evolving into a much more complex organism.

NOTES

1. William A. Gamson, "The Social Psychology of Collective Action," in *Frontiers in Social Movement Theory*, ed. Aldon D. Morris and Carol McClurg Mueller (New Haven: Yale University Press, 1992), 60.

2. Bert Klandermans, "The Social Construction of Protest and Multiorganizational Fields," in *Frontiers in Social Movement Theory*, ed. Aldon D. Morris and Carol McClurg Mueller (New Haven: Yale University Press, 1992), 89.

3. Gamson, "The Social Psychology of Collective Action," 73. He writes, "It is insufficient if individuals privately adopt a different interpretation of what is happening. For collective adoption of injustice frame, it must be shared by the potential challengers in a

public way. This allows the participants to realize not only that they share the injustice frame but that everyone is aware that it is shared."

4. *A/PLG Newsletter*, no. 16 (December 1981).
5. *A/PLG Newsletter*, no. 12 (August 1981).
6. *A/PLG Newsletter*, no. 16 (December 1981).

6

The Next Generation

NOT THAT KIND OF ORGANIZATION

It is not uncommon for members to join an organization for different reasons. But if the reasons are not compatible, they can prevent the organization from moving ahead in a cohesive way. Terry Gock observes that the white members of A/PLG usually did not see the organization as more than a social space or see the need for it to become more vocal and active in the community, "especially since there were so many groups that would represent their [political] interests." Even Reggie Bogan, who was more supportive than the average non-Asian member and who understood that A/PLG was essentially an Asian organization, nevertheless saw the organization as something that could facilitate Asian–Caucasian relationships by familiarizing the Caucasian partners with Asian cultures. Reggie might have been reacting to a prominent, though partial, reality of the prevalence of interracial relationships. Having a Japanese lover at that time, it is reasonable that he would be interested in better communication and understanding between Asians and Caucasians; his intentions were benevolent. But privileging the Asian–Caucasian relationship over other possibilities meant replicating the familiar pattern of racialized desire in the organization, and sometimes the process was quite unconscious. Reggie Bogan recalls the similar kind of conflict and competition would start arising in A/PLG. He says, "Sometimes some Asian got a raw deal with a Caucasian. Caucasian got a lover and Caucasian is out cruising, you know what I'm saying? And the Asian finds out about it, or it might be one of his best friends. That can happen. You get those kinds of conflicts within a club." In an article published in the A/PLG September 1981 newsletter (which was re-published a month later by Association of Lesbian and Gay Asians in San Francisco), Clark I., a Caucasian member, writes,

> During my years at the R.C. [River Club], I became acquainted with a number of Asians, most of them as sex partners, a few as friends. I was aware that there were Caucasians there too, but they might as well have been painted into the "waitin' fo de Robert E. Lee" tableau above the pool table for all I cared. As I watched them leering at the same people I was after, I developed a peculiar kind of contempt for these "old faces." I was different, I told myself: I didn't treat Asians as sexual objects. I even convinced myself that there were physical differences between me and these "rice queens."
>
> Occasionally, it became apparent even to me that I was treating the Asians I met as sexual objects; that I, too, was becoming an "old face"—and I was certain that this was obvious to everyone else as well. At these times I would disappear from the R.C. for several months, fully intending to be gone forever. When I eventually re-emerged, I fancied that I had again become a new face. Of course, I was still an old face. And I was alone in the crowd.
>
> Unconsciously, I started to bring my River Club mentality into A/PLG. Quickly I realized that to do so would be to relive the past six years [of going to the River Club]. I couldn't do that. What to do? I began to look around me at the people who were taking responsibility for A/PLG. Here were people who really cared about what they were doing, and about the people they were doing it for. I decided I wanted to assist them, to make some kind of contribution.
>
> As I began to participate, I noticed that there were Caucasians around me, and that they too cared about what they were doing. And I began to care about them.
>
> For me, the wising-up process has been slow and painful.

Despite Clark's genuine introspection, however, many white gay men still hadn't wised up. Instead, they wore the label "rice queen" as a badge of honor. June Lagmay remembers that one of the men she knew "actually had 'Rice Queen' put on his personalized license plate." The mere existence of A/PLG could not by itself convince others of the nobility or necessity of its missions. By having an inclusive membership policy, A/PLG saw its roster grow by leaps and bounds in its first few years. However, this seeming accomplishment camouflaged the problem that was to come. And as the organization began to expand, fewer and fewer members, both Asians and non-Asians, knew or shared the priorities of the founding members. Instead, they were more interested in taking than giving back.

Andy C.

We came up with A/PLG on the strength that it would be an Asian club, but somehow during the interim . . . it wasn't so much the club's doing. I think it was the expectations of people. Like people would call us or tell us, "I'm really interested in finding an Asian lover." I can't speak for other people, but Tak and I just said, "Well, you're looking for an Asian lover? You're in the wrong place. But if you have more to offer, maybe we'll have you come around to a few meetings and see for yourself." And you also had Asians who would say, "This is the place where I can probably find me a lover." That contributed to that expectation as well. Things used to flow freely, but after a while, we decided to take action and form an educational committee to tell these people the purpose governing this organization, that A/PLG was not a dating club. I'm sure there are groups that come together for the sole purpose of socializing. I'm not objecting to that. What I'm saying is, those are clubs, but A/PLG is an organization, with a different focus.

Paul Bautista

I remember Dennis Akazawa at one time gave a speech at a meeting. He said, "Some of you are only coming here to cruise and to meet people. Well, A/PLG is not that kind of organization. I really would appreciate it if you don't show up. Go to the bars if you want to do that. We're not that kind of organization." I remember that distinctly. Half the room was cheering, and the other half was just totally shocked that it came out of his mouth, that he was asking people to leave. That was a major concern, and still is. But how are you going to . . . ? It's always seemed to be so silly a concern for me, because if the Asian guy is attracted to Caucasians, he's attracted to Caucasians. If the Asian guy is attracted to Asians, he is attracted to Asians. It's sort of like trying to put parameters on who can meet whom. It seems rather silly.

Fortunately, time and understanding kept the balance. The response to Dennis' speech was that, for whatever reason you were in A/PLG—whether you were there to cruise, or you had no family and A/PLG was the only family you had, or you had nothing better to do on a Sunday afternoon—whatever the reason was, that was fine. It wasn't about being an exclusive organization. That's why it was never Asian-only. That's what I've always liked about it. You know, I'm very supportive of GAPSN [Gay Asian Pacific Support Network] and other [Asian-only] organizations, but as soon as I found out they were excluding other people, then they'd find out where I was at. To me, that's like you haven't learned the lesson. When GAPSN started, someone came up to me at our Christmas party at home, "Oh, Paul, we're going to start this new organization for gay Asians. We're going to meet this Sunday. So why don't you come?" I said, "Oh, great. I think Bill and I will be having lunch. We'll be late."

He said, "Oh, you can't bring Bill with you."

I couldn't believe he said it, right in front of Bill. It was so rude. It broke my heart to have my lover having to listen to that.

I understand there is a need for it. That was like a 180-degree turn from what we thought we were doing. See, A/PLG never lost that. It has always welcomed everyone, which was what was so nice about it.

Paul Chen

I don't think any of us had any delusions about what we really were, when we were really sort of an alternative to bars. Yes, we were some place where we could meet other Asians and find camaraderie and find family. But we were also a pick-up area, some sort of a dating service. Yes, we protested loudly and longly about how we didn't want to be that. At times, I think half the membership were rice queens. Our socials were really popular. We had membership up to three, four hundred for a while. We were the largest gay Asian organization in the country. Probably the world for a while. That's why we went to [Metropolitan Community] Church for our meetings. We got so big that we just ran out of room and couldn't meet at people's homes. I think that hurt us, too, because it became kind of sterile. Having it at people's home was really fun, but nobody's home could handle it.

I remember Doug saying that he didn't want to be a dating service, that we needed to educate people. We had aspirations of making a mark, of being counted in the community. And there was the number. But when it really came down to it, we really didn't have enough people that were out enough then to do something. God, it took a lot of pushing and shoving just to have a contingent in the Gay Pride Parade. So many people were afraid, but they would come to the socials. We provided something for everybody. At least we tried. I know we made a conscious effort to always include social time in meetings and whatever else we did. We recognized that that was our drawing card. If we wanted to educate or politicize, we had to have the people there. And in order to get the people there, we had to offer them some sort of social outlet.

Did people in the leadership warn members about the cruising that went on, so people wouldn't get hurt?

Well, we never said we were a dating service. It wasn't overt.

Right, but if you know certain people were coming into the organization with the express purpose . . .

Oh, you mean the slimos?

[*Chris:* Who was it that had the house in Silverlake?]

Jim? Jim was so obvious, Chris, that no one had to warn anybody about Jim. Actually, Jim was cute and he was intelligent. He was just . . .

[*Chris:* Leering and rubbing his hands on people.]

You know, I don't think you really had to warn anybody about those slimos. Slimos are slimos. They are obvious at fifty yards. And really some of the Asians that were attracted to them we thought were kind of funny, too. There's somebody for everybody, even for the slimos. Everybody's got to get love somewhere. Actually, Jim had that Asian guy—what's his name?—who lived in his basement, who was in love with him for years and years and years, and who was an alcoholic because of it. Jim had a house that basically had two halves, the top part and the bottom part. And this guy lived in the downstairs of Jim's house. Jim sort of played him for years. We all talked to him, and he knew he was doing self-destructive things. But he just drank himself into oblivion every night. He was self-destructive, and Jim was a slimo. Hey, I just felt sorry for him. Jim is Doug's ex-lover. When I first met Doug, Jim used to live in Hawaii. And the reason why they lived in separate places was supposedly Jim had a career in Hawaii and Doug had his career over here in California. But actually Jim wanted to fuck around, and Doug was much too big to push around. [Laughs] Doug would've slugged him. They got divorced and Jim moved to Silverlake. Jim still went to A/PLG after that. I mean, they were friends, more or less. Not close, though. Doug was never possessive, as far as I could tell.

[*Chris:* With his friends, he is very easy-going, very forgiving.]

Tak Yamamoto

After I was no longer president [after 1982], my telephone number was still listed [as a contact]. I would get calls, even from places like Texas: "Oh, I want an Oriental to be my houseboy." I said we didn't provide that kind of service. "Well, can you connect . . . ?"

I said, "No, we don't do that. If you want, you can come out and do that yourself. We don't do that." I would just tell them to go to certain bars.

One of the other things we found was that the new immigrants who came, who were limited in English, were looking for older Anglo types to have them take care of them. That's why Dennis was saying we didn't want a dating service. As it turned out, the ones that availed themselves at that particular kind of a dating thing were more of the older Anglos looking for younger Asian/Pacifics and the younger Asian/Pacifics were almost always foreign-born. The Anglos had a way of having more leverage. They had more money and they got the time, while the Asian kids were going to school or something. So that's how these Asian kids were squeezed into position like that. I guess they utilized the bars until the bars weren't working for them any longer. A/PLG was another way of having these encounters. I know several couples who had developed from that. I can't say it's wrong, but that was not the initial intent of the organization. It was somewhat political. I think we showed that by going to a lot of different groups, explaining who we were.

So there were non-Asians joining the organization for the purpose of looking for a certain type of Asians? Did you want to discourage that?

If they didn't join, they came to the meetings. In some cases, yes. We would discourage them if that was all they were going to do and they weren't going to give nothing back. But there were people who were sincerely interested in sharing what knowledge and talents and time they had. So we didn't want to discourage them. They might ultimately date someone in the organization. That's fine. But if a person was just going to sit there and take everything, you know, just use you up, that wasn't going to help the organization at all.

There was no way to discourage those people completely because there were many couples who did meet through A/PLG. Therefore, you would presume that it was a good dating service. Not everybody met that way, but people who did would pass that information on. I didn't want to discourage that at the time because I felt, whatever ability we had to do outreach, if we could get them in, maybe we could work with them in some fashion. That was my initial attitude. Where else could they go? The bars? We were safer. I think many of us felt that way, and we knew that we were not necessarily going to get people who were the best support for the organization. We knew that, but we were the only Asian group then. What else could we do? We wanted some place for gay Asians to go and feel good other than a bar.

You said that was your initial attitude. Did it change later on?

When I started seeing a lot more of that than anything else, it was kind of discouraging. It was becoming a rice organization. It was becoming social, more than I had initially thought it would be.

Leo Joslin

I don't remember what year that was [before or around 1984] when I ran into Tak and Roy. Roy was handing out flyers for A/PLG at the Frontiers, the gay rodeo in San Fernando Valley. They were recruiting people for A/PLG, so Roy invited Ross and me to the meeting. We just said thank you and got the information. But then we decided we didn't want to go because it'd be nothing but rice queens. That was actually the perception. I went to a party before. I don' t think it was an official A/PLG function, but just a gathering of people who hung out at A/PLG. I was really turned off by what I saw. It's kind of like the same power dynamics. It was so clear that the white guys were running the show, and the Asian guys were like the pretty things that were hanging around them. That quenched it for me. I never went to an A/PLG meeting because of that, even though I always knew about them. I never took them seriously.

But I didn't associate people like Tak and Roy with A/PLG. I don't know why. I think when I thought of A/PLG, in my mind I had this conception of a dating service for white guys who wanted to meet Asian guys. Even though there might be people there that wanted to make it into something else, that's really what it turned into. So I didn't see anything other than just a social, which is okay. I just didn't feel interested. I didn't see it as having any sort of a significance for any gay Asian community.

Hoang Phan

After I graduated from college, I got a job and started to go out to dance clubs. This was the beginning of 1983. I went to clubs with a very distinct, specific, and practical reason. I went there to connect with other men. I was looking for a relationship. I did not go there for sex. That was not the purpose of my trips. I went to Faces a lot. I found out about it from reading *Frontiers* and *Edge*, the gay rags. Back then, there was another gay Asian club called Mugi's. But I liked Faces better because Mugi's was a lot older and just a little bit quieter, not as fun. Going to a Caucasian club would be scary for me. I felt safe in a gay Asian bar because they were more like me than unlike me. I was attracted to Caucasians who liked Asians. Therefore, it was only natural that I went there.

I did get into situations where I would basically tell the white guy off. They would say something like, "Oh, God, look at the ass on that one." They would make physical comments. Right in front of me. I'd say, "You know you're very insulting. Did you notice I have a brain also?" I would never consider dating someone like that. It's almost as if they thought it was complimentary. I just thought it was rude.

When I graduated from college, I did not want to date a student. It was like, been there, done that. I was looking for maturity, someone that I could learn something from or respect. I wanted to date someone who had been out there for five, ten years, out in the real world. And at that time, the choices of college-educated Asians, gay, comfortable with themselves, were so small. I didn't have a lot of choices. And trust me, I picked some really losing candidates to date.

The first time at Faces, I'm sure I was a nervous wreck. It was like, I want to meet my prince tonight, so I don't have to do this anymore. I was going through a pretty typical, romantic, and idealistic phase. What I would do was, I would talk to different people throughout the night, and we would exchange numbers. I would call, or they would call, and we would go out on dates. It would take me a month or two to recycle the people that I met at the bar. And once I ran out of dating partners, I'd go back. I wasn't there to socialize. I was there to find a partner, to find a relationship, which is kind of sad. Looking back, I wish I had eased up on it and had a good time.

By then, I started to join A/PLG. One of the men I dated introduced me to it; he was a member. At that time, I said, "I don't need A/PLG." I was pretty independent and successful. I didn't need them to tell me how screwed up I was. I didn't know anything about A/PLG. To me, they were like AA [Alcoholics Anonymous]. I just presumed if you have to go to a group, then something is wrong with you. But when he took me there, I was fascinated. I was hooked. I thought, "Oh, my God. I don't have to go to bars anymore. I can meet nice people in nice environment." That was my impression.

At the meeting, we were divided into small groups to have discussion. I remember being very forthright and outspoken. I think the board recognized that right away. It was within months that I was recruited to become a board member. Then I became the vice-president. And I was the president in 1986 and 1987.

A/PLG—and you probably have heard this before—was my family. It was the first environment in which I felt accepted in total. It was a long journey that I took and I was finally home. They were just like me. We got the same feelings and we talked about the same things. That identification was a breakthrough. The organization created an environment in which you can speak and be who you are and truly build your leadership skills. It allowed that quality to come out. If I were in a white organization, I would've never grown as much as I did because I would not have the chance. In a white organization, Asians aren't really respected. A/PLG really allowed us to do that.

When I first joined, it was run by the older group. I hate to call them that, but that's what they were. Tak, Dean, they were our elders. They ran the organization faithfully and strictly, and we were like little kids. We were all over the place. We wore shorts and tank tops to the meetings. We didn't follow any rules of the meetings. I remember being chastised constantly. The younger ones were excited. We wanted to do things.

When I became president, the first thing I wanted to do was to change the stationery because I couldn't stand the way it looked. It was so old-looking, just awful. I wanted to present a more professional, more business look, so that we could be recognized as an organization on a higher level.

Typically our installation dinner would be in a very moderate restaurant, like a little banquet room. So when I became president, I said, "Well, we're going to do it different this year. We're going to do it at a hotel." So we did it a Crown Plaza Hotel by the airport. We had 250 people coming to our dinner, all dressed in tux. It was really a beautiful event. We would have politicians attending our events. I think that's when the organization went through a great growth period of becoming a well-known entity. In my term, we created an advisory board. We had lawyers, real estate developers to help us out with some things.

My philosophy was very different from the older group. I think there was some prejudice within the organization against whites. It was almost like, "It's our organization. What are you doing trying to run it?" But you know what? I needed volunteers. I don't care what color you were. Tell me what you got, and here's what I need you to do. The expectations were very high. I remember the guilt that the board would generate on our members. "If you don't devote twenty hours of your life a week, then you're not truly a good member." I was like, "Fuck that shit. These people are very busy. They got their own lives. So if they gave us two hours a week, our response is thank you. That's the proper response." I was very outspoken about that. I remember the first year that I was president, almost all of the older group resigned, out of respect. They just felt this was a new regime. You really need to have your own board to run things. So they said, "I've done this so many years. I don't want to do this anymore" or "They're new. They're young kids. Let them do what they want to do. I'm too old for this." We then basically recruited and got a brand new board. Very talented. Very smart. Very enthusiastic. We did so much in my two years.

A/PLG had this reputation of being like a pick-up place for white men who had an Asian fetish. Did you think that was justified?

That's a very limited caricature of the situation. When I first joined, I thought Asians were given more freedom or range to roam in because it was an Asian organization essentially. Like if you were Asian, you could put a personal ad in the newsletter. But if you were Caucasian and did that, you'd be dead. You'd be really chastised. I thought that was kind of stupid. A/PLG was an environment in which you could have relationship, you could find someone to date, be it Caucasian or Asian. We could also say the reverse. A/PLG was a place where Asians with white fetishes went to look for dates. So what if it's true? The ultimate goal is to find relationships, to find people of like tastes, that you're attracted to and who are attracted to you. That's the real purpose.

But we saw a lot more than that. We saw A/PLG as an education, as a cultural piece. We saw it as a way to—and I hate to use the word—empower Asians. We learned about all the cultures. I didn't know anything about Malaysians and Thais, but then I got quite an education from that. I think that's really important. Yes, members would date each other and their meeting place would be an A/PLG function. I absolutely thought it was wonderful. I didn't see that as a negative thing.

I also began to see more Asian–Asian relationships in the mid- to late 1980s, which was kind of cute for me. It was delightful. I thought it was about time. But I saw a lot of resentment toward Caucasians from Asians who liked other Asians only because they were competing with these white people. I saw a lot of separation. I didn't see that from the Caucasians. They were fascinated. The weird thing was—this is the analogy I can draw—you know how straight men would not mind if their lovers want to have a lesbian lover? Similarly, the Caucasians in A/PLG didn't have that threat, so they saw two Asians as non-threatening to them personally because there wasn't another Caucasian there. It was an interesting twist. If there was another Caucasian there, then they would see that as competition. But with another Asian, they didn't see that as competition.

I'm sure A/PLG had something to do with that development [of Asian–Asian relationships]. If you are scraping by, trying to hide who you are and scared, you'll never have time to think of anything else. And once you've gone beyond the coming out stage, then you can start thinking about all the possibilities and really assess what you're attracted to and why. And maybe at that time, the Asian men were saying to themselves, "You know what? It's okay to be attracted to other gay Asian men, and truly I'm attracted to them."

ARE YOU "STICKY"?

The rapid growth of A/PLG membership and the presence of rice queens contributed to the dilution of the founders' ideal of an autonomous gay Asian man. The leaderships felt their hands were tied; they understandably refrained from policing other people's desire, however problematic it might be. As Harry Park says, "It [the cruising] bothered me to a degree because that was not the purpose of A/PLG. It was not formed as a cruising ground. But by the same token, we had to be adult about this. It's going to happen no matter. We tried to discourage it." The resentment was brimming just underneath, but Harry was still surprised when Dennis Akazawa made the speech about A/PLG not being a dating service. He says, "I understood to a degree the anger. I do not agree or disagree with it. I believed that person had a right to express himself whenever he felt was necessary. People who live in glass houses, they should not throw stones." Harry's quiet disapproval exemplifies the tightrope that many in the A/PLG leadership found themselves walking on. According to sociologists Debra Friedman and Doug McAdam, "From the point of view of the leaders of the SMO [social movement organizations], the kind of collective identity they shape for consumption will, in large part, determine both the number and the kind of people who are likely to be attracted."[1] The A/PLG leadership mastered this theorem. They understood that, by insisting on not being a "dating service," they would alienate at least half their membership. Conversely, leaving the gay Asian identity open to competing interpretations swelled their membership rolls. So they turned a blind eye to the cruising. At the same time, A/PLG fell victim to the disease that plagues other successful organizations. Their accomplishment resulted in a collective identity that was so ambiguous that it "cease[d] to be exclusive property of the movement, thus losing [its] power to compel participation."[2] Friedman and McAdam continue,

> The most important strategic decision to be made is one that defines the boundaries of the group: how inclusive or exclusive do the organizers want their group to be? The range, the specificity, and the action orientation are the foundations upon which the collective identity may be constructed. . . . The usual view is that if an SMO extends its mission . . . it casts a wider net. . . . Our view, however, is that by extending the scope of its missions, an SMO actually narrows the field of potential participants. . . . A broader conception may also lead to conflict within the organization itself. . . . The more inclusive the collective identity, the harder it is to control, and thus the less powerful it is as a selective incentive [to participate].[3]

The murkiness of identification allowed many A/PLG members to partake of a collective gay Asian identity without making a substantive commitment to the founding principles of gay Asian autonomy and liberation.

After all this Monday-morning quarterbacking, however, it is understandable why early A/PLG leadership was slow to bring on the offensive. There were no other gay Asian organizations around. The founders didn't want to leave anyone out, and they harbored for a while the optimism that they could change the old attitudes. While A/PLG did not vanquish the old hierarchy, it certainly presented a formidable first strike.

A new generation of gay Asian men also began to imagine a new possibility for themselves. Their arrival is captured colorfully in a 1984 article in *Stallion: The Magazine of the Alternative Lifestyle*.[4] The article is written by Blade, a self-identified "Occidental." Like many gay publications, this magazine features numerous pictures of nude male models but also serious articles, such as "Fighting the FBI for Gay Rights." Blade's own article is entitled "Hard Boiled Rice [in Oriental typeface]: Are the Days of 'Rice Queens' & 'Geisha Boys' Giving Way to a Tough New Breed of Oriental Men?" In this article, Blade confronts the dilemma presented by a new generation of "young Orientals" on the edge of losing their "authenticity": "a college-bred body builder with an elegant wardrobe including the smoothest of black leathers, who collects

Forties jazz, Deco furniture, and erotic art for his show-place loft apartment, who attends plays, concerts and opera, plays bridge with experts and gives great small parties. He has a large circle of friends, but prefers other Asian men near his own age as lovers. He works out at a couple of martial arts schools and does his Nautilus exercises at a popular health spa."[5] In other words, this new breed of gay Asian men were supposedly doing everything opposite of their predecessors. As more and more Asians gained access to higher education and better job opportunities, not only did they become more independent individually, but they also looked to each other, and not just to white men, as partners of more stable relationships. Roy Kawasaki explains the phenomenon in a similar way. He says,

> In the past, when an Asian was looking for a white lover, it was because of, number one, status; and number two, security. A white person was more fluid in society, more established. But today, Asians have really come up status-wise. A lot of Asians are educated. They have more confidence within themselves, and they do a whole lot. They make a lot more money. Now, it's not so much money that's a problem. I think Asians now think about happiness in long-term relationships, coming into some understanding between two people. So to have an Asian lover is a lot better because then there is more understanding between the two culturally. And that makes relationships a lot easier.

Blade, writing as an expert in white–Asian relationships, is astute enough, too, to point out how class factors into the transformation of this new generation, though in stereotypical terms:

> In earlier times, one might meet a houseboy, gardener, or chauffeur (positions for which uneducated young Orientals most often used to immigrate). This was only a step up the social ladder from the traditional laundry man, railroad laborer, or cook, the only jobs open to him for many years here . . .
>
> Today, the accepted "in" public meeting places . . . still often yield handsome young Orientals looking for a broad, understanding, appreciative older man's shoulder (invariably white) for support, since it has long been an unwritten assumption that these winsome beauties bow and scrape to do the bidding of some powerful lord and master, yet almost never to a man of the same age or ethnic background. It is as if they have conditioned and disciplined themselves to a life of service, entertainment and pleasure for the dominant male, a traditional Asian female function. For too long, Oriental gay youths have been thought of as "geisha boys."
>
> In societies such as China's or India's, where one is born to a certain caste or class, and one seldom if ever changes it, the idea of subservience dies hard. The father image is very strong and a young fellow who finds himself growing up gay often adopts the female role, learning from his mother and sisters the "language of the

> fan"—from the way they treat their fathers to all the ways of pleasing and catering to other men.[6]

This all changes in America because, as he concludes, "[t]he men of the Orient are gradually changing, growing . . . taller, stronger and more muscular, due in part to diet and to more active styles of life. . . . [They] are now attaining a formidable hunkiness along with their liberation, away from accepted custom."[7]

Blade notices a shift in how gay Asian men related to each other. Interestingly, he appeals to Asian history—such as the tradition of Japanese samurais and certain tribes in Asia that are hairy and well-endowed—to inscribe this new masculinity among gay Asian men within a "natural" history and, in essence, to diffuse the Asian/feminine stereotype as just that, a stereotype. Like an anthropologist, he unearths the new gay Asian man as a recovered piece of historical archetype. In the end, Blade is able to offer a comforting conclusion to his fellow rice queens: "Though the salary he [the new Asian] makes is more than enough for him to look down on the majority of us Occidentals, he has never lost the warmth and the polite manners he learned early. We heartily welcome the new Eastern butch image (bringing us tasty rice dishes such as the one pictured here [an accompanying photo spread of a young, nude, tan-skinned, tight-bodied, mustached Asian lying side-ways on a bamboo-wicker chair, grabbing his own penis] and, with our chop-sticks poised at the ready, we'll be on the look-out for more great-looking men of the East."[8] He further cautions that "Americanization" is "the only drawback" for this new generation because it "breaks down those basic differences that through the years have always made Easterners and Westerners so attractive, through contrast, to each other . . . [O]ne just hopes that certain fine ethnic values may remain, if not completely constant, then certainly as part of an even finer mix." The article illustrates how an "authentic" East figures most prominently in some rice queens' obsession with gay Asian men. That this "new" gay Asian masculinity needed explanation to reassure Blade's status as a rice queen shows how much the masculine ideal has been eluded for gay Asian men in previous generations. Blade and other rice queens delight in the fact that gay Asian men finally are catching up with the rest of the gay community. Instead of a feeling of threat, Blade advocates a response of fascination, with chopsticks poised and appetites whetted. Interracial attraction such as Blade's is a dangerous kind because it is deceptively couched in anti-racist terms at the same time when it was perpetuating a stereotype. He writes, "Despite the many myths like 'the inscrutable Oriental mind' and 'unspeakable Asian cruelty,' myths created by bigots who were dead set against races mixing, East and West keep cozying up together very nicely. Half the population of a lovely place such as Honolulu is blended (Occident with Orient), and anyone who's been there must agree, its citizens are some of the most beautiful people in the world."[9] The old racialized ideology changed its shape and managed to stay alive. But this Rice Queen's Manifesto also documents a second tale. It tells of a gay Asian community in transition where the white–Asian relationship was no longer hegemony.

But this "new" gay Asian man is not merely a product of the masculinist gay culture overwhelming accepted customs of the natives. Yes, some Asian men did adopt the dominant culture's style, dress, and mannerisms. But they were only able to do so because years of A/PLG organizing had opened up new possibilities of what being a gay Asian man means, possibilities that had eluded generations past. Before A/PLG was founded, white gay men were integrated into the lives and spaces of many gay Asian men. Many personal and emotional relationships inevitably developed from this interaction. Therefore, it was rather inconceivable for A/PLG founders to exclude non-Asians entirely. Many Asians actually found out about A/PLG through these white men, just as a previous generation discovered gay bars—even the rice bars—with their white counterparts as their guides. But in its first years, the organization sought to assert a gay Asian identity that was less dependent on their relationship to their white counterparts, but one that was more about how they related to each other. Despite some laments of what A/PLG was turning into, it was clear that new paradigms were emerging in the gay Asian community, even though the old one was far from being eradicated.

In 1984, the same year that the Blade's article was published, a small group of gay Asian men began to meet informally in Long Beach. Co-founded by Steve Lew and Prescott Chow, the group called itself Gay Asian Rap Group, or GARP. Its formation was not a reaction against A/PLG. Some GARP members were not even aware of such a group. A few, like Leo Joslin, had attended A/PLG meetings or functions and were dissatisfied with their experience. As they organized GARP, they would try to avoid what they considered to be A/PLG mistakes. Although in the beginning GARP did not advertise itself as an alternative to A/PLG, its growth could be partly attributed to the growing internal strife of A/PLG. Some A/PLG members became GARP participants while maintaining their membership and role in their first organization, but later on left the organization completely and devoted their time in organizing GARP into a more formal entity. Dennis Akazawa, who made the scalding speech at an A/PLG meeting that brought the simmering tension to a boil, eventually defected to GARP. Meanwhile, with most of the older membership gone and many younger and vocally political members defecting to GARP, there was less of a push for A/PLG to be more political. While they were never a majority on the A/PLG board, Caucasian members did take on more leadership roles, including the presidency one year. Indicative of this escalating split, the internal debate about the role of white men in A/PLG shifted to an inter-organizational debate between A/PLG and GARP over their different membership policies.[10] Consequently, GARP (incorporated as Gay Asian Pacific Support Network or GAPSN in 1988) and A/PLG (which in 1997 changed its name to Asian/Pacific Gays and Friends, or A/PGF) became quite different organizations.

David Hong

I moved to L.A. in May 1981. I started getting involved with A/PLG and became a delegate-at-large. Then I went on to do their newsletters. Then in December of 1984, I joined GARP. I was not one of the pioneers, since GARP started in October of 1984. I was still part of A/PLG. I drifted in and out of GARP until 1986 when I really got involved. I felt my evolution was based on what my needs were. At that time, I was interested in meeting other people that were more API [Asian/Pacific Islander] than A/PLG, which had a lot of non-Asians in it. I was interested in other APIs and looking for a life partner. So GARP fulfilled a void that A/PLG couldn't, although it met my expectations in terms of [cultivating] my organizational skills. The non-Asian members of A/PLG at the time I was involved were, number one, much older; and number two, their presence there was to leech upon the younger Asians. I felt that A/PLG was a tool for white people to obtain their sexual fantasies in their encounters. I always let them know that I was interested in other Asians, and not non-Asians. So I never had that problem with them, being part of their beef rack, so to speak. They called me a lesbian, incestuous, et cetera. But then I responded, "Well, how come when I was at Studio One, I'd see other whites with other whites? What do you call that?" I put them on the spot and they had no response. Other Asians I talked to felt the same way, that their presence there in A/PLG made them flee.

Eventually over time, the non-Asians overwhelmed the old guard. They were upset at the all-Asian rap. I kept saying to myself, "What is wrong with them? We need our own safe space." And that's what GARP is all about. Safe space. A lot of people were upset with the politics that was going on and they moved into GARP, but GARP was not formed because of A/PLG.

For me, what I've learned from A/PLG gave me some background on how to organize GARP. I brought some management skills into GARP and eventually into GAPSN, like how to have different committees, how to put together social events. I did the newsletter for A/PLG, so I used those skills as well.

The Caucasian membership of A/PLG was really upset because GARP was a threat to them. We were taking the Asians away from them.

Was the idea of an gay-Asian-only organization a strange concept?

To the non-Asians, yes, because they were not accustomed to it. That never existed around them. But the all-Asian concept was not new at all, because in other cities, like Boston and Toronto, it's always been all-Asian. If you even go beyond that, like Japan and Hong Kong, it's all Asian. Those people were not exposed to that environment. GARP became a learning process for them.

Prescott Chow

I went to Cal State Long Beach in 1983 with Steve Lew. He was an art major as well. We met at the gay and lesbian student group on campus. One of our initial conversations was about what groups were out there and what it was like to be a gay Asian person. To be honest, when it first came about, part of me had not really looked at the issue of my being Asian as something I needed to deal with. Being away from my family, I think, threw me into a situation where I then had the opportunity. I mean, I was living with four straight white men at the time. It was becoming clear to me that I was very different. I think I was just beginning to understand what it meant to be a minority in this country. Steve, also, was involved in a lot of Asian American student activities. That was a big eye-opener, not because it was Steve, but because he had a similar background to me.

So when we started thinking about GARP, we didn't really think about it as an organization. It started out as a desire to talk with others [about what Steve and I would discuss]. It was funny. The other day I rented "The Stepford Wives." I guess this is appropriate because it's the 1970s or early 1980s. There is this one scene where Katherine Ross is freaking out because she's in this town and all the women are drones. And she wanted to start a consciousness-raising group. I was laughing at it, and then I got to thinking that was very similar to what the impetus was for Steve and me starting the group. I don't want to equate that with indoctrination or making people think the same way. What it was about was getting folks the opportunity to look at an area that they hadn't looked at before. At the time, I didn't think, "Oh, ten years down the line, they're going to have a banquet and I'm going to speak there about the organization's history." It was just a chance to talk with other folks about our experience. College is the time when you stay up late. For us art majors, there were a lot of all-night painting sessions. So you sit and gab, shoot the shit. That to me was the beginning of the rap group. Those kinds of discussions were a little more introspective than I would have with other folks.

Did you hear anything about A/PLG at that time?

Yes, I heard enough to make me not have that much interest in going. Partly, it was the distance again. I was pretty much based in Long Beach. There was the stereotype of what many people said about older white men. I was also wanting to be in a place where other Asians were American-born. So I didn't think I would have that much in common. I eventually met some people who had started A/PLG, but I didn't know any folks that were actively involved who were my age. The men I knew were about fifteen years older than I was. So that was the other thing. I felt it was for older Asians. A/PLG, being an open group or being one that was open to non-Asians, it always had the impression that it was a dating group or about meeting white guys. I think with GARP, and eventually GAPSN, that wasn't the intention. There was some criticism like, "Why do you exclude?" or "If you discriminate against them, you're no better than . . . blah, blah, blah." I think some really, to be honest, naive views in my estimate. I just don't think it's as simple as that. The funny thing was, GARP also was a place to meet guys, meet other Asian men. So part of it was depending on what you liked, whether you were "sticky" or not "sticky."

Steve Lew

I had gone to an A/PLG meeting when they were already organized. Not knowing anyone at all, I never felt comfortable because it always felt like a social group, and definitely a lot of older, white gay men and most Asian guys who were not Asian Americans, like more recently immigrated. I didn't feel like it was the group that I would feel comfortable with. It also seems as if the white men were more vocal and they dominated the meeting. There wasn't anything politically interesting about what they were talking about. I can't say I spent enough time there to really capture what was going on. It just wasn't right for me.

I should say, too, that I knew Tak in the Japanese community because he was involved in JACL and I had been active in the student organizing around Little Tokyo redevelopment. I knew he was playing a similar role as me, being gay and active in the Asian American community. But he was also a slightly different generation from me. There wasn't the immediate connection to want to seek him out and get to know him. Same with Roy [Kawasaki], too. Not many years later, I ended up feeling like we had much more in common.

I had wanted to organize a group like GARP for a while. I was dating this guy for a while and we eventually just became very, very good friends. So in 1984, we started GARP. That's when it really felt like there was a very good integration of my political interest—at least interest in organizing—and my sexual identity.

I think the main difference between A/PLG and GARP was that we wanted to create an environment where gay Asian men could focus on themselves, by creating an organization just for gay Asian men. At the same time, we wanted more emphasis on talking about what it was like to grow up Asian and gay. It was to address social, political, and cultural issues. The Asian American movement was, I think, much more of an influence on what a lot of us in GARP wanted to do, which was to really be out in our Asian American communities, to be able to feel comfortable claiming both identities. And visibility in the gay community wasn't as strong of a desire, although it was a big deal for us to get a group to go into Christopher Street West parade. But it was primarily how do we become more visible in our families and in our Asian/Pacific Islander community.

We were very clear about who could be members of GARP. We had a few duplicate A/PLG/GARP members. As a matter of fact, one organizer who came on board of GARP in the beginning was Dennis Akazawa, who was active in A/PLG as well. There were a couple others. They were primarily Asian Americans also. The first couple of years there were only around twelve of us, so it wasn't a huge group. But some in A/PLG, once they heard about GARP, were very hostile toward it. I don't know about the leadership. Some of the white men were very offended by it, like we were exclusive or we were against white and Asian relationships.

Did the relationship improve between the two organizations?

Yes, yes. GARP started out to be only a rap group. But by the second or third year, we wanted to build community. We did a fundraiser for Minority AIDS Project and we wanted to hook up with other types of organizations. Then later on, we did a West Coast Asian/Pacific Islander Gay, Lesbian and Bisexual Conference. By then, relations were friendly. That was the first thing we ever tried to do together. Roy and Tak were very supportive. They really wanted to see it happen also. It was a good experience.

Charles Chang

Back then, my love life was not a big smash in the gay community. If I had wanted a white boyfriend, I'd probably go to A/PLG instead. But I was interested in meeting other gay Asians. I think most of us were brainwashed in thinking that white is the best, that the way to validate ourselves is to have a white boyfriend, and that having sex with another Asian is just like having sex with my brother or my cousin. Back then, you didn't see Asian movie stars, or Asian models in magazines and fashion ads. So we weren't promoted as something with sexual interest. And if an Asian happened to have a boyfriend, the boyfriend would probably be white, and the Asian would be seen as something exotic.

So when I met people at GARP, that was really nice. People just respected each other's sensitivities. I didn't find that in any predominantly white kind of social network. I developed a sense that Asians are attractive, physically and sexually. I saw Asians having Asian boyfriends. It was very erotic.

And GARP was an active and lively group. I had been politically involved in the gay white population for a while. They had gotten a lot out of the gay civil rights movement already, and I just didn't feel like I was growing personally. So GARP really attracted me. They were interested in going places. They had directions. They had a mission. Seeing that other Asians can be leaders, can make something happen and have an impact in the community, that was very empowering.

Leo Joslin

This guy named John M.—I guess it was in 1985—called Ross and said, "Can I come over and talk to you about GARP?" So he came over and brought a bottle of white wine. I liked him right away. [Laughs] He started talking about this all-Asian group. He said, "We heard that you're an Asian couple. We'd like to meet you. We'd like to see an Asian couple." So we said okay.

So we went down to this meeting. Steve Lew was the facilitator. There were about twenty-five gay Asians at this house. I've never seen so many gay Asians in one group by themselves. That's what did it. That night something crystallized in my mind: "Wow, this is my group. This is where I belong." It hit me right away that we needed this, with what was happening with the HIV/AIDS crisis. This was survival. We went around and did a check-in. They were asking why we were there and stuff. I remember saying that we really needed each other, something along those lines. That's when I realized that there could be a gay Asian community. We still didn't understand the virus. My friends dropped right and left. A lot of people I hung out with died in the early 1980s or mid-1980s. I survived it. Had I liked anal sex, I could've been infected just by getting around because I was hanging out in the orgy room in the 8709 [a bathhouse in L.A.]. I was in there with the best of them. It could hit any of us at any time. As far as we knew, we were all going to get sick. HIV really changed us. Big time. On one level, that might have helped create the community.

LOVE YOUR ASIAN BODY

In 1987, Paul Bautista, right out of law school at age twenty-seven, took the bar exam. The very next day, he and his forty-seven-year-old partner Bill took the HIV test. "We wanted to know where we were," he explained the back-to-back tests. "Am I going to keep doing law? Is he going to retire and we could enjoy our lives together?" Perhaps he should've taken the HIV test the same day as he took the bar exam, since that seemed to have been a luckier day for him. Paul found out both Bill and he were positive before he finally received the good news about passing the bar. It was a good thing. Had he failed, he didn't think he would have the strength to take it again.

Paul and Bill started their AZT regimen. "It seemed like we had at least a couple of years of health," he reflected, often glancing at the picture of Bill on the wall as we talked, the same way you would acknowledge other people's presence in the room when you are talking to someone else. "And after putting all that time in law school, I wanted to be a lawyer, even just for a little while. So we thought, 'Okay, then go ahead and be a lawyer.' " But Paul was only an attorney for a year before Bill became really sick, a couple weeks into his retirement. "It was too soon. We totally miscalculated it," said Paul. Bill was hospitalized for a year before he passed. During that time, Paul dropped out of his practice and took care of him full-time.

"When Bill was sick that year, I felt so important. Everything was in my hands. Everything I was groomed, educated to be came into play. Me being an attorney, me knowing science, having good social skills to get the nurses to do us one more favor. All that came into play. When Bill died, he left a humongous hole of what I was about. What was I going to do? There was this scathing wound," Paul said. "That was when Dean [Goishi] asked me to facilitate the [HIV support] group [for A/PLG, which later became the Asian Pacific AIDS Intervention Team]. So the A/PLG support group rested on my shoulders. We had been meeting at my house. It just made sense. Plus, I was so into the research and the news materials. I was the question and answer man anyway.

"So they could borrow the house as often as they want. It's very easy. It's very easy for me. It always astonished me when people say, 'Oh, it's so nice for you to share your house. You're so trusting, blah, blah, blah.' How can you not? At what point in time do human beings and good cause mean less than whether your china was moved or your crystal bowl was misplaced. Do you know what I mean? All the time I've opened up my home to the organization, I've never had anything stolen. Ever. Ever. In fact, the place usually ends up cleaner than before they came here.

"It kept me alive, those first couple of years after Bill died. It kept me focused. The only thing that got me over the pain of losing Bill was, at any given time whatever I was doing, I was saving someone else's lives, or helping someone else's lover save their lovers' lives because I had been there before.

They were very lonely times. I was actually allowed to be part of their lives, to fight the disease."

After taking a hiatus of more than half a decade, Paul returned to practicing law in 1996.

* * *

A/PLG and GARP represented, respectively, the first and second points of a changing consciousness of gay Asian men in how they related to each other. The AIDS epidemic accelerated this transformation process by forcing the community to put aside some internal differences and come together. Ironically, it also opened up old wounds about stereotypical white–Asian relationships. If before, the most *laissez faire* among them believed that desire—no matter what form it takes—is never problematic and that some Asians are submissive and some Caucasians are dominant and that's just the way they naturally are, the AIDS epidemic compelled them to re-examine the implications of this dynamic. Safe sex education is more than awareness of risky behavior. It also provokes us in taking a more assertive role in determining the terms and limits of our sexual relationships. One could still be a master or a slave in bed, but safe sex advocates a more equal status between lovers, whether they are in a long-term, exclusive arrangement, or something more transitory, in outlining and negotiating the parameters of their sexual boundaries. In the early 1990s, I was a volunteer for the Asian Pacific AIDS Intervention Team, doing outreach in the streets of West Hollywood. I would still see a lot of white–Asian couples, and quite a few white partners would resent me and other volunteers for trying to educate their Asian partners about safe sex. Some even took the liberty of answering questions for the Asian partners. Although that made outreach difficult, our experienced volunteer coordinator had already prepared us for that kind of situation. We managed to pass the basic information on to our target audience without embarrassing them too much. Later on, when the Asian Pacific AIDS Intervention Team came up with their "Love Your Asian Body" campaign, the images they promoted in the advertisements and the outreach literature were those of Asian–Asian eroticism. If those images did not reflect a changing consciousness of the gay Asian community, they projected a message to which the community was at least receptive. This was not the same sexual and political landscape that A/PLG founders had been operating in anymore.

NOTES

1. Debra Friedman and Doug McAdam, "Collective Identity and Activism: Networks, Choices, and the Life of a Social Movement," in *Frontiers in Social Movement Theory*, ed. Aldon D. Morris and Carol McClurg Mueller (New Haven: Yale University Press, 1992), 164.

2. Friedman and McAdam, "Collective Identity and Activism," 157.

3. Friedman and McAdam, "Collective Identity and Activism," 164–65.

4. Blade, "Hard-Boiled Rice: Are the Days of 'Rice Queens' & 'Geisha Boys' Giving Way to a Tough New Breed of Oriental Men?" *Stallion: The Magazine of the Alternative Lifestyle* (May 1984), 48–53.

5. Blade, "Hard-Boiled Rice," 53.

6. Blade, "Hard-Boiled Rice," 48.

7. Blade, "Hard-Boiled Rice," 53.

8. Blade, "Hard-Boiled Rice," 53.

9. Blade, "Hard-Boiled Rice," 48.

10. In the late 1980s, some A/PLG members publicly accused GAPSN of being racist because it was an Asian-only organization. (Incidentally, GAPSN did accept non-Asian membership but designated a separate category—"supporter"—for them.) See www.gapsn.org/project2/racism1.asp, www.gapsn.org/project2/racism2.asp, and www.gapsn.org/project2/racism3.asp.

Afterword

The last conversation I had for this oral history project is with Patrick Mangto. Patrick was born in 1965 in Karachi, Pakistan, and came to Los Angeles in 1980. It would be another decade before he set foot in a gay bar for the first time and became active in the gay and lesbian community. Patrick's story was just beginning where the last chapter left off, and I wasn't planning on including him in this history of pre-AIDS Los Angeles. But as I was nearing the end of my manuscript, in my elation of glimpsing what I thought to be the light at the end of the tunnel, I began telling people about my imminent return to normal life. Inevitably, they asked me this one question (or its many reasonable variations): What have I learned about this history that can be applied to the gay Asian community at this turn of the century?

It is a fair question, I suppose, and I am not without opinions. At first, my answer was that I, in my role as an oral historian, should not be imposing one specific lesson out of these polyphonic narratives. Although I have presented my analysis unequivocally in the previous pages, I still believe that the format I have chosen to present these narratives leaves room for readers to have alternative interpretations. It's a fine line, for sure, and every time I put pen to paper, or fingers to keyboard, I had to think about this line. (For more elaboration of my agony, see Appendix I.) My methodological restraint—if you can call it that—however, failed to satisfy my inquirers. I see their point: as an active member of the queer Asian community in Los Angeles, and having finally put this history together, I would be skirting my responsibility if I didn't offer some last words.

That light at the end of the tunnel was beginning to dim.

Nevertheless, I want these last words to be consistent with the rest of the book and not to be prescriptive. This is where Patrick comes in. At the time of our interview, I have known him for about five years. (He insists that we had met in 1994 when he was working for Californians for Justice to defeat

Proposition 187, an anti-immigrant ballot initiative in California, and I was doing the same for Asian Pacific Islanders for Immigrant Rights and Empowerment.[1] According to my memory, we met more than a year later when he was organizing the South Asian community against Proposition 209, an anti-affirmative action initiative. I was peripheral in that struggle, but because Patrick wanted to make connections between this proposition and other attacks on immigrants, he invited me to a community forum to talk about welfare reform that was impending in Congress at that time. Perhaps it was a sad sign of the times when activists had to plot their introductions along a timeline of conservative politics. It was sadder still when we couldn't agree on the date of our first meeting because the onslaught had been so seamless in the 1990s.) Since we met, and especially since he had become GAPSN co-chair in 2000, we have had numerous conversations about the state of the gay Asian community in Los Angeles. However, I did not decide to interview Patrick because I agreed with all his politics or his strategies. In fact, it would probably take about half a glass of wine before we'd start telling each other what we really thought. Nevertheless, there are four reasons why I feel his story will make a compelling afterword.

Patrick was an Indian born in Pakistan and went to boarding school in England from age six to fifteen. Then he came to Los Angeles as a foreign exchange student in 1980. His host family—whom he still considers his own family to this day because that was really the first time in his life when he lived with an actual family—is German American, born-again Christians. They were living in a lily-white, well-to-do suburb in the San Fernando Valley at that time. His experience and relationship to colonization is at once overt and complex. Patrick's eventual acceptance of his gay identity is inextricably bound with his acceptance of his identity as an Indian or an Asian, and vice versa. In this post–A/PLG Los Angeles, it is neither possible nor desirable for many to develop these two identities independently.

Second, Patrick contributes to the continuing conundrum of panethnicity. As a "brown" Asian, he had a hard time finding acceptance in both A/PLG and GAPSN. Patrick couldn't even fit in at Trikone, a gay and lesbian Indian organization. In the Los Angeles chapter, Trikone's membership was mostly immigrants. Although Patrick entered the United States at the age of fifteen, he was more Westernized than a typical Indian immigrant due to his ten years in England. So at Trikone, he "wasn't Indian enough." Patrick illustrates the difficulty of any one organization to satisfy the needs of everyone in its community, however it is defined. His racial and sexual coming of age in the 1990s coincided with the proliferation of smaller, ethnic-, gender-, and/or language-specific gay and lesbian Asian organizations in Los Angeles.[2] Furthermore, Patrick's eventual rise to the leadership in A/PLG and GAPSN, respectively, underscores the need of these panethnic organizations to adapt to the changing realities of the community, lest they lose relevance.

Third, Patrick had leadership experience first with A/PLG in 1997 and then with GAPSN in 2000. Although he served on the boards of these organizations under different circumstances, his agenda had not changed significantly for each period. The degree of success he had with either organization gives credence to the divergence between the two organizations that I only have begun to hint at in the last chapter.

Finally, although Patrick is not speaking officially for GAPSN, having been its co-chair in 2000 and a seasoned organizer in general gives him a vantage point to look to the future. Specifically, Patrick addresses how our community can and must move beyond a "safe space" model under which every gay Asian organization in Los Angeles has operated in the last twenty years. Many progressive queer Asians, particularly those who are educated and politicized in universities and colleges, have already gone through the self-empowerment process that safe spaces like campus organizations have afforded them. They are more interested in working beyond identity politics and on larger issues of economic justice and racial and sexual equality. Understandably, they are not joining these traditional queer Asian organizations. Clearly, it is time to try something new. Having worked at the Gay and Lesbian Center, Patrick is envisioning a "social service" model for the gay Asian community. This is just one strategy and cannot be the only one. While I continue to harbor reservations about the role of professionals and how sometimes their relationship with the community denies opportunities for grassroots organizing,[3] I recognize that substantial social change takes all fronts. The trick is to find a way for different strategies to complement each other. In this sense, Patrick's vision is not prescriptive; nor should anyone else's be. Rather, it is another idea that evolves as it bounces around the community.

So, in the spirit of the primacy of oral narratives, someone other than me will have the last word.

Patrick Mangto

I was born in 1965 in Karachi, Pakistan. I was five and a half or six years old when I went to England for school. And I was in a boarding school. I only went back [to Pakistan] every summer during vacation. I remember [Pakistan], but it's like a very childish memory. I was fifteen when I came here [Los Angeles]. I had graduated my secondary school [in England], and I was in this exchange program for the final year. It was 1980, actually, March 20. It was a big date. Ever since I was a kid growing up, I had this fascination about Los Angeles. I have always thought even as a kid that there would be much more freedom in Los Angeles, because it's in the movies. Anybody that was famous used to be in L.A. Even though I did not think I was going to be able to stay longer, in the back of my mind, I always wanted to remain here. And at the end of that year, my host family basically went out of their way to make sure that I can stay. And it's because of them that I actually stayed. It was the first time that I had lived in a family situation. I had three host brothers. It was a nice family situation.

I was going to Chatsworth High. When I first came here, I qualified for the twelfth grade. It was a culture shock to some extent. When I went to Chatsworth High, bussing was not there. There were a lot of foreign students because of the exchange [program]. Chatsworth was a very affluent area, so most of the families had their exchange program for their kids for their final year. And I was the only brown foreign student. The majority of the foreign students were from England, France, and all that stuff. I was the first brown foreign student there. You know, growing up in England and growing up in Western society can be such a big shock, but America was a much bigger shock. I thought L.A. would be a lot more sophisticated. It turned out it was as provincial as the rest of America. Even now, I don't find myself fitting in at times. I actually came to this area in Chatsworth when a mixed couple moved in, and there was a conversation about, oh, the house pricing is going down. And this was in the 1980s. So sexuality was just not there. I mean, it was there probably, but nobody was willing to talk about it. And then my [adopted] family, they were German Americans, born-again [Christians]. One of my brothers was on the football team and he was captain in his last year. So it was difficult at that time to be openly gay. So it was a very closed community. I think it forced me to prove to everybody that I wasn't gay by actually, in a sense, becoming homophobic at times, and acting homophobic, so people would think that I'm not.

I think getting married was to prove to myself [I was not gay]. I actually knew her from high school. We lasted six months. At that time, I don't think [we split up] because I thought I was gay. We were just not compatible. It was one thing when you date somebody; living with somebody was difficult enough. And also she was Jewish and her family was less accepting of me because technically Pakistan is a Muslim country. There was still a lot of backlash in the community. I sort of remember walking in the street, people were yelling [at me], Iranian or whatever. I don't think they knew what Iranian or Pakistani or Indian looks like. It was just, let's lump them together because you're all brown.

I think my own coming out started in 1988, 1989. Before that, I've done my share of destructiveness in not accepting myself, I think, which is normal. My [adopted] mother asked me to go to therapy because she thought I was being self-destructive. I did some stupid things. I did drugs and got wasted and all that stuff. Coming out was a huge step for me. I always thought that my family wouldn't be able to deal with it. And my own real family wouldn't be able to deal with it. So having these two families . . . it was a hard enough to be brown and fit into a white community and add gay to it, I did not think I would survive that.

In 1990, I went to my first gay bar. This is one of the few gay bars in the [San Fernando] Valley that has been around. The bar has been around since the 1970s, and everybody [who]'s grown up in the Valley knew that this is a gay bar. Now it's called Banana. At one point, it used to be called Incognito. Everybody knew it was a gay bar. I mean, It's on a major thoroughfare in the Valley. What do I do if people see me park my car?

I think the hardest part [about coming out] was realizing that I was a little different not only just because I was gay but also because I was Asian. One of the things I can say about my coming out is that it's also coming back and understanding what it is to be Indian and Asian. I was really looking to understand what was it that was annoying me. And I used the word "annoying" because I don't know what the word is, because I used to have this anger when I can't explain to people how I felt no matter how much they were trying to accommodate [me]. They just couldn't get the concept, and that would really get me angry. And I went through my share of going out and getting drunk.

I think it was the cultural shame, the cultural embarrassment. And I actually sat down and read a lot of books on the Indian culture. In England, I grew up with the perception that Indians were so stupid the British had to come and colonize them, to make them civilized and all that stuff. I grew up with that perception of Indians being backward, and all Asians being in the same category, from the historic point of view of the Western culture. In England, the worst word is Paki as an insult. You know, growing up with that, I always felt that Asians were not at the same level with the whites, or the Western community. In a way, growing up in England and then here, I always thought it was unfair for me not to be white because I didn't have the privileges. So I needed to act white, to fit in. So when I started actually reading and understanding what Indian was, what was Asian, what was heritage, what was the culture, I realized that what I learned as history as a kid was in a sense somebody who conquered a land and justified it by making up stories. I came from a culture that was very open about homosexuality up until the British, when it became a taboo issue. Since the Western culture conquered the Asian culture, they took what they didn't understand, chalked it up as uneducated. You know, stereotypical, since-we-conquered-you-you-can't-be-that-bright attitude.

As I was seeking the gay Asian community, I went to GAPSN, and I also went to A/PLG. And also I started volunteering at the [Gay and Lesbian Community Service] Center. This was like 1992. Within the Asian community, there was a stereotype of who's a better Asian, and I think Indians were not, to still some extent, considered Asians. I went to GAPSN's rap, even though I didn't feel Asian with them. But there was one thing different from A/PLG. It was that actually walking into Chinatown Annex [the building where GAPSN used to hold its raps]: there were forty gay men, all Asian. I think the first thing somebody said to me was, "Oh, come in. Do you want to eat?" (I had walked in just before the rap. At that time, they used to have potluck.) I don't know how to explain it. I think maybe it was a subconscious thing growing up Indian or Asian that—you know, food and acceptance—in our culture, we give you food if we like you. If we don't, you don't eat anything. Food in our culture has played a part of acceptance. I walked in and here's a group of people who said, "Come eat with us." And at the same time I felt a little uncomfortable because I was the brownest one of them. There were some people who said to me, "You're not Asian." And some people said, "Yes, he is." It was out loud. It was at the first meeting. Actually I do remember one of the board members saying that I wasn't Asian. So after dinner, I felt that I wasn't invited, and I got up and left. At that time, I wasn't willing to get into discussions with people on what Asian is because I was actually going through my own coming to terms with being Indian and being Asian, in addition to coming out at the same time. I told my adoptive parents. They didn't react well. It was the end of 1992 that I was telling people I was gay. And some took it well. I lost a lot of friends. My old adopted family did not speak to me. (Well, they still don't speak to me at the same level, though things have changed.) So there was all the drama, and I just did not want to get into a discussion with GAPSN at the time.

And then I went to A/PLG. Again, I was very uncomfortable. There were not very many Asians at the raps. It was mostly a white community. A/PLG was just having fun, parties. I mean, there were some things that happened, but they were still fun. I used to go because all my friends went there and I used to go with them. I think getting involved in A/PLG at that time would be uncomfortable. They had a white president.

So then I went to Trikone, which was supposed to be the [gay and lesbian] Indian group in L.A. It turned out to be a social group, rather than a support group. It was more like having parties and people would drink. It was no different than any social parties. In Trikone, I was called a white boy because growing up with Western culture, I did not relate to their standard [of Indian] because they were all recent immigrants. It was a hard time fitting in. So I think in early 1993, I basically had given up on everything. I was just volunteering at the Center and working and going out clubbing. I had a few friends. All of my gay friends were white at the time. So I hung out with them. We hung out, had a few drinks, had a great time. I had relationships, mostly with whites. It was very hard. I wasn't able to define what I was looking for.

In 1993, 1994, one of my friends ended up committing suicide. He was a foreign student from Pakistan. He came, and I think it was one year after he was tested [HIV-] positive. So he was either going back home or reapplying for his visa but ended up committing suicide. A group of us Indian gay men came together and approached APAIT [Asian Pacific AIDS Intervention Team] to write a South Asian project [proposal]. This is some of the people I met in Trikone. I think we were all kind of disturbed about it, and we always couldn't fit in. I wasn't the only Indian man who didn't fit into Trikone, but I think they fit in a little bit better in Trikone at that time because their families were here, so they were much more Indian than I was. We looked at the services that were missing. We wrote a grant outside of APAIT and went to them and said this is the grant we want to carry out. I did the work but I did not get involved in the leadership part of the community. I was able to help them.

I met Jeff also during that period: Jeff Kim, who was at that time membership chair of GAPSN. He had just moved here from Chicago and he got involved with GAPSN, and he was working at the Center at the time. We never ran into each other. And then one day we went to a club, and we ended up talking and I told him why I didn't go [to GAPSN]. Then he said to me, how dare they, that kind of thing. And he was very instrumental in getting me involved. I think after him, I started going to raps and talking to people. By that time, I had reached a point [where] I didn't care what people thought. Also at that time, I had swung from the other side of being Asian-phobic to being white-phobic, to some extent. I was really willing to embrace my Asian-ness. I was trying to know what it meant to be Asian, particularly what was it to be Indian, and I think I'm still looking for that answer. But that was the time I started identifying myself as Asian.

I think Jeff was [GAPSN co-]chair, 1994, 1995. And I actually was involved. I never joined the board, but I was very actively involved in what he was doing. After Jeff became [co-]chair, the issue [of whether I am Asian or not] never came back up again. He actually gave me a free membership to make up for what was said. And I actually was surprised how many of them would get up and defend me, if somebody said something. This was also the time when the community was looking at creating organizations based on specific language, culture, or region. Barangay, JUST came out of that. CRA came out of that.[4] They actually started a couple years after, but there was a conversation going on. The seed of the idea was planted. It was a very exciting period. At the same time, I also started looking at political issues, joining Californians for Justice. I think that's about the time when you and I met also. So during that period I was actually coming to terms with not only being a gay Asian man, but also being a man who is willing to look at the politics, how politics affected how I am, who I am, or what I am. I started looking at issues that affected Asians, in particular, immigration equality and stuff. With Proposition 187, we all learned what grassroots mobilization is. I didn't expect that to be that difficult. I just thought people [in our community] would agree with us because it was the right cause. And I was mistaken. I actually was amazed that that many people were for it. It was shocking to me. I remember the first time we had a poll in the API community, it was sixty or seventy percent [for Proposition 187] and we were the minority. People like you and me kept talking and going out and doing stuff. I remember going into the South Asian community, and they were like, "Oh, it's good for all Americans." No, it's not good for all of us! It was also the HIV issue. We had a lot of people who were HIV-positive or AIDS symptomatic. I think it was all those issues. I would say 1994, 1995 was when I started relating all that to my being a gay Asian man. Until then it was all separate issues.

In 1996, some of the API members of A/PLG were asking me if I wanted to join the board. We all met for dinner, and the conversation came up that Richie [Selva] was going to run for president of A/PLG. And he came with all these proposals of making A/PLG an Asian organization for Asians. He wanted to know if I would want to be involved and also to do some political work, which was missing in the gay API community. I think it's because of 187 and he had seen us [that he asked me to join the board]. I just dismissed it because at that time I was not ready to join a board. Then after Thanksgiving—Richie had been elected at that point because A/PLG's election is always on Thanksgiving [week]—he asked me again. Richie and I went to have dinner and we talked about it. Sounded like he was looking at the same empowerment for APIs as I was, and I agreed to join. So I joined the board finally in January. They actually created a new position for me because none of the old positions was satisfying for what I wanted to do, which was more political activism in the Asian community. My friend Rudy was chair of social events at that time. So Rudy and I used to talk a lot. So we were looking at creating an Asian organization out of A/PLG.

There was a lot of internal dissent between some of the membership that was entrenched who was still on the board and the new APIs who came on the board. I mean, bluntly, it was the difference between the white men and the Asian men on how things should be. I think there were some members who were there for ten years, twelve years or fifteen years, and did not like people who had the same argument whether or not I was Asian. Because I'm

Indian. Because I wasn't their version of what Asians should be. I never fitted that. So I never felt that I got the support of the white membership. But there were also new members, who were standing on the outside, who actually I worked with, who were looking to have a political agenda. I think we all felt that it should be to mobilize the API community. And since we were joining the organization, and we were willing to do this, we should be able to proceed with this. Some of us felt that it would be more acceptable in some way to move the political agenda forward. I don't think there was much support from the non-Asian members. I think most of them had been very involved and had done their work, but their motivation was different because A/PLG or A/PGF [the name was changed by that time] was more a social organization, not political. That was the source of the friction.

I was quite aware of what A/PLG was, but I really went in with the firm conviction that things would change. It was a time when I used to be more idealistic. There was a whole core of people who came with that board who felt the organization should be an Asian organization, moving with Asian issues, with Asian empowerment. And I thought we could. I think the tension was too high. We did make very active strides. At that time we joined the Freedom to Marry [Coalition]. I think we were the first Asian group to come on board, and that's because I was working on Freedom to Marry [Coalition] from the Center and I made an issue of forcing Freedom to Marry to look at immigration as part of it. On that level, I thought A/PGF could've taken the leadership on that. I think most of us got disillusioned. There was a lot of politics and fights. I actually resigned because I just couldn't deal with it anymore. I resigned in July, less than six months. It became an issue of, is this a social organization or is it a political organization? I think my decision was that it was a social organization. It was no different than a club environment for non-Asians and Asians to meet, and I don't think that was what I was looking for. I resigned based on that. I still kind of feel betrayed by the A/PGF experience. My "favorite" was the [A/PGF's annual] Fourth of July [picnic] before I resigned. There was an A/PGF prominent member giving a young Asian kid marijuana to smoke and having sex with him in the bathroom. This happened at Griffith Park. That was a shock. I brought that up to the board. My impression from the board was, "Oh, it was a social thing. No big deal." That was the end of it. And I think nobody thought of it as an issue as seriously as it needed. There were a couple of other board members who felt very betrayed—I wasn't the only one—because we worked very hard to increase the API members. The majority of us who saw that was basically disenchanted. I mean, I resigned right away because to me that was just not where I wanted to be. I think the other two board members finished the year but did not run again. And the majority of the people who came with us—

some were activists, some were just there because we were all friends—most of us were not part of A/PGF anymore. That is when I came to the realization that A/PGF is a social group. That's what they are, and that's what they are best at. If I was looking for political empowerment, or whatever, you know, then I needed to find something else.

But at that time, my immigration thing started. [I had a student visa when I was enrolled at UCLA, and it expired after I was no longer attending classes.] I never finished at UCLA, because I couldn't afford it. They had given me a work visa then, which was very easy up to that point. I was working retail, you know, at UCLA Store. It was a visa to work on campus. That category was called something like "work experience." All you had to do was send it in and they would grant it. Thousands of people have done that. They just approved it. We mailed it in; they mailed it back. But in 1997, when the immigration law changed, my category was eliminated. So I went from being legal to illegal. Then I filed for asylum [on the grounds that I would be persecuted in Pakistan because of my sexuality]. And I basically disappeared [from the gay Asian community] for two and a half years because of the struggle for asylum. I mean, to qualify for asylum was one of the hardest parts of my life. Intellectually I thought it was just a visa category, but subconsciously I was very much awed by the whole thing. And I was denied at one point, and I had to fight to get it. It was a struggle. They first denied it on the ground that I had grown up here. And if I did go back, nobody would realize that I'm gay (as long as I stay in the closet). And not only stay in the closet—this is what I found shocking—the immigration officer said to me that my mannerism would just imply that I'm an American and not gay. I think the hardest part was knowing that if I got denied, I would be deported. I think it became my whole life at that time.

My friends at GAPSN were very helpful. They called me, you know, just checked up on me, heard me cry. GAPSN wrote an official letter [on my behalf], and Dean Goishi or APAIT wrote an official letter to immigration. You know, Jeff, whether he wants to accept it or not, was my legal counsel. I was very pissed off at my attorney most of the time. She just explained the asylum process. The lawyer doesn't do anything. You have to make your own case to the officer. She just takes care of the paperwork and sits next to you to make sure your civil rights are not being violated. That's all the lawyer does. And my lawyer was in it for the money. I mean, it's when I needed the most help, the people that came to help were the people that I culturally related to. Even if the person did not go through the experience of immigration, somebody they knew went through immigration, either their boyfriend or girlfriend or cousin or nephew. So they could relate better. They could understand how the frustration was.

It was early 1999 when my asylum was granted. At this point I'm on what they call a work visa. I'm waiting for my green card, which has been two years. And then I'll apply for citizenship. I quit my retail job in April [1999] and for six months I didn't work at all after I got my asylum. That was the time I just tuned out of the whole universe. It was a really good time. And then I came back. I didn't start at the Center until October 1. But during the immigration thing, I still did volunteering at the Center for major events. Then I created a program for HIV-positive youth at the Center. I created the grant and took the position in October.

I joined the GAPSN board the year 2000. Actually the conversation started in 1999, after I was at the Center. Knowing that services were lacking [in the gay Asian community], and working at the Center and seeing services could be made available to the community, knowing all that, you know, I would say I'm not different than some of the other people at GAPSN, who always said, "You need to do that. You need to do this." Until Pei[-Chi Chang, GAPSN co-chair-elect for 2000 at that time] said to me, "Then why don't you get up and do it?" That was when I just sat back and said, "Are you asking me to be co-chair?" It's kind of surprising. Pei and I had had long conversations about this issue: we felt basically alike in what we thought was the missing component in the gay Asian community. The time has passed to just giving a safe space to our community. The time has come to look at providing services to the API community. L.A. County, if they are all counted, I would say seventeen, if not twenty percent of L.A. County now is Asian Pacific Islander. And looking at it, there is nothing except social groups. I don't think we can meet anymore and have potlucks and look at issues and say, "That's nice. Let's go walk in the parade." And looking at our own Asian community being so homophobic, there is a lot of work to be done. That's one of the goals of the [GAPSN's] media tolerance campaign next year. We're going to run ads in seven different language-specific groups. And the ads would run about once every two months in each paper in each community. So we [Pei and I] talked. We talked a lot about what we saw. I don't think raps is what we needed in our community anymore. I don't think having an event, having a pool party . . . those things were in the past. Internet has now become the bathhouse of the year 2000. So I don't think we need to provide a rap for people to come out because they are already coming out in anonymous chat groups. Whether they are facilitated by a group that is supportive or unsupportive, it's happening. The community is much more sophisticated, but it's still lacking services. Counseling, for example, I think, is a needed component.

I think one of the changes that is happening also is that, just based on the demographics in Los Angeles, 65 percent of all APIs are recent immigrants. There is a great strength in being pan-Asian, and also a great weakness in being pan-Asian, too. I think the weakness is simply that people who are looking to identify sometimes find it harder to identify with the pan-ethnic organization, but they were much more into identifying with somebody that speaks their language. China Rainbow Association is the best example of this. I go to their events and I see all these Chinese men speaking Mandarin, which is really a nice thing to see. I see that at Barangay, which is a predominantly Filipino organization. I think the evolution is a natural component of the community. Sometimes people are more afraid to come to a bigger group than with their friends who speak their language. GAPSN is in a unique position of not having the time to be everything to everybody. And with all these smaller organizations, GAPSN can actually take the leadership on policy issues, social services and programs that are missing in the community, and let the social organizations on specific regional language base to come together within their own community and support the community on that level. So on this level, it has been a great evolution.

NOTES

1. For a discussion of Proposition 187 and gay and lesbian Asians, see Ignatious Bau, "Queer Asian American Immigrants: Opening Borders and Closets," in *Q & A: Queer in Asian America*, ed. David L. Eng and Alice Y. Hom (Philadelphia: Temple University Press, 1998), 57–64.

2. For a discussion of this development of the queer API community in Los Angeles, see Eric C. Wat and Steven Shum, "Queer API Men in Los Angeles: A Roundtable on History and Political Organizing," in *Q & A*, 166–84.

3. See Wat and Shum, "Queer API Men in Los Angeles," 166–70.

4. These are some of the ethnic-specific gay Asian organizations that came into existence in Los Angeles in the mid-1990s. Barangay is Filipino; JUST is Japanese; and China Rainbow Association (CRA) is Chinese.

Appendix I

On Methods and Methodology

Locating narrators was at first a scary task. I knew instinctually that there were a lot of gay Asian men out there who had lived in Los Angeles before the early 1980s. In the beginning, however, I only knew two: one of the anonymous narrators and Dean Goishi. I had heard of David Hong, Steve Lew, and Prescott Chow from my GAPSN peers because David had been active in GAPSN until recently and remained a valuable advisor even in his "hiatus," and Steve and Prescott were revered co-founders. However, I knew them only by names and had never talked to them or even met them before this project. Fortunately, around the same time, GAPSN was sponsoring a group for self-identified mature members, called GAPSN Classics. Dale Murakami, one of its organizers, introduced me to some of its members, many of whom had been active in A/PLG, such as Tak Yamamoto and Roy Kawasaki. I got more names with each interview. In addition, Milt Owens, who at that time was still part of Asian/Pacific Gays and Friends, opened up the A/PLG archives for me, which was basically a public storage space. I found early A/PLG newsletters, which contained more names that those narrators I already met had forgotten or lost touch with. In a local library, I looked some of these names up in telephone directories of their last whereabouts. I had some successes this way. I also had announcements printed in both GAPSN and A/PGF newsletters and local gay publications. No one responded to them. Nevertheless, in a few months, the names outgrew my one-page contact sheet, and I had to make a posterboard to keep track of whom I had called, whom I had interviewed, and whose interviews I had transcribed or sent out for revisions.

From October 1997 to June 1998, I conducted twenty interviews with twenty-one individuals (not counting four follow-up interviews). Afterward,

I started working on a manuscript based on these interviews that would eventually become my Master's thesis. I finished the thesis in October 1998. As I was readying the thesis for publication a year later, I conducted interviews with four more individuals between April and November 2000 (not counting one follow-up interview). Of the twenty-five narrators, all are Asians except two, who are Caucasians (Reggie Bogan and Chris Gaynor). One of them (Chris) was only present for part of the interview I was conducting with his partner (Paul Chen). There is only one woman among the narrators (June Lagmay). Seven out of twenty-three Asian narrators are immigrants (Paul Bautista, Andy C., Terry Gock, Patrick Mangto, Hoang Phan, Stanley Rebultan, and André Ting). I am not counting as immigrants the two narrators who were born overseas but whose fathers had belonged to the U.S. military (Leo Joslin and June Lagmay). I interviewed each narrator individually, except the couple (Paul and Chris) and a group interview with four narrators I had previously interviewed individually (Andy C., Doug Chin, Roy Kawasaki, and Tak Yamamoto). The interviews ranged from a little over an hour to over two hours. Most were conducted at the respective narrator's residence; the rest took place either in the narrator's workplace or in public spaces. Four of the narrators currently live in Northern California, three in the Pacific Northwest, and one in Riverside County, California. Everyone else has stayed in Los Angeles.

Before I began each interview, I entreated each narrator to treat it like a normal conversation: They didn't have to answer any questions if they didn't want to; they were free to change the direction of the interview; if they didn't think I was asking the right questions that strike at the heart of gay Asian life in the period that I was looking at, they should tell me so; and they should not worry about tangents. It was usually in these conversational detours that I discovered new information, new questions, and new ways of seeing. If I felt they were not doing justice to a topic or if I wanted more details of a specific event or ritual, I could always go back and ask them to elaborate later. And finally, they should not worry about whether the information they were giving me would be useful for the project. In one instance, a narrator was giving me really truncated answers in the beginning. When I kept asking him to elaborate his answer, he said that he was worried that longer answers might make it difficult for me to transcribe later. I assured him that detailed answers would help me much more in the long run and allow me to present him as a fuller human being. The last thing I wanted was a narrator that second-guessed or censored herself or himself.

I transcribed each interview verbatim for the most part. Aside from some false starts and clutch words, such as "you know" or "hmmm," I did not edit the first draft heavily. Not having the time and resources as a graduate student to hire someone else to transcribe the interviews, I had to do that all by myself. It was a tedious process, but in hindsight it was a blessing. It forced me to pore over the transcripts slowly and become more intimate with their stories. The nuances of their word choices and the nonverbal cues would not have come across if I were just reading the transcripts that someone else had prepared for me. Many insights and new questions emerged from this process, and I often had to interrupt the transcribing to record them.

I then sent each transcript to the respective narrator for clarifications and corrections. They also had the opportunity at that time to retract comments that they did not want included in the final transcript. Most narrators left the first draft "as is." A few were appalled by the grammatical mistakes they had made in their speech and the lack of coherence in their narratives. In those cases, I assured them that very few people, whether English is their first language or not, speak grammatically all the time, and that there is nothing wrong if the interview does not follow a chronological or thematic order. Everyday speech generally comes off a little awkward on the page, anyway. For the oral history, I explained, I wanted to preserve a certain voice that makes each narrator distinctive. So even if a sentence could be better articulated, or a word or a phrase was overused, I would rather not change it unless the spirit of what was said was so muddled that it would confuse the readers. I promised that no one would sound unintelligent in the final product; I would work my editing magic. (I was not convinced that they sounded "unintelligent" in the first place. We are often our own worst critics.) Most eventually relented.

The magic turned out to be a little complicated. Any act of editing is to some degree a compromise on authenticity, that is, if authenticity is narrowly defined. On the one hand, I dismissed the narrators' quest for language purity. Sure, a glaring grammatical mistake can distract and confuse the readers, especially when it occurs continually. And if, for example, it is not clear which antecedent a pronoun is referring to, or if the change in tense alters the sequence of events, I would wave my editing wand without hesitation. Even when I added something for clarification, however, I put it in brackets. But an occasional subject-verb disagreement never harms anybody. I certainly am not going to correct a narrator for using *continual* when he means *continuous* or change a passive voice to an active one so the sentence's impact is more forceful and dramatic. I am neither Strunk nor White. Excessive meddling borders on condescension and may result in a collection of narratives in which everyone speaks the same way: my way. On the other hand, as an ESL speaker myself, I sympathized with the narrators, and not just the immigrants, either. Everyone can make a grammatical mistake, but when an Asian does it, even if she or he was born in the United States, others would stereotype her or him as an inassimilable foreigner. Asian Americans often have to watch what they do so that they won't be made to feel like aliens in American society, and I didn't want to add to that burden because of some rigid sense of an authentic voice. At the same time, if I overhauled each transcript with a heavy hand so that in the end it no longer resembled the narrator's speech, would I be reinforcing the inferiority of those who don't speak standard English?

This was just the beginning: the line between narrator authority and editorial interference became finer. Many oral historians hold fast to the principle that the narrators are the masters of their own stories. In its purest form, we don't tell their stories for them, we don't summarize them, we don't quote from them, and we don't take them out of their natural order in the larger narrative to help us make a point in our own stories. In many an oral history book, even though it almost always bears the name of the oral historian as author, the historian only writes a brief introduction to set the context and purpose of the book and sometimes a conclusion. The body of the work is a sequence of whole life histories that are written "in the narrators' own words." Sometimes, the author provides relevant biographical information at the beginning of each narrative, but aside from that, in this extreme case, the academic is missing. Historian Judy Yung, for instance, had written *Unbound Feet*, a pioneering study of Chinese American women in San Francisco. Although she used oral history as a method for this book, the stories of the women she interviewed did not stand on their own, but rather served as evidence to support Yung's own analysis of their history. To explain the format she decided on for this book, she writes a few years later, "Because I intended *Unbound Feet* to be a synthesis of Chinese American women's history based on a variety of primary and secondary sources, I could not include anyone's full life story, interesting and significant as it might be. Instead I selected excerpts from different interviews to make certain interpretive points about their collective history. In the process of interspersing my analysis with excerpts from the interviews, it was inevitable that I would end up cutting people off and omitting the natural flow of the interviews."[1] Although this format had served its purpose for this book, Yung, a community historian, still felt it was incomplete. She writes, "Although I had quoted extensively from these sources in my published works, I felt that my selective use of them had not done them justice. The full range of the women's voices deserved to be heard."[2] A few years later, in 1999, she published *Unbound Voices: A Documentary History of Chinese Women in San Francisco*. In this new volume, the oral interviews of Yung's narrators appear in their entirety along with other primary sources on the subject—a format more "natural" to Yung's methodological training, which complements her previous book.

One can argue rightfully that the historian asserts her influence by the way questions are posed to the narrators, the way she orders the narratives, and what she leaves in or out in the final published form. Therefore, she may be invisible but hardly absent. And some historians do make commentaries in the body of their work. Even when they do so, however, most are careful not to impose their analysis as the one and only possible reading of the narratives. Giving up our claim of omniscient mastery of the research subject runs contrary to an academic orthodoxy in which the academic's authority and credibility depend on her objectivity and distance from the subject. Instead, oral history is a collaboration and the authority is shared. This is why most oral historians refer to people they interview as *narrators*, who actively tell the story, and not *interviewees*, who passively answer questions.[3] More than that, the narrators can change the research agenda.

This occurred early on in this project. In the very beginning, I did not want to include anything about A/PLG. When I came out in the early 1990s, A/PLG had a reputation of being a playground for rice queens who wanted to meet and cruise Asian men. Not unlike some of the narrators who were active in GARP in chapter 6, when I thought about A/PLG, I had this image of these white gay men leering or brushing against me in the most inappropriate places. So did I really want to spend a year of my time interviewing a group of people who were willing to tolerate and include these rice queens in their milieu? I thought I could cleverly avoid this unpleasantness by focusing only on the period before 1980, the year of A/PLG founding. I drew up a list of questions, none of which had to do with A/PLG. By the third interview, I realized to ignore A/PLG in this history would be like telling a story without the ending. A/PLG was either the reference point to which the narrators compared the rest of their lives or the mark that separated their lives from before and after. In one interview, a narrator interrupted his own answer about gay life in the 1970s and asked me if he could start talking about A/PLG then. That was the exact moment when I realized I couldn't impose my biased timeline on their life histories. This realization at first disappointed me because it meant I had to change the entire conceptual framework of my proposed study. The blow was softened by the incredible generosity and openness that the narrators had shown me. They had dispelled the stereotypes I had of A/PLG. What they had envisioned in the early 1980s was very different from what I knew the organization had become. Imagine how stagnant our conversations would be if I had not let them talk about A/PLG. Handing over some of my power in defining the parameters of knowledge yielded very positive results. Later on, when I interviewed other younger narrators who were active in GARP, I encouraged them to talk about GAPSN as well for the same reason, even though I would not have time to discuss GAPSN in the book.

It was one thing to make my research design more responsive to the narrators. It was another, however, to refrain from making definitive analysis about this history. I rewrote two of the chapters in this book and submitted them as one essay to an academic anthology on community fieldwork. Because of space limitation, I adopted Yung's strategy in writing her *Unbound Feet*: I interspersed my analysis with selected excerpts from the interviews. The editors were interested in publishing the essay, but they had some suggestions for revisions. First, the "quotes" were too long. Perhaps I could summarize some of the more lengthy ones. Second, I needed to be clearer in what I wanted to say. After all, if I wouldn't make specific conclusions out of my own research, who else would be qualified to do that? Not understanding that the purpose of the anthology was very different than that of my thesis, I was frustrated by their comments. I wrote back. I told them that the interview excerpts themselves were taken out of much longer narratives and that I was very uncomfortable in making them any shorter. As for their other suggestion, I already felt like there was too much of me in the essay. I vaguely promised a revision in my reply to the editors, when privately I began to nurse reservations about the idea of getting published in this anthology.

My memories fail me in regards to what spurred me to the following reflection, but around the same time, I remembered one of the first oral history books I had read as I was embarking on my research in 1997. It was called *The Children of Los Alamos* by Katrina R. Mason. I picked it as one of the texts that I would discuss in my oral history seminar. I had liked the book, but my comments in class were mostly negative because the author frustrated me. The insights in this oral history work were many and surely the author must have known them. Yet, she made no attempt to state what she had learned from that history. A case in point: There is one particular chapter where a few narrators recall their childhood experience of race relations. The white narrator does not remember any incidents of racism in the Los Alamos community, and although he lived in the same neighborhood at the same time, the black narrator's memories are very different. As a reader, I wanted the author to tell me who has the truth—obviously the black narrator, no?—and what it means when different races define and experience racism differently. I read the entire chapter, but Mason was nowhere to be found. I reserved my disappointment and continued reading the book, thinking that she would have to make some sort of conclusion by the end of it. She didn't. In another word, I was as frustrated by *The Children of Los Alamos* as the editors of the anthology were by my own work. I began to develop sympathy for them. After all, I had felt their frustration before.

As I immersed deeper into oral history, I began to appreciate the subtlety of *The Children of Los Alamos* and the strategies Mason uses to assert herself without compromising her respect for her narrators or the readers. *The Children of Los Alamos* would become one of the heuristic models for this book, although my format differs significantly. On the other hand, I also began thinking how the purpose of my anthology piece is different from the larger oral history. I realized that I had made a mistake. In adopting a format that privileges my analysis (which is not in itself a bad thing) but not clearly stating what that analysis is, I had created a hybrid that looked as messy as a failed genetic experiment. I insisted that the narrators tell their own stories, but the narrators could not do that when their narratives were truncated and dispersed. In my blind allegiance to the ideal of shared authority, I had actually given the narrators short shrift.

Deciding on a format for this larger oral history took a little more thought. Without space limitation, I should devise a format that allows the narrators to come forward as fuller human beings than I had presented them in the short anthology essay. Instead of whole life histories, I decided to organize this history in discrete chronological and thematic units and use a combination of extended excerpts to move the larger narrative along. It did mean that I would have to cut each transcript into pieces. But since most of the narrators knew each other and often referred to the same events, I would have to excise from each narrative to avoid repetition anyway. The benefit of this patchwork approach is that I could have the narrators "talk" to each other, by juxtaposing their narratives strategically. By having longer excerpts, I hoped to avoid the problem of taking their words out of context. When I had finished my thesis in 1998, I sent or delivered a copy to each narrator. All the narrators had approved the transcripts long before that time already, but this gesture was more than a matter of courtesy. They knew what they had said, but they had no idea how their transcripts were severed and juxtaposed to each other to tell a version of a history according to someone who had not lived it. Therefore, I felt it was important to give them each an entire thesis, and not just the portions where their respective interview excerpts appeared. In 2000, after I received confirmation that Rowman & Littlefield was interested in publishing the manuscript, I again asked the narrators to review the thesis and let me know if they would like me to correct anything. No one had any objection. However, I was still careful not to equate their tacit approval of my narrative arrangement with an uncontested endorsement of my analysis.

I could not resist my deconstructive impulse, as I am very much present in the presentation of this history. I included my analysis not so much because of my role as an academic. But as a community activist and organizer, I have a stake in envisioning a community that I am a part of. To me, this project is more than reclaiming history or giving voice. Like I have stated in the introduction, the racism that is documented in this book is still very much with us today, but the narratives stopped at the mid-1980s.[4] A device is needed to connect this history with its legacy. Besides its contextualizing function, my analysis can also be read like cautionary tales, about some things that have stayed the same, about our generation, who are blessed with unprecedented opportunities, resources and support, being a little too content with the racism and homophobia that still exist in our lives. Academic activism is a harrowing tightrope in any discipline, but more so in one that tries to decentralize the power of knowledge production away from the academic. In this book, I tried to accomplish this balancing act indirectly by manipulating the book's structure. For example, in some chapters, I withheld major interpretive points until after all the narrators had spoken on the subject. Or I highlighted the importance of political consciousness in community building by separating the political experiences of the narrators into their own chapter right before the one on the formation of A/PLG. I refrained from directly analyzing or deconstructing specific comments by individual narrators. Since it would be unethical for me to attribute words to narrators that they had not used, I had to be more ingenious with my editing. In these instances, I found my training as a creative writer very helpful. Let me offer an example. Take the first excerpt I used for this book (in the introduction) that was taken out of the interview with anonymous narrator Ernest Wada:

> I never thought about it actually. At school, when I used to have these crushes and physical attraction, it was a mixture of Asians, Mexicans, whatever turned me on. But once I became gay, I guess I was looking for . . . I don't want . . . I want someone that is masculine.

Based on this short excerpt, an active reader might ask the following questions: How had his desire changed? What did "becoming gay" have to do with it? Did he not consider Asians to be masculine categorically? Why not? Ordinarily I would excise the false starts ("I guess I was looking for . . . I don't want . . ."). In this case, I left them in, but not for the sake of authenticity. The false starts are valuable because they indicate he was having difficulty stating his thoughts on this subject. And they give us even more interesting questions: Was he not aware of this change, even in his sixties? If that's the case, how did this happen unconsciously and uncontested? I only stated some of these questions implicitly for the purpose of the introduction, not all, and I certainly didn't offer any answers authoritatively, which I suppose I could have. I'd rather address these questions through a fuller transcript of Ernest Wada* and other narrators who had gone through similar experiences like his. Eventually, I did have my say. My deconstructive impulse was not so much denied but delayed. And in that time of delay, I hope I had allowed interpretive room for the readers to interact with the narratives in their own way, so that by the time they reached my analysis, my last words did not have to be the last word.

* * *

I picked Los Angeles for this study because I have been living in it for most of my life. I thought its gay history has always been eclipsed by that of New York or San Francisco. I also picked Los Angeles because I had conceived this study in the very beginning as a political project. I came out both sexually and politically in Los Angeles since my early twenties around the same time I became involved in its gay Asian community. It bothered me that even I, a self-identified politically progressive activist, didn't know "my own" gay Asian history in Los Angeles at all. In addition, I was having a hard time organizing the gay Asian community around issues that I was working on, like immigrant rights and affirmative action. At that time, I didn't attribute my difficulties to my own novice organizing skills. Instead, I became frustrated with the community and viewed them as "apolitical." Instinctively I knew that community does not appear magically like eggs out of a hen (spoken like a city boy). I truly believed that, by excavating this history, I could convince other people that community building is an act of (political) will, and not a teleological historical progression, and then I could motivate them to become more politically involved. It was naïve of me: organizing is a lot more than political education. Nevertheless, this memory is still important to me because it reminds me that even in this suspicious beginning I was already thinking about "giving back" to the community.

Many academics who are grounded in community research scoff at the idea of "giving back." To them, it reinforces the boundary between town and gown: you have to leave the community to give something "back" to it. They see their research as legitimate as any work that is done in the community. On that level, I agree with them wholeheartedly. However, I'd still like to think of this research, this book, as an act of "giving back." I was raised to believe that when someone gives something to you, you should return in kind. Reciprocity is one of the bases of a good relationship. The narrators allowed themselves to be subject of my scrutiny (even if it was polite and diplomatic scrutiny), and in the process handed over to me the most intimate details of their lives. I needed to give something back.

On a superficial level, I promised to propagate their collective stories, so that my research and their interview transcripts would not be buried in the dusty shelves of the ivory tower (even if it's just the ivory tower of a state college), waiting for some other academics to "use" them again. In May 1999, months after the completion of my thesis, on which this book is based, I organized two community presentations. Asian Pacific AIDS Intervention Team co-sponsored the first one, and I worked with GAPSN on both events.

The first took place in the Japanese American National Museum in Los Angeles, with an attendance of more than fifty people. Three weeks later, we held the second one at the Gay and Lesbian Center. For both events, rather than having me read what I had written about the narrators, I involved them by having some of them speak in a panel discussion format, with me in the role of the moderator. Foolishly, we scheduled the second presentation during the Memorial Day weekend. (That event eventually attracted about thirty people.) Realizing that most people wouldn't be able to make it, I elaborated the flyer for the second event. Unlike the first one, there was more text on this second flyer and it covered some of the major points in the thesis. Also, by that time, I discovered that most people are not interested in attending community forums; those of us that do are the abnormal ones. However, more people would read what you give them. I was distributing some of these longer flyers at a film screening of "Bishonen" co-sponsored by a few gay Asian organizations as well as Visual Communications, which runs the annual Los Angeles Asian Pacific Film and Video Festival. I could see people reading the flyers. Once I was passing it out to a gay Asian man who asked me what the flyer was for, and his friend, apparently having read it previously, explained it to him. I began to see the flyer having not only promotional value but community education value as well.

In the beginning of 2000, I began contributing to the GAPSN's newsletters. I serialized my thesis into shorter, individual articles in its monthly newsletters to its members. Instead of narrating the history chronologically, I tried to give a historical context to whatever was going on in the community. When narrator David Hong received an award from the city of West Hollywood, I excerpted from his interview portions that would highlight his contributions to the gay Asian community. When someone was complaining about discrimination in West Hollywood, I wrote an article relating the narrators' experience with racism in gay establishments in the city to contextualize these current incidents as legacy of exclusion of anyone who doesn't fit a certain gay mold. In the summer of 2000, I was contracted by Rowman & Littlefield to publish the oral history in book form. Because I had to revise the thesis, I hadn't been able to contribute to the newsletter since then.

Obviously, this book is a logical extension to my mission of propagating the narrators' collective story. But this book also epitomizes the fallacy of a grounded researcher as someone who is no different than any community worker. Although I am carrying out my promise of "giving back" to the community by publishing this history, it is I, the academic, who reap the most fruits from this publication. Academia is still an institution that rewards academics the glory of knowledge production, even when we acquire this knowledge from somebody else. In this case, the more I "give back," the more recognition I attract. Although the narrators and I do not play a zero-sum game—I am not taking any more from them than I already have—the irony does not escape me. It is delusional then to think that community research can be devoid of the exploitative dynamics between researcher and community just because the researcher can identify as part of the community. If anything, as grounded researchers, we should acknowledge the many subtle and not-so-subtle ways we benefit from this research. In oral history, this research can mean people's private lives.

I am not sure there is anything I can "give back" that would be equivalent to the rewards I have gained from the last three years. Nor do I believe that the admission that nothing would be enough is enough. Oral historians have debated continuously the proper relationship between narrators and them, and that debate is not going to end in this paragraph. In return for the narrators' brave frankness and generosity of spirits, I hope what I have offered them, though intangible, is valuable. For those narrators who have lost touch with each other, I hope that in the course of the interviews I have helped in renewing these friendships. I also hope that I have offered them a new perspective on their experience. I don't think any of them has thought of him- or herself as a pioneer. When they began organizing in the early 1980s, they were just doing what they thought needed to be done. They didn't do it because they wanted to be honored decades later. I admire and learn from their humility, a mark of great leaders. At the same time, I want this book to confer a sense of importance on them: not self-importance, but the kind with which they can see a continuity between what they did and the shape of the community now. They matter.

At the first community presentation at the Japanese American National Museum, the partner of one of the narrators came by himself and sat with the audience. It was great fun for him meeting up with old friends and reminiscing old times. At the end of the presentation, I asked him if he thought his partner, the one I interviewed, would consider speaking at the next presentation. He seriously doubted it. "He didn't even want to come to this," he said. Then he added, "But you should ask." We hadn't really gone too deep into it in the interview, but I got a distinct feeling that, while this narrator spoke fondly of A/PLG in the interview, he didn't leave the organization on a good note. His partner's comment confirmed for me that he might not be in a hurry to catch up with these old friends. I called, anyway. Even though I had expected him to say no to me and this was just a courtesy call, I came up with a couple reasons why he should be one of the speakers at the next event and decided, even before I made the call, how much I would push the issue. So when the time came, I'd be ready and neither one of us would feel uncomfortable. I began by telling him about the first presentation. He replied that his partner had told him that he had a wonderful time. Then I continued with a simple question, "We are holding a second one later this month. Would you be interested in speaking in this one?"

And he said, "Yes."

He might not be able to tell I was surprised, but I did stop for a second before his answer sank in and I duly gave him the information. At the event, he was more animated than he had been with me in the interview. He talked to people he had not seen in years. He was demonstrably appreciative of what I had done. All the time I wanted to ask him why he had changed his mind. I had some inkling, but I wanted him to confirm it for me. But I didn't ask him.

I didn't have to be an oral historian all the time.

NOTES

1. Judy Yung, *Unbound Voices: A Documentary History of Chinese Women in San Francisco* (Berkeley: University of California Press, 1999), 515.

2. Yung, *Unbound Voices*, 2.

3. After completing my thesis, I sent it out to a number of academic presses as well as submitting part of it to be included in anthologies. One consistent feedback is the objection to the use of the word "narrator." Many editors found it confusing and preferred more conventional terminology, such as "interviewee" or "subject." However, if I insisted on and explained my choice, their objection would abate.

4. Indeed, the racialization of desire in the gay community continues to be a contentious debate even in the 1990s. For a discussion of this in the North American context, see Tim McCaskell, "Towards a Sexual Economy of Rice Queenliness: Lust, Power, and Racism," in *Rice: Explorations Into Gay Asian Culture + Politics*, ed. Song Cho, (Toronto: Queer Press, 1998), 45–48; and Wayne Yung, Ming-Yuen S. Ma, Winston Xin, and Song Cho, "Racy Sexy: Round Table Discussion," in *Rice: Explorations Into Gay Asian Culture + Politics* ed. Song Cho, 59–67. For a discussion of Asian–white dynamics in the gay scenes in Australia, see Damien Ridge, Amos Hee, and Victor Minichiello, " 'Asian' Men On the Scene: Challenges to 'Gay Communities' " *Journal of Homosexuality* 36, no. 3 (1999): 43–68.

Appendix II

Interviews

Paul Bautista*

January 26, 1998, Los Angeles, California
Paul Bautista was born in Quezon City, Philippines, in 1960 and came to the United States with his family in 1970. When A/PLG started in 1980, Paul was one of the youngest members of the organization. A one-time actor, he has appeared in *M*A*S*H, Fantasy Island,* and *Magnum, P.I.* Because of this, he was known to A/PLG members as "Mr. Entertainment." He graduated from law school, which he hated, in 1987. It was also the same year that he and his partner Bill, whom he had met in 1978, tested positive for HIV. Bill died in 1990, and Paul has only resumed practicing law since 1996. Though never an A/PLG board member, Paul volunteered to facilitate its HIV support group since 1989, for which he was honored by A/PGF in 1998. He has opened his home in Los Angeles for many A/PLG meetings and events.

Reggie Bogan

March 24, 1998, Riverside, California
Reggie Bogan is a Caucasian man who was born in 1931 in Bangor, Maine. He first came to Los Angeles after he was discharged from the U.S. Navy in 1955. But he did not finally settle in Los Angeles until 1968, after his marriage ended. He has two sons from that marriage. From 1973 to 1977, Reggie owned a gay bar in Hollywood called the Stopover. He was a bartender for Mugi's, off and on from 1983 to 1988. Reggie was the fundraising chair for A/PLG in its early years and was one of the very few Caucasian members who served on its steering committee. He is now retired and lives in Riverside, California.

Andy C.

February 25, 1998, Panorama City, California
May 2, 1998, Panorama City, California
Andy C. is an ethnic Chinese born in Ipoh, Malaysia, in 1940. He is third among seven children in his family. He left for Hong Kong on his own in 1967 and then for the United States in 1969 to study in a business college. He has lived in Los Angeles ever since. In Penang, Malaysia, where he spent most of his twenties, Andy participated in many drag contests, something that he continued to do in Los Angeles when he first came here. He joined A/PLG in its early years, and although he was never a steering committee member, he was both vocal and active. Andy is also known to be an excellent cook.

Charles Chang

February 16, 1998, Long Beach, California
Born in 1940, Charles Chang is a third-generation Chinese American from Honolulu, Hawaii. He received his M.A. in Social Work from the University of Hawaii and then moved to Los Angeles in 1970, where he has worked as a psychiatric social worker ever since. Charles was one of the earliest members of GARP. He also became active in Lambda Democratic Club in Long Beach serving as its treasurer and vice president, respectively. One of Charles' favorite activities is singing. He had sung with the now defunct Gay Men's Chorus of Long Beach for about ten years. In the 1990s, Charles was among the first members to join Asian/Pacific Crossroads, a gay Asian men's organization serving Long Beach and Orange County, California.

Paul Chen and Chris Gaynor

March 31, 1998, Vashon Island, Washington
Paul was born in Jacksonville, Florida. His maternal great-grandparents were originally from Toisan, China, and the family has owned a farm in Florida since the 1890s. His father was also from Gwangdong, China. He speaks "Toisanese with a Southern accent." When Paul was nine, his parents moved the family to Orange County, California, to escape racism in the South. Paul attended California State University, Fullerton, where he met his current partner, Christopher Gaynor, in 1976. Both became leaders in the Gay Student Union on campus and Orange County Against the Briggs Initiative. Paul went to graduate school at California School of Professional Psychology. He was head of the Speaker's Bureau at the Gay Community Services Center in Hollywood, where he met June Lagmay. Both served together as the co-

chairs of A/PLG when it first formed. He joined the staff of AIDS Project Los Angeles in 1984, and became the first Asian Pacific Islander case manager in the nation there. In 1991, Paul relocated with Chris to Washington State and worked at Northwest AIDS Foundation, again as the API case manager. He is currently the HIV/AIDS Program Coordinator at the International Community Health Services, a non-profit medical clinic serving the Seattle API community. Chris and Paul live happily on an island with a horse, a cow, two sheep, dogs, cats, and lots of assorted poultry.

Doug Chin

February 16, 1998, Long Beach, California
May 2, 1998, Panorama City, California
Born in 1949 in Hawaii, Doug Chin is fourth-generation Chinese-English. He is sixth of nine children in his family. In the late 1960s, Doug enlisted in the U.S. Army for three years, two of which he was stationed in Japan. He moved to Los Angeles in 1974. He received his bachelor's degree in accounting from California State University, Dominguez Hills. As a co-founder of A/PLG, he first served on the board in 1981 as its treasurer. Doug has also been a member of the Lambda Democratic Club and the Long Beach chapter of Dignity, a gay and lesbian Catholic organization. He currently resides in Long Beach, where he has his own consulting business.

Prescott Chow

January 21, 1998, San Francisco, California
Prescott Chow was born in 1962 in Honolulu, Hawaii, and grew up in suburban Northern California. He moved to Los Angeles in 1983 to study art. In 1984, he co-founded GARP, which started out as an informal discussion group among gay Asian men. Prescott met his partner Jesse in 1987, and returned to the Bay Area in 1988. He is a program coordinator at an Asian and Pacific Islander health advocacy organization. From 1997 to 2000, he helped to run Jaded, a dance club that attracted hundreds of gay and lesbian Asian Americans every month.

Terry Gock

December 9, 1997, Rosemead, California
April 7, 1998, Rosemead, California
Terry S. Gock was born in 1951 in Hong Kong and came to the Unites States in 1970. He obtained his B.A. degree in psychology from California State

University, Chico, in 1974. He then completed his Ph.D. in clinical psychology in 1980 from Washington University, St. Louis. He relocated to Los Angeles in 1980 to begin his post-doctoral fellowship in forensic psychology at the USC School of Medicine, and became active in the founding of A/PLG. He was the Vice-President of that organization in 1982. In addition to his part-time clinical practice, Terry is presently the Director of the Asian Pacific Family Center of Pacific Clinics in the San Gabriel Valley area of Los Angeles County. He is active in the American Psychological Association (APA), and has served previously as the Chair of its Committee on Lesbian, Gay, and Bisexual Concerns as well as its Board for the Advancement of Psychology in the Public Interest. He is currently the President of Division 44 of APA (Society for the Psychological Study of Lesbian, Gay, and Bisexual Issues). In 1997, he married David, his partner, at All Saints (Episcopal) Church in Pasadena.

Dean Goishi

October 24, 1997, Los Angeles, California
Dean Goishi is a third-generation Sansei, Japanese American born in 1943 in the internment camp at Poston, Arizona. After the war, his family settled in Reedley, which is in the Central Valley of California. Dean attended the University of California, Berkeley, and then entered the military. After his discharge, he worked for a national insurance company that eventually transferred him to Los Angeles in 1979. Dean was an early supporter and member of A/PLG. He became its first membership chairperson. From 1987 to 2000, he was the founding Director of the Asian Pacific AIDS Intervention Team, a project that was initially started with A/PLG. Dean and Tom, his partner of ten years reside in Los Angeles with their two four-legged children, Keiko and Bruno.

David Hong

February 25, 1998, West Hollywood, California
David Hong was born in the 1950s in Chicago Chinatown. Since coming to Los Angeles in 1981, David has become a mainstay of gay Asian activism. In the early 1980s, he joined A/PLG and quickly became its delegate-at-large and newsletter editor, respectively. In December 1984, he became active with GARP. A few years later when GARP became incorporated as GAPSN, he was one of its co-founding members who wrote the bylaws for the new organization. He and his partner Nid have been together for sixteen years.

Because of his long history of activism, David was honored by the City of West Hollywood in 2000.

Ted Hune*

October 30, 2000, Burbank, California
Ted Hune was born in Los Angeles in 1935. In the mid-1970s, he became active with the Gay Rights Chapter of the American Civil Liberties Union in Los Angeles. He was in a ten-year relationship with his partner, Tommy, until Tommy died of pneumonia in 1988. Shortly after that, Ted joined GAPSN as a member and later served on its board for more than two years. Ted works for the entertainment industry and lives in Thousand Oaks.

Leo Joslin

January 20, 1998, San Francisco, California
Leo Joslin was born on a U.S. Air Force base in Nagasaki, Japan, in 1955. He grew up in Atascadero, a small town in Central California. In 1973, he came to Los Angeles to study at Occidental College. He then moved to the Bay Area in 1992. Leo has worked in banking for two decades and for several years was a Vice President for a major bank. He returned to school in middle age and received an M.A. in Psychology, which he uses as a counselor and HIV educator in a drug rehab center in San Francisco. His extensive volunteer background includes board positions with GAPSN in Los Angeles and Gay Asian Pacific Alliance in San Francisco (GAPA), peer counselor at GAPA Community HIV project, and spiritual support volunteer at Maitri AIDS Hospice. He and his partner Gary were married in 1992 at Glide Methodist Church in San Francisco by the Reverend Cecil Williams. They live in San Francisco.

Roy Kawasaki

January 6, 1998, Los Angeles, California.
May 2, 1998, Panorama City, California.
Roy Kawasaki is a third-generation Japanese American. He was born in 1941 in Hawaii, where he grew up in a sugar plantation community. In his family, he is the youngest of six children. He moved to Los Angeles in 1961 to attend Los Angeles City College. He has been a teacher in the Los Angeles Unified School District since the mid-1960s. For more than fifteen years, he has specialized in special education, working with hearing-impaired children. A co-founder of A/PLG, Roy was its third president in 1984 and 1985.

June Lagmay

April 6, 2000, Los Angeles, California
June Lagmay was born in 1954, in Yokohama, Japan, where her father, a Filipino American serviceman, had met and later married her mother, a Japanese national. He brought his family back to the United States when June was just a few months old. They settled in the Echo Park/Silverlake area of Los Angeles. In high school, June met her partner Rita Romero, and they have been together for almost thirty years. In the late 1970s, June worked at the Gay and Lesbian Community Services Center, where she met Paul Chen, who would later serve with her as the co-chairs of A/PLG. She became involved in politics in 1980 when she joined the campaign for Don Amador, an openly gay candidate for the Los Angeles City Council. After Amador lost, June was invited by his opponent, Councilwoman Peggy Stevenson, to be her Silverlake field deputy. June then went on to work in the Office of Assemblywoman Gloria Molina, then returned to the City of Los Angeles as a legislative assistant in the City Clerk's Office. Until 2001 June worked for Los Angeles Mayor Richard Riordan as his legislative coordinator.

Steve Lew

January 19, 1998, San Francisco, California
Steve Lew is a fifth-generation Chinese American born in 1958 in Watsonville, California, but he grew up in Sacramento. Steve aspired throughout high school to be an artist and revolutionary, especially after he went to a concert given by Chris, Jo, and Charlie, Asian American folk singers, and pored over a bright yellow boxed set of poetry and political illustrations called "Yellow Peril." He was a student organizer at different colleges from 1975 to 1986, helping to found the west coast Asian Pacific Student Union, and supporting Asian and Pacific Islander community organizations. He moved to Los Angeles in 1977, after he graduated from high school. In 1984, he co-founded the Gay Asian RaP (GARP) and was involved in the organization of two major conferences in Los Angeles—the International Lesbian and Gay People of Color conference in 1986 and the first west coast conference for Asian and Pacific Lesbians and Gays in 1987. Testing HIV positive in 1985, Steve became involved in early HIV/AIDS work in gay Asian and Pacific Islander communities. In 1987, he moved to San Francisco and co-founded the GAPA Community HIV Project, where he served in various staff positions as the organization grew into a nationally recognized AIDS service organization, eventually becoming the Living Well Project, and in 1997, merging with the Asian AIDS Project to become Asian and Pacific Islander Wellness Center. Steve has served on local and national HIV policy bodies in San

Francisco and Washington, D.C. Over the years of community arts and HIV work, Steve has also been involved in nonprofit organizational development and currently works at CompassPoint Nonprofit Services.

Patrick Mangto

November 25, 2000, Van Nuys, California
Patrick was born in Karachi, Pakistan, in 1965. He went to a boarding school in England from age six to fifteen. In 1980, he came to Southern California as an exchange student at Chatsworth High School. He then went to Pierce College and transferred to UCLA. His sponsor family helped him petition to stay in the United States. However, in 1998, his visa category was eliminated. Patrick petitioned for asylum, and after two tumultuous years of court hearings, his petition was finally approved in 2000. Patrick was a board member of A/PLG in 1997 and co-chair of GAPSN in 2000. Until 2001, he worked with HIV-positive youth at the Gay and Lesbian Center in Los Angeles.

Harry Park

March 7, 1998, Los Angeles, California
Harry Park is a Korean American born in Hawaii in 1935. He came to Los Angeles in 1958. An early A/PLG steering committee member, Harry served as its fundraising chair. In the late 1980s, Harry also co-founded with his partner Herb the Uptown Gay and Lesbian Alliance, which serves Highland Park, Eagle Rock, Pasadena, and surrounding areas. He and Herb have been together for twenty-eight years, and in 2000, they successfully adopted a fifteen-year-old son named Chase.

Hoang Phan

March 30, 1998, Brush Prairie, Washington
Hoang Phan was born in 1960 in Saigon, Vietnam, where his father worked for the U.S. government. His family migrated to the United States in 1975 just before the fall of Saigon and settled at first in Oklahoma and then in Garden Grove, California. Hoang graduated from Claremont Men's College in 1982. He served as A/PLG president in 1986–1987. He left for Washington in 1992. Currently, he works for the largest publishing firm in the world.

Stanley Rebultan

January 29, 1998, West Hollywood, California
June 4, 1998, West Hollywood, California
Stanley Rebultan was born in 1951 in Northern Luzon in the province of Ilocos Sur in the Philippines, where he started training as a teacher. He came

to Los Angeles in 1972. He was briefly married to a woman in the 1970s before he came out. In 1979, he attended the first March on Washington. When he returned to L.A., his activism significantly increased. A year later he co-founded A/PLG, and in 1983 Stanley was elected its second president. Soon after, he reduced his involvement with A/PLG because he found a new relationship, which lasted seven years until his partner, Thomas, died of AIDS complications in 1990. Stanley himself tested positive for HIV in 1988. Since then, he has been a staunch advocate for alternative treatment for AIDS. Stanley uses a bitter melon therapy and has testified on its effectiveness in international AIDS conferences in Berlin in 1993 and in Yokohama, Japan, in 1994. Stanley admits that his smoking habit poses a greater threat to his health than HIV. Not without irony, he has found a new career in 1998 as a respiratory therapist. He lives in West Hollywood and is currently working on a book about his experience with the bitter melon treatment.

André Ting

October 1, 2000, La Habra Heights, California
October 21, 2000, La Habra Heights, California
André Ting was born in Soochow, China. His family moved to Hong Kong (then a British colony) when he was three. When he was thirteen, his family moved to Malaysia (then called Malaya). When he turned twenty, he moved to Brazil. A year later, he went to Austin, Texas, to start his college education. He stayed in Texas for seven years, getting his B.S. degree from St. Edward's University and his M.A. from the University of Texas at Austin. In 1971, he came to live in southern California. In 1981, he was one of the founding members of A/PLG. He did the first art demonstration in an A/PLG meeting and held a workshop at their first retreat. In 1981, he was nominated for the vice secretary of A/PLG. In 1990, he became a board member of Que Viva (a.k.a. VIVA!), a queer Latino performance group. In 1998, he joined China Rainbow Association (CRA). In 1999, he became the social event coordinator of that organization. In 2000, he was elected its chair. André is a tenured instructor in a community college district.

Virgil Vang*

October 23, 1997, Los Angeles, California
Virgil Vang is a third-generation Chinese American born in 1950 in San Francisco Chinatown. He was a community artist at the Hop Jook Health Fair from the age of fifteen and a member of the Kearny Street Writers' Workshop. He attended San Francisco State College. He spent a couple years in

Asia during the early 1970s. In 1977, he relocated to Los Angeles, where he worked as a designer of new age interior spaces, and has been living there ever since. His poetry and prose work has been widely published in the United States, and translated in Taipei, Shanghai, and Nanjing.

Ernest Wada*

December 4, 1997, Los Angeles, California
Ernest Wada was born in 1935. His family had belonged to the fishing community in Terminal Island before they were sent to the internment camp in Manzanar during World War II. When he was nineteen, Ernest joined the U.S. Army and was stationed in Korea for sixteen months. He is now retired and lives with his partner Jim, whom he met in 1995.

Tak Yamamoto

November 7, 1997, Arleta, California
February 18, 1998, Arleta, California
May 2, 1998, Panorama City, California
Tak Yamamoto is a second-generation Japanese American born in Los Angeles in 1938. When he was just three, his family was sent to the internment camp in Poston, Arizona. When the war ended, they moved back to East Los Angeles. Tak joined the U.S. Air Force when he was eighteen, and he was stationed in Germany for four and a half years. After he was discharged, he enrolled in California State University, Los Angeles, where he obtained a B.A. in sociology in 1969. For almost thirty years, he has worked for the Los Angeles County Voters Registrar Office. In 1975, he joined the Manzanar Committee, and to this day he continues to coordinate the annual pilgrimage to what used to be the internment camp in Manzanar. In 1981, he was elected the first president of A/PLG. Around that time, he also became the president of the San Fernando chapter of the Japanese American Citizens League. Tak moved to the San Fernando Valley in 1976, where he still lives with Carl, his partner since 1967.

Stan Yogi

January 24, 1998, Los Angeles, California
Stan Yogi is a third-generation Japanese American born in 1962 in Inglewood, California, and raised in nearby Gardena. He holds degrees from UCLA and UC Berkeley. He was active in the National Coalition for Redress and

Reparations. He left Los Angeles in 1986 and currently lives in Berkeley, California. Stan has held positions with the ACLU Foundation of Northern California and the California Council for the Humanities. He is the editor of *Highway 99: A Literary Journey Through California's Great Central Valley* and co-editor (with King-Kok Cheung) of *Asian American Literature: An Annotated Bibliography*. Stan is the author of numerous articles and reviews on Asian American literature. He is a former president of the board of Horizons Foundation and has served on the board of the Northern California Grantmakers.

NOTE

Names followed by an asterisk indicate pseudonyms.

Bibliography

A/PLG Newsletter. No. 12 (August 1981).

———. No. 16 (December 1981).

———. No. 1B (January 1982).

Barrus, Tim. *Anywhere, Anywhere*. Stamford, Conn.: Knights Press, 1987.

Bau, Ignatius. "Queer Asian American Immigrants: Opening Borders and Closets." In *Q & A: Queer in Asian America*, edited by David L. Eng and Alice Y. Hom, pp. 57–64. Philadelphia: Temple University Press, 1998.

Berube, Allan. *Coming Out Under Fire: The History of Gay Men and Women in World War II*. New York: Free Press, 1990.

Blade. "Hard-Boiled Rice: Are the Days of 'Rice Queens' & 'Geisha Boys' Giving Way to a Tough New Breed of Oriental Men?" *Stallion: The Magazine of the Alternative Lifestyle*. (May 1984): 48–53.

Butler, Judith. *Gender Trouble*. New York: Routledge, 1990.

Champagne, John. *The Ethics of Marginality: A New Approach to Gay Studies*. Minneapolis: University of Minnesota Press, 1995.

Chan, Jeffrey Paul, Frank Chin, Lawson Fusao Inada, and Shawn Wong, eds. *The Big Aiiieeeee: An Anthology of Chinese American and Japanese American Literature*. New York: Meridian, 1990.

Chauncey, George. *Gay New York: Gender, Urban Culture and the Making of the Gay Male World, 1890–1940*. New York: Basic Books, 1994.

D'Emilio, John. *Sexual Politics, Sexual Communities: The Making of a Homosexual Minority in the United States, 1940–1970*. Chicago: University of Chicago Press, 1983.

Dower, John W. *War Without Mercy: Race and Power in the Pacific War*. New York: Pantheon Books, 1986.

Edwards, Tim. *Erotics & Politics: Gay Male Sexuality, Masculinity and Feminism*. New York: Routledge, 1994.

Eng, David. "Managing Masculinity: Race and Psychoanalysis in Asian-American Literature." Ph.D. diss., University of California, Berkeley, 1995.

Espiritu, Yen Le. *Asian American Women and Men: Labor, Laws and Love*. Thousand Oaks, Calif.: Sage Publications, 1997.

Faderman, Lillian. *Odd Girls and Twilight Lovers: A History of Lesbian Life in Twentieth Century America*. New York: Penguin Books, 1991.

Fanon, Frantz. *Black Skin, White Masks*. New York: Grove Press, Inc., 1967.

Foucault, Michel. *Discipline and Punish: The Birth of the Prison*. New York: Pantheon Books, 1977.

Friedman, Debra, and Doug McAdam. "Collective Identity and Activism: Networks, Choices and the Life of a Social Movement." In *Frontiers in Social Movement Theory*, edited by Aldon D. Morris and Carol McClurg Mueller, pp. 156–73. New Haven: Yale University Press, 1992.

Fung, Richard. "Seeing Yellow: Asian Identities in Film and Video." In *The State of Asian America: Activism and Resistance in the 1990s*, edited by Karin Aguilar-San Juan, pp. 161–71. Boston: South End Press, 1994.

Gamson, Joshua. "Must Identity Movements Self-Destruct? A Queer Dilemma," *Social Problems* 42, no. 3 (August 1995): 390–407.

Gamson, William A. "The Social Psychology of Collective Action." In *Frontiers in Social Movement Theory*, edited by Aldon D. Morris and Carol McClurg Mueller, pp. 53–76. New Haven: Yale University Press, 1992.

Haggerty, George, ed. *Gay Histories and Cultures: An Encyclopedia*. New York: Garland Publishing, 2000.

Hagland, Paul EeNam Park. " 'Undressing the Oriental Boy': The Gay Asian in the Social Imaginary of the Gay White Male." In *Looking Queer: Body Image and Identity in Lesbian, Bisexual, Gay and Transgender Communities*, edited by Dawn Atkins, pp. 277–93. New York: Haworth Press, 1998.

Healy, Murray. *Gay Skin: Class, Masculinity and Queer Appropriation*. London: Cassell, 1996.

Ho, Fred. "Fists for Revolution." In *Legacy to Liberation: Politics and Culture of Revolutionary Asian Pacific America*, edited by Fred Ho with Carolyn Antonio, Diane Fujino, and Steve Yip, pp. 3–13. Brooklyn, N.Y.: Big Red Media, 2000.

hooks, bell. *Black Looks: Race and Representations*. New York: Routledge, 1992.

Hwang, David Henry. *M. Butterfly*. New York: Plume Books, 1988.

Jeffords, Susan. *The Remasculinization of America*. Bloomington: Indiana University Press, 1989.

Julien, Isaac, and Kobena Mercer. "True Confessions." In *Male Order: Unwrapping Masculinity*, edited by Rowena Chapman and Jonathan Rutherford. London: Lawrence and Wishart, 1987.

Klandermans, Bert. "The Social Construction of Protest and Multiorganization Fields." In *Frontiers in Social Movement Theory*, edited by Aldon D. Morris and Carol McClurg Mueller, pp. 77–103. New Haven: Yale University Press, 1992.

Ling, Jinqi. "Identity Crisis and Gender Politics: Reappropriating Asian American Masculinity." In *An Interethnic Companion to Asian American Literature*, edited by King-Kok Cheung, pp. 312–337. New York: Cambridge University Press, 1997.

Lowe, Lisa. "Decolonization, Displacement, Disidentification: Writing and the Question of History." In *Immigrant Acts*. Durham: Duke University Press, 1996, pp. 97–127.

Mangaoang, Gil. "From the 1970s to the 1990s: Perspective of a Gay Filipino American Activist." In *Asian American Sexualities: Dimensions of the Gay and Lesbian Experience*, edited by Russell Leong, pp. 101–111. New York: Routledge, 1996.

McCaskell, Tim. "Towards a Sexual Economy of Rice Queenliness: Lust, Power, and Racism." In *Rice: Explorations Into Gay Asian Culture + Politics*, edited by Song Cho, pp. 45–48. Toronto: Queer Press, 1998.

Morgan, Tracy D. "Pages of Whiteness: Race, Physique Magazines, and the Emergence of Public Gay Culture." In *Queer Studies, A Lesbian, Gay, Bisexual & Transgender Anthology*, edited by Brett Beemyn and Mickey Eliason, pp. 282–90. New York: New York University Press, 1996.

Nguyen, Viet Thanh. *Writing the Body Politic: Asian American Subjects and the American Nation.* Ph.D. diss., University of California, Berkeley, 1997.

Nung, Hung. "Letter to the Editor." *Bridge* 1, no. 5 (May/June 1972): 51.

Okihiro, Gary. "Oral History and the Writing of Ethnic History." In *Oral History: An Interdisciplinary Anthology*, edited by David K. Dunaway and Willa K. Baum, pp. 119–214. Walnut Creek, Calif.: AltaMira Press, 1996.

Racelis, Felix. "Bill Matsumoto Finding Community, Fighting Discrimination." *The Advocate*, no. 363 (March 17, 1983): 24–25.

Ridge, Damien, Amos Hee, and Victor Minichiello. " 'Asian' Men On the Scene: Challenges to 'Gay Communities,' " *Journal of Homosexuality* 36, no. 3 (1999): 43–68.

Schudson, Michael. *Watergate in American Memory: How We Remember, Forget, and Reconstruct the Past*. New York: Basic Books, 1992.

Stallybrass, Peter, and Allan White. "The Grotesque Body and the Smithfield Muse: Authorship in the Eighteenth Century." In *Politics and Poetics of Transgression*. Ithaca, N.Y.: Cornell University Press, 1986, pp. 80–101.

Stoller, Ann Laura. *Race and the Education of Desire: Foucault's* History of Sexuality *and the Colonial Order of Things*. Durham: Duke University Press, 1995.

Sturken, Marita. *Tangled Memories: The Vietnam War, the AIDS Epidemic, and the Politics of Remembering*. Berkeley: University of California, Press, 1997.

Takazawa, Yasuko I. *Breaking the Silence: Redress and Japanese American Ethnicity*. New York: Cornell University Press, 1995.

Thompson, E. P. *The Making of the English Working Class.* New York: Pantheon Books, 1963.

Ting, Jennifer. "Bachelor Society: Deviant Heterosexuality and Asian American Historiography." In *Privileging Positions: The Sites of Asian American Studies*, edited by Gary Okihiro et al. , pp. 271–79. Pullman: Washington State University Press, 1995.

Tsang, Daniel Chun-tuen. "Gay Awareness." *Bridge* 3, no. 4 (January/February 1975): 44–45.

Van Den Berghe, Pierre L. *The Quest for Other: Ethnic Tourism in San Cristobal, Mexico.* Seattle: University of Washington Press, 1994.

Wat, Eric C. "Preserving the Paradox: Stories from a *gay-loh*." *Amerasia Journal* 20, no. 1 (1994): 149–60.

Wat, Eric C., and Steven Shum. "Queer API Men in Los Angeles: A Roundtable on History and Political Organizing." In *Q & A: Queer in Asian America*, edited by David L. Eng and Alice Y. Hom, pp. 166–84. Philadelphia: Temple University Press, 1998.

Wei, William. *The Asian American Movement*. Philadelphia: Temple University Press, 1993.

Yanagisako, Sylvia. "Transforming Orientalism: Gender, Nationality, and Class in Asian American Studies." In *Naturalizing Power: Essays in Feminist Cultural Analysis*, edited by Sylvia Yanagisako and Carol Delaney, pp. 275–98. New York: Routledge, 1995.

Yung, Judy. *Unbound Voices: A Documentary History of Chinese Women in San Francisco*. Berkeley: University of California Press, 1999.

Yung, Wayne, Ming-Yuen S. Ma, Winston Xin, and Song Cho. "Racy Sexy: Round Table Discussion." In *Rice: Explorations Into Gay Asian Culture + Politics*, edited by Song Cho, pp. 59–67. Toronto: Queer Press, 1998.

Index

About the Author

Eric C. Wat received his M.A. in American studies from California State University, Fullerton, in 1999. He has taught Asian American Studies at California State University, Northridge, and UCLA. His writing has appeared in various literary and academic journals and anthologies. He is a 2000–2001 Sundance Writing Fellow. Currently he works as a research analyst for the Los Angeles County Proposition 10 Commission.

Wat is an active member of Asian Pacific Islanders for Human Rights and Liberty Hill Foundation. He lives and writes in Los Angeles.